Egypt Travel Guide 2024

Everything you need to know, When to go, what to see, and what to do in Egypt vibrant destinations - Your 2024 travel companion

Bobby L. Knowles

Copyright Page

Copyright © [Bobby L. Knowles] All rights reserved. 2024 No part of this book may be reproduced, stored in a retrieval system, or transmitted in any form or by any means, electronic, mechanical, photocopying, recording, scanning, or otherwise, without the prior written permission of the publisher

Table of contents

Introduction to Egypt..3
Chapter 1. Historical Background......................12
Chapter 2. Practical Information........................19
Chapter 3. Dining and Cuisine...........................33
Chapter 4. Nightlife and Entertainment............45
Chapter 5. Top Attractions.................................57
Chapter 6. Day Trips and Excursions................71
Chapter 7. Museums and Galleries....................83
Chapter 8. Technology and Travel.....................92
Chapter 9. Beyond the Tourist Trail..................101

Introduction

Welcome to Egypt, a country of ageless wonders where the dynamic pulse of modern life blends with the echoes of ancient civilizations. Permit me to be your guide as we set off on this historical, cultural, and adventurous tour around this fascinating country as I tell you stories based on my own experiences and findings.

When I first laid eyes on the Great Pyramid of Giza, its imposing silhouette rising against the desert sky like a monument to human intellect and ambition, it was an experience beyond description. I was dumbfounded by the enormity of the pyramids, which were constructed more than 4,000 years ago, and felt humbled by the history of our ancestors.

However, Egypt is a tapestry of stories waiting to be discovered; it is more than simply its famous structures. Every corner of this country offers a wealth of experiences, from the busy streets of Cairo, where the scent of spices permeates the air and the call to prayer reverberates through tiny alleyways, to the serene banks of the Nile, where feluccas glide silently along the water and time seems to stand still.

The evening I spent stargazing in the Western Desert is among my favorite recollections of Egypt. I was deeply connected to the land and its people as the campfire blazed and the solitude of the desert around me. As I sat under a blanket of stars and heard stories of old Bedouin customs, I came to understand that Egypt is an invitation to explore the secrets of the past and create important connections with the present, not just a place to go to.

However, Egypt is also a country of opposites, where modernity and tradition live together. Ancient customs and modern artistry converge in the thriving marketplaces of Khan El-Khalili, providing a window into the rich fabric of Egyptian culture. Egypt is a country where history is engraved in every stone and every smile, and as the sun sets over the Nile, illuminating the ancient temples of Luxor in a golden glow, I am reminded of this.

I hope this handbook inspires you to go on your Egyptian voyage and experience the sights, sounds, and sensations of this amazing country as you flip the pages. Egypt promises to capture your imagination and make a lasting impression on your spirit, whether you are driven to the country by the romance of the ancient monuments, the friendliness of the Egyptian people, or the excitement of adventure.

So let us go off on this adventure together, driven by passion, enlightened by Egypt's mystique, and directed by curiosity, dear traveler. Let us cruise the ageless waters of the Nile, meander through maze-like passageways, and gaze in wonder at structures that have lasted the test of time. And may we explore the infinite depths of our soul as well as Egypt's secret riches as we make our way across its dunes.

Come, let's visit Egypt—the birthplace of civilization, the home of the pharaohs, and a source of inspiration. Awaiting you is your journey.

Come along with me as we set off on a once-in-a-lifetime adventure across the pharaonic realm. Together, let's discover Egypt's mysteries and create lifelong memories. Are you prepared to go on an adventure? Flip the page and go on an exciting journey.

- **Welcome to Egypt**

Welcome to Egypt, where the Nile River winds through the center of history and the sands of time whisper tales of ancient civilizations. A unique kaleidoscope of sights, sounds, and experiences awaits you as you enter the legendary realm of the pharaohs.

Here, between the timeless Saharan landscapes and the fast-paced metropolises of Cairo and Alexandria, you'll find a region of paradoxes and contrasts, where modernity and tradition coexist in a harmonic symphony of legacy and culture.

Smiles as plentiful as the sun's golden rays await you in Egypt, where you will be welcomed with the kind embrace of Egyptian hospitality from the time you arrive. Egypt's inhabitants are as colorful and hospitable as the country they live in, whether you're sailing down the Nile at twilight, enjoying delicious mint tea in a neighborhood café, or haggling over finds in a busy souk.

Egypt is a country of limitless opportunities and undiscovered treasures that lie beyond its well-known sites and historical marvels. Every moment spent in Egypt is an adventure of discovery and joy, whether you're plunging into the lively underwater world of the

Red Sea, exploring the maze-like labyrinths of Islamic Cairo, or taking in the magnificence of Luxor's temples.

Allow the spirit of discovery to pull you off the main road and into the heart of this remarkable country as you set off on your Egyptian trip. Egypt has plenty to offer everyone, regardless of your interests—history buffs, thrill seekers, or those just looking for a little downtime.

I so send a warm welcome to you, my visitor, to Egypt—a country full of enchantment, mystery, and wonder. I hope you have a wonderful time here and that you have many treasured memories and happy times. Welcome to Egypt, a country where smiles are a tribute to the continuing spirit of this amazing place and where every corner offers a fresh adventure. Have fun while visiting, and then start your adventure.

- ## Brief Overview of Egypt's History and Culture

Egypt, which is tucked away along the banks of the enormous Nile River, has a millennium-long history and culture that has left a lasting impression on the fabric of human society. Egypt's tale is one of perseverance, ingenuity, and enduring legacy, from the earliest days of ancient civilizations to the contemporary metropolises that dot its terrain.

Egypt in Antiquity: The Birthplace of Civilization The heritage of ancient Egypt, sometimes called the "cradle of civilization," is crucial to Egypt's history. Magnificent pharaohs dominated the region for more than 3,000 years, building magnificent structures like the Great Sphinx, the Luxor and Karnak temples, and the Giza Pyramids. The skill and inventiveness of the ancient Egyptians, who accomplished amazing feats of engineering and building without the help of contemporary technology, are demonstrated by these colossal monuments.

Heavenly Monarchs and Pharaonic Dynasties Ancient Egypt's history is separated into dynasties, which were distinguished by a line of pharaohs who served as both religious and governmental leaders. Egypt's pharaohs, who were heavenly rulers thought to possess godlike abilities, had an everlasting effect on history, from the mythical King Narmer, who united Upper and Lower Egypt in the First Dynasty, to the famed Queen Cleopatra, who famously associated herself with Julius Caesar and effect Antony.

Egyptian Mythology and Religion A deep and intricate religious system based on the veneration of gods and goddesses connected to the natural world, animals, and celestial bodies was fundamental to ancient Egyptian civilization. Egypt's mythology, with its sun god Ra and goddess of writing and knowledge Thoth, offered a framework for comprehending the universe and the afterlife. Extensive funeral customs, including as mummification and the building of ornate tombs and pyramids, demonstrated the Egyptians' deep regard for the afterlife.

Literature, Language, and Art's Legacy of Influence Ancient Egypt had a profound impact on language, literature, and the arts in addition to its colossal building and religious rituals. One of the first written languages, hieroglyphic writing, was used to embellish temple walls and royal tombs. It provides insights into the everyday activities and religious beliefs of the ancient Egyptians. Meanwhile, the Egyptians' mastery of artistic expression and workmanship was demonstrated by magnificent works of art, including wall reliefs, sculptures, and elaborate jewelry.

Egypt in the Modern Era: An Innovative and Traditional Tapestry Even though ancient Egypt may have vanished from the pages of history, its influence can still be seen in the country's rich present culture and identity. Egypt is a country of paradoxes and contrasts, from the busy streets of Cairo, where contemporary skyscrapers and ancient bazaars coexist in a flurry of activity, to the tranquil villages of the Nile Delta, where long-standing customs and traditions persist.

I hope the ongoing heritage of this amazing place inspires you as you learn more about Egypt's rich history and culture. Egypt's tale is one of tenacity, ingenuity, and everlasting beauty, from the majestic pyramids of antiquity to the humming metropolis of today. Come along with us as we set off on a voyage through time, discovering the glories of Egypt's history and the opportunities that lie ahead.

- **Tips for Traveling in Egypt**

Traveling to Egypt may be an exciting experience that offers the possibility of adventure, exploration, and cultural absorption. To guarantee a seamless and delightful journey, take into account the below advice for traveling in Egypt:

1. Pick the Ideal Time to Go: Egypt has a harsh desert environment, with summertime highs sometimes reaching sweltering degrees (June to August). Visit in the cooler months of spring (March to May) or fall (September to November) for a more enjoyable experience, with more temperate temperatures and fewer tourists.

2. Dress Properly: Egypt is a popular tourist destination with a largely Muslim population, but tourists are typically allowed to wear whatever they choose. However, while visiting places of worship or more conservative locations, it is courteous to dress modestly. Men should refrain from wearing shorts in certain areas, while women may choose to cover their knees and shoulders.

3. Drink Plenty of Water: Egypt's weather is harsh, particularly in the summer, therefore it's critical to drink plenty of water. Always have a reusable water bottle with you, and make sure you stay hydrated, especially while seeing outdoor sites or traveling through a desert.

4. Honor Local Customs and Traditions: Egypt is a traditional country with strong cultural ties, thus it's essential to honor local etiquette and customs. Avoid showing love in public, especially in more traditional settings, and always get someone's permission before snapping pictures of people, especially ladies.

5. Be Ready to Bargain: In Egypt, especially at markets (souks) and bazaars, bargaining is a widespread activity. Haggling over costs is nothing to be frightened of, but always remember to do it politely and with a smile. A good agreement for both sides may frequently be reached with a little polite negotiating.

6. Beware of Scammers: Egypt, like any other travel destination, has its fair share of touts and scammers, especially in the vicinity of well-known tourist attractions. Be wary of excessively cordial people who offer uninvited help or tour services. Use common sense and only go with trustworthy tour operators to prevent being a victim of fraud.

7. Keep Up to Date on Safety: Although Egypt is a generally secure vacation destination, it's important to keep up to date on any advisories or security issues. Keep an eye on regional news sources and follow your hotel's or tour operator's recommendations for safety measures and any hazards.

8. Show Respect for Archaeological monuments: Egypt is home to some of the most famous archaeological monuments in the world, such as the Luxor temples and the Pyramids of Giza. Make sure you abide by any stated guidelines when visiting these locations, particularly those prohibiting taking pictures and climbing on historic buildings. Assist in protecting these treasures so that future generations might enjoy them.

You may make the most of your vacation to Egypt and fully immerse yourself in its rich history, lively culture, and breathtaking scenery while also making sure that you and your fellow travelers have a safe and unforgettable time by adhering to these suggestions and rules.

Chapter1. Historical Background

- Ancient Egypt: Birthplace of Civilization

Tucked away on the lush banks of the Nile River, Ancient Egypt is a reminder of the resourcefulness, tenacity, and enduring heritage of one of the oldest civilizations on Earth. A rich tapestry of invention, culture, and great accomplishments can be seen throughout Ancient Egypt's history, which spans from the establishment of the Old Kingdom to the collapse of the New Kingdom.

The Nile: Civilization's lifeblood The Nile River, whose yearly floods ledivineft rich silt along its banks and produced lush soil ideal for cultivation, was essential to Ancient Egypt's prosperity. Because of their plentiful resources, the ancient Egyptians were able to build a highly developed civilization that included trade, agriculture, and centralized governance. This civilization is considered to be one of the longest-lasting in history.

Pharaohs and Divine Rulers: The pharaohs, who were seen as rulers with unrestricted power over their subjects, were at the center of Ancient Egypt's social and political system. Egypt's pharaohs made an enduring impression on history as emblems of divine power and authority, from the fabled King Narmer, who united Upper and Lower Egypt in the First Dynasty, to the mythical Queen Cleopatra, who famously allied herself with Julius Caesar and Mark Antony.

Engineering marvels and colossal architecture: The pyramids of Giza, the Sphinx, and the temples of Luxor and Karnak are only a few examples of Ancient Egypt's enduring architectural legacy. The Egyptians' expertise in engineering and construction is demonstrated by these amazing structures, which are still a source of amazement to historians and archaeologists due to their accuracy and inventiveness.

Religion and the Afterlife: The worship of gods and goddesses connected to the natural world, animals, and the heavens was the focal point of an intricate and sophisticated belief system that pervaded ancient Egyptian civilization. Egypt's mythology, with its sun god Ra and goddess of writing and knowledge Thoth, offered a framework for comprehending the universe and the afterlife. Extensive funeral customs, including as mummification and the building of ornate tombs and pyramids, demonstrated the Egyptians' deep regard for the afterlife.

Legacy of Influence: Ancient Egypt left a lasting impact on the fields of art, language, and literature in addition to its imposing architecture and religious rituals. One of the first written languages, hieroglyphic writing, was used to embellish temple walls and royal tombs. It provides insights into the everyday activities and religious beliefs of the ancient Egyptians. Meanwhile, the Egyptians' mastery of artistic expression and workmanship was demonstrated by magnificent works of art, including wall reliefs, sculptures, and elaborate jewelry.

We are reminded of the permanent imprint that this extraordinary civilization left on the fabric of human history as we look at the ruins of Ancient Egypt's splendor. Ancient Egypt is a tribute to the lasting legacy of one of the greatest civilizations in history, a beacon of creativity, culture, and timeless beauty that still inspires surprise and amazement today. It can be seen from the banks of the Nile to the majestic pyramids of Giza.

- **Pharaohs, Pyramids, and Temples**

Few civilizations in Egypt, with history have captivated the mind as much as Ancientits mysterious pharaohs, breathtaking pyramids, and magnificent temples. Let's explore the mysteries of these famous Egyptian symbols as we travel through the sands of time. They are all monuments to the strength, creativity, and spirituality of a bygone age.

Pharaohs: Nile's heavenly lords The pharaohs were the highest authority in Ancient Egyptian civilization, held in high regard as divine rulers with unquestionable power over their followers. Egypt's pharaohs, from the powerful Ramses II, dubbed the "Great Builder" for his extensive building projects, to the mysterious Queen Hatshepsut, who broke with custom to become a sovereign in her own right, made a lasting impression on history as representations of heavenly strength and terrestrial authority.

Pyramids: Pharaohs' Tombs The pyramids may be the most iconic building that captures the majesty and mystery of ancient Egypt. These colossal constructions, which were created as ornate tombs for the pharaohs to secure their safe transition into the hereafter, are a tribute to the Egyptians' extraordinary engineering and building prowess. Every pyramid offers a tale of aspiration, commitment, and enduring legacy, from the famous Pyramids of Giza, which include the Great Pyramid, one of the Seven Wonders of the Ancient World, to the lesser-known pyramids of Dahshur and Saqqara.

Temples: Doors to the Spirit World The ruins of Egypt's magnificent temples, which were constructed in homage to the gods and goddesses of the prehistoric pantheon, are strewn along the banks of the Nile River. Every temple provides an insight into the spiritual practices and beliefs of ancient Egypt, from the majesty of Luxor's Karnak Temple with its enormous sculptures and tall columns to Aswan's tranquil Philae Temple, which is perched on an island in the Nile. These temples, which were decorated with colorful wall reliefs and elaborate hieroglyphic carvings, functioned as hallowed places where the worlds of the gods and humans met, enabling believers to communicate with the gods and ask for direction.

Legacy of Influence: The pharaohs, pyramids, and temples of Ancient Egypt have had a profound cultural impact on the world, even beyond their stunning architectural design. Generations of historians, artists, and explorers have been captivated and inspired by the heritage of Ancient Egypt, from the pyramids of Mesoamerica, which were modeled by the massive tombs of Egypt, to the ongoing obsession with Egyptian art and mythology.

We are reminded of the continuing heritage of Ancient Egypt as we are in awe of the soaring pyramids, take in the tranquil beauty of the temples, and wonder at the secrets of the pharaohs who once controlled this region. These iconic images of Egyptian culture, which can be seen everywhere from the banks of the Nile to the desert's dunes, bear witness to the inventiveness, spirituality, and resourcefulness of a people that has fascinated the globe for millennia.

- **Key Historical Periods: From Pharaonic Egypt to Modern Times**

Egypt's history spans thousands of years and encompasses a multitude of civilizations and cultures. It is a fascinating tapestry woven with threads of victory, strife, and change. Egypt's history, from the time of the pharaohs to the present, is one of tenacity, inventiveness, and enduring legacy.

Egypt under the Pharaohs: The Golden Age of Egypt's Kings One of the first civilizations in history, Pharaonic Egypt, was a powerful and inventive society that lasted for more than 3,000 years along the banks of the Nile River. The building of magnificent monuments, the creation of an advanced writing and administrative system, and the flourishing of art, literature, and religion were all witnessed in Pharaonic Egypt, from the unification of Upper and Lower Egypt under King Narmer in the Early Dynastic Period to the illustrious reign of Queen Cleopatra in the Ptolemaic Period.

Roman and Hellenistic Domination: The Hellenistic and Roman Eras After Alexander the Great conquered Egypt in 332 BCE, Egypt was ruled by the Greeks and then the Romans, ushering in a new age of political and cultural dominance. Greek and Egyptian customs were combined throughout the Hellenistic Era, which resulted in the establishment of Alexandria as a hub of scholarship and culture. Egypt flourished as a province of the Roman Empire under Roman administration, and Alexandria became a thriving center of commerce, trade, and learning.

Egypt under Islam: The Period of Caliphs and Sultans Egypt went through a period of change when Islam arrived in the seventh century CE and it joined the growing Islamic Caliphate. With the establishment of Cairo as its capital during the 10th century, the Fatimid dynasty brought an era of unparalleled Islamic art, architecture, and learning. Egypt's cultural environment was further shaped by other dynasties, such as the Ayyubids and Mamluks, who left a legacy of magnificent mosques, madrasas, and monuments that remain to this day.

Egypt in the Modern Era: From Colonization to Freedom Egypt came under the rule of European colonial powers in the late 19th and early 20th centuries. The French, led by Napoleon Bonaparte, initially occupied Egypt in 1798, and the British took over in 1882. Egypt was ruled by the British until 1922 when it attained nominal independence despite occasional moments of resistance and uprising. However British influence remained, and eventually, a constitutional monarchy headed by King Farouk was established.

Egypt is still navigating the challenges of modernity, political unrest, and cultural shift as it moves into the twenty-first century. Egypt's rich past serves as a reminder of the lasting spirit of a country that has survived the tides of time and risen stronger and more alive than ever before, from the famous monuments of ancient times to the busy streets of modern Cairo. Egypt's tenacity, inventiveness, and ageless beauty serve as constant reminders of this remarkable country as we consider its major historical eras

Chapter 2. Practical Information

- **Planning Your Trip: When to Go, What to Pack, and Travel Essentials**

Traveling to Egypt is an exciting trip that promises fascinating cultures, historic sites, and life-changing experiences. A well-planned journey is necessary to guarantee a trouble-free and joyful experience. This guide will assist you in navigating the nuances of organizing your trip to Egypt.

When to Go: Your tastes and level of heat tolerance will determine when is the ideal time to visit Egypt. Between October and April, when the weather is warmer and more appropriate for touring historical buildings and outdoor attractions, is usually the busiest travel period. But it also means more people and more expensive costs. Visit during the shoulder seasons of late spring (May to June) or early autumn (September), when temperatures are still bearable but crowds are less if you prefer fewer visitors and don't mind the heat.

What to Bring: When packing for Egypt, keep in mind the country's temperature, customs, and planned activities. The following are some necessities to put on your packing list:

1. Lightweight, breathable clothes: To keep cool and comfortable in the heat, choose loose-fitting, light clothing made of breathable materials like cotton or linen. When attending places of worship, bring modest attire such as long skirts or slacks and shirts with sleeves.

2. Sun protection: Carry sunglasses, a wide-brimmed hat, high-SPF sunscreen, and a lightweight scarf or shawl to shield your head and shoulders from the intense Egyptian sun.

3. Comfy walking shoes: If you intend to explore and walk a lot, bring strong, comfy shoes that can withstand uneven surfaces and long days of touring.

4. Shawl or scarf: A thin scarf or shawl can be used for a variety of things, such as covering your shoulders and head at places of worship, adding extra warmth on chilly nights, or shielding you from the wind and dust in the desert.

5. Travel adapter and voltage converter: To charge your electronics, make sure you bring along a travel adapter that is compatible with Egypt's Type C and Type F electrical outlets, which are European standards. Additionally, if your electronics aren't compatible with the local power (220-240V), think about carrying a voltage converter.

6. Medication and first aid kit: Bring along any prescription drugs you might require in addition to a basic first aid kit that includes bandages, painkillers, and antidiarrheal medication.

Travel Essentials: To guarantee a hassle-free and seamless vacation, you should have the following items on hand in addition to packing appropriately for clothes and equipment:

1. Valid passport and visa: Verify that your passport is valid for at least six months beyond the date you want to leave Egypt and that you have obtained any required visas in advance of your trip.

2. Travel insurance: To guard against unforeseen circumstances like trip cancellations, medical crises, or misplaced luggage, think about getting travel insurance.

3. Cash and credit cards: For minor purchases and transactions, it's a good idea to carry some cash (ideally in Egyptian pounds), even if credit cards are routinely accepted in large cities and tourist destinations.

4. Maps and guides: To help you traverse Egypt's attractions and discover more about its history and culture, download travel guides or guidebooks.

5. Language and communication tools: Although most people in tourist regions speak English, it might be useful to download translation apps or learn a few simple Arabic words to help you communicate with locals.

Planning and packing sensibly will help you have an amazing vacation to Egypt that is full of life-changing events and fascinating cultural discoveries. So gather your belongings, get set for travel, and get ready to discover the delights of this ancient country. Egypt is on the horizon!

• Visa Requirements and Entry Formalities

To guarantee a simple and hassle-free travel experience, you must acquaint yourself with the prerequisites for obtaining a visa and the entrance procedures before setting off on your vacation to Egypt.

What you should know is as follows: Most visitors to Egypt must have a valid visa to enter the nation, although there are a few exceptions for nationals of specific nations who can enter the nation without a visa or who can obtain one upon arrival. Your nationality, the reason for your travel, and the length of your stay will all determine the kind of visa you require. The following are the primary types of visas required for visitors entering Egypt:

1. Tourist Visa: This kind of visa is appropriate for vacationers who want to visit Egypt for tourism, sightseeing, or to meet friends and relatives. Tourist visas can be obtained upon arrival at Egyptian airports and seaports, or before your trip from Egyptian embassies or consulates overseas. They are normally valid for 30 days.

2. Transit Visa: You might be able to obtain a transit visa if you're passing through Egypt on your way to another location and won't be remaining there for more than 48 hours. With this kind of visa, you can spend a little time in Egypt while traveling to your ultimate destination.

3. Business Visa: A business visa could be necessary for those who are going to Egypt for business, such as to attend conferences, meetings, or negotiations. Business visas are normally granted for predetermined periods and may need accompanying paperwork, such as an invitation letter from an Egyptian host firm.

Formalities for Entry: Arriving in Egypt requires visitors to fulfill specific entrance requirements in addition to securing the required visa. Here's what to anticipate:

1. Passport Requirements: Make sure your passport is valid for a minimum of six months after the day you want to exit Egypt. Make sure you have enough blank pages for entry stamps and check the expiration date.

2. Visa Application: You must complete an application for a visa and pay the necessary visa fee in cash (typically in US dollars or euros) if you're getting one upon arrival. Be ready to share facts regarding your trip schedule, lodging, and contact information with Egyptian officials.

3. Customs Declaration: You must fill out a customs declaration form as soon as you arrive in Egypt to declare any valuables, including cash, gadgets, and expensive products. Make precise and truthful declarations to prevent any problems with customs officers.

4. Health Screening: Due to concerns about public health, passengers may be subject to temperature checks and health questionnaires when they arrive in Egypt. Be ready to assist health officials and adhere to their directions.

It's possible to guarantee a seamless and stress-free arrival in Egypt by being aware of the country's visa requirements and admission procedures. Before your journey, make sure you are aware of the most recent travel warnings and entry requirements. If you have any questions or concerns, don't hesitate to get in touch with Egyptian authorities or the Egyptian embassy or consulate that is closest to you. If you plan before and prepare well, your trip to Egypt will be an unforgettable and fulfilling experience.

- **Transportations: Getting Around Egypt**

A key component of any trip is navigating Egypt's enormous and varied terrain, which provides chances to discover historic sites, vibrant cities, and stunning scenery. From the crowded streets of Cairo to the placid Nile River banks,

This is a map that will help you navigate Egypt:

Domestic Flights: Especially for long-distance travel, domestic flights offer a practical and effective means of getting between Egypt's main cities and popular tourist locations. Regular flights are offered by EgyptAir, the national airline, connecting Cairo and well-liked locations including Luxor, Aswan, Sharm El Sheikh, and Hurghada. Domestic travel is a convenient and fast method to see the many parts of the nation at a reasonable price.

Train Travel: Egypt's vast train network provides a reasonably priced and picturesque means of getting from one city or area to another. Regular rail services between Cairo and important cities including Alexandria, Luxor, Aswan, and Port Said are provided by the Egyptian National Railways. The trains come with a range of facilities and levels of luxury, from standard economy class to more opulent sleeper cabins on overnight trains. Traveling by rail offers the chance to view the countryside and engage with people while saving time compared to flying.

Public Transportation: Buses, metro trains, and microbuses (shared minivans) are the available modes of public transportation in cities such as Cairo and Alexandria. With two lines servicing important parts of the city, the Cairo Metro is among the most effective methods to get about the busy metropolis. Buses and microbuses are similarly affordable and generally accessible, however, they can be congested and unorganized, particularly during rush hours. In addition to taxis, ride-hailing services like Careem and Uber are also well-liked means of transportation in cities.

Private Transportation: Rental vehicles and private drivers are examples of private transportation solutions for passengers looking for greater convenience and flexibility. Major towns and popular tourist destinations have plenty of rental vehicle options, but driving in Egypt may be difficult because of the country's crowded roads, aggressive drivers, and unaccustomed driving conditions. For a safer and more comfortable way to see Egypt's sights, consider hiring a private driver or scheduling guided excursions that include transportation.

Nile Cruises: Take a trip down the Nile River for a genuinely exceptional and life-changing experience. With all the comforts and facilities of a floating hotel, Nile cruises provide a relaxing way to discover Egypt's historic monuments, including temples, tombs, and archeological finds. Usually, cruises sail from Luxor to Aswan, stopping at famous sites including the Temple of Philae, the Valley of the Kings, and the Temple of Karnak.

Traveling around Egypt is an experience in and of itself, whether you're riding a camel safari over the desert dunes, taking a classic felucca down the Nile River, or taking the metro through the bustling streets of Cairo. It's never been simpler to discover Egypt's delights with so many transportation alternatives to fit every taste and budget. So gather your belongings, get ready for an exciting voyage, and get set to see the classic scenery and dynamic local culture of this alluring location. Egypt is on the horizon!

- ## Accommodation Options: From Luxury Resorts to Budget Hostels

Any travel experience must include finding the ideal location to stay, and Egypt has a wide variety of lodging alternatives to fit every taste, budget, and style. From luxurious resorts on the shore of the Red Sea to little boutique hotels in old cities The following is a list of lodging choices in Egypt:

Luxurious Resorts: Egypt's seaside resorts provide a plethora of sumptuous lodging options and top-notch services for those looking for the utmost in comfort, elegance, and leisure. In locations like Sharm El Sheikh, Hurghada, and Marsa Alam, you can discover opulent five-star resorts with expansive accommodations, exclusive beaches, infinity pools, and a variety of recreational options including diving, snorkeling, and spa services along the Red Sea coast. Sophisticated tourists seeking a calm and luxurious getaway in a breathtaking beachside location are catered to by these resorts.

Boutique Hotels: As a more individualized and intimate option to standard resorts, boutique hotels may be found in Egypt's ancient cities and cultural hotspots. Boutique hotels blend traditional local character with contemporary comforts and services, whether they are located in the quiet havens of Luxor and Aswan, the busy streets of Alexandria, or the winding lanes of Islamic Cairo. Egypt's rich history and culture may be fully experienced at boutique hotels, which provide a variety of selected experiences, individualized service, and elegantly equipped rooms with panoramic views.

Budget Accommodations: Egypt has a range of reasonably priced lodging alternatives, such as budget hotels, guesthouses, and hostels, for tourists on a tight budget. Budget hotels and guesthouses provide cozy, reasonably priced housing with standard services like free breakfast, Wi-Fi, and clean rooms in destinations like Luxor, Cairo, and Alexandria. Hostels, on the other hand, provide reasonably priced dorm-style lodging that is perfect for those traveling alone, backpackers, and groups looking to network and share advice.

Traditional lodging: If you want to have a very authentic Egyptian experience, think about booking traditional lodging on the Nile River, such as a felucca (a traditional sailing vessel) or riad (a traditional courtyard dwelling). Discover Egypt's rich architectural legacy through the exquisitely restored riads in towns like Luxor and Cairo, which include elaborately carved wooden furniture, mosaic-tiled floors, and elaborate courtyards. A romantic and unique way to take in the everlasting splendor of the Nile River is to spend a night beneath the stars on a felucca.

For your Egyptian vacation, there are plenty of lodging alternatives to choose from, including magnificent seaside retreats, quaint boutique hotels in the middle of the city, and affordable hostels. Egypt's accommodations are just as fascinating and varied as the nation's. Egypt has a wide variety of lodging options to fit any traveler's preference, taste, and style, from the historical attractions of Cairo to the Red Sea's sun-kissed beaches. Select your ideal haven, make yourself at home, and get ready to travel around this timeless location's captivating scenery and dynamic culture.

- **Health and Safety Tips for Travelers**

To have a wonderful and worry-free trip to Egypt, it is essential to ensure your health and safety. From navigating the busy streets of a metropolis to touring historic archeological sites, Here are some crucial safety and health advice to remember:

Remain Hydrated: It's important to remain hydrated in Egypt because the country may have a scorching and dry summer. Throughout the day, sip on lots of water, particularly if you're visiting outdoor activities or spending time in the sun. Keep a reusable water container with you and fill it up frequently with purified or bottled water.

Take Care of Yourself in the Sun: The Egyptian sun may be very strong, so take precautions to avoid sunburn and heat exhaustion. To protect your face and neck from the sun's rays, use wide-brimmed hats, sunglasses, and sunscreen with a high SPF. Whenever feasible, seek for shade, especially in the warmest portion of the day.

Adopt Good Food and Water Hygiene: Steer clear of tap water, especially ice cubes in beverages, to prevent foodborne infections and upset stomachs. When consuming street food, exercise caution and choose freshly prepared meals from reliable restaurants. If you don't have access to soap and water, use hand sanitizer instead of routinely washing your hands with it.

Be Alert with Personal Property: Pickpocketing and small-time theft are common in Egypt, as they are in any tourist destination, particularly in crowded tourist locations and when using public transit. Use a money belt or covert pouch to carry valuables, keep your possessions safe at all times, and be aware of your surroundings, especially in busy marketplaces and tourist attractions.

Respect Cultural Norms and Customs: Given Egypt's conservative society and ingrained cultural traditions, it's critical to observe appropriate local behavior and manners. When visiting places of worship or more conservative locations, dress modestly and refrain from making public shows of affection. Before taking pictures of people, especially ladies, get their consent, and be aware of cultural sensitivities.

Keep Up with Current Events: Keep up with local news sources and travel warnings from your home country to stay updated about current events and any possible safety or security issues in Egypt. Steer clear of regions experiencing political upheaval or civil upheavals, and heed the guidance provided by local authorities, your embassy, or consulate.

Seek Medical Advice and Insurance: Speak with a healthcare provider before your trip to Egypt to make sure you are up to date on your regular vaccinations as well as any additional shots advised for the area. Think about getting travel insurance that covers trip cancellation, evacuation, and medical situations.

You may reduce hazards and have a happy and safe trip to Egypt by paying attention to these health and safety precautions. You may confidently and with peace of mind discover the beauties of this ancient nation if you prepare yourself and exercise prudence.

Chapter 3. Dining and Cuisine

- Introduction to Egyptian Cuisine: Flavors and Ingredients

Take a culinary adventure into the savory and rich realm of Egyptian cuisine, where many influences and age-old customs come together to produce a tapestry of mouthwatering tastes and fragrant spices. Egyptian food represents the colorful culture, rich history, and varied terrain of the nation. Dishes like aromatic rice dishes and robust stews are served alongside savory pastries and sweet desserts.

An overview of the tastes and components that characterize Egyptian cuisine is provided here: The fundamentals of Egyptian cuisine are the use of seasonal, locally produced foods and a well-balanced combination of tastes and textures. Grains like rice, wheat, and barley; legumes like lentils and fava beans; and an abundance of fruits, vegetables, and herbs like tomatoes, cucumbers, eggplants, parsley, cilantro, and mint are examples of staple foods. Fish, lamb, and chicken are examples of foods high in protein that are frequently prepared in Egyptian cuisine.

Aromatic herbs and spices: Egyptian cuisine heavily relies on spices to enhance the flavor and scent of food while giving it depth and complexity. Cumin, coriander, cinnamon, cloves, nutmeg, and cardamom are among the often used spices. Local delicacies like Bharat, a spice blend, and dukkah, a concoction of nuts, seeds, and spices, are also made with these spices. Aromatic herbs like mint, dill, cilantro, and parsley are also frequently added to give food a vibrant, fresh taste.

hallmark Dishes: The wide range of hallmark dishes seen in Egyptian cuisine highlights the nation's geographical differences and culinary history. Among the famous dishes are:

1. Koshari: A filling and substantial dish topped with hot garlic vinegar and a tangy tomato sauce, layers of rice, lentils, pasta, chickpeas, and crispy fried onions.

2. Ful Medames: Traditionally eaten with hard-boiled eggs and flatbread, Ful Medames is a classic Egyptian morning meal prepared with slow-cooked fava beans seasoned with garlic, lemon juice, and olive oil.

3. Mahshi: Savory rice, herb, and ground beef mixtures cooked in a tasty tomato sauce, stuffing vegetables like grape leaves, eggplants, and bell peppers.

4. Molokhia: Served with rice or bread, this wholesome and reassuring soup is prepared with molokhia leaves, also referred to as Jew's mallow, and simmered with garlic, coriander, and chicken or lamb stock.

5. Kofta: Seasoned meatballs cooked on a grill or skewer from ground lamb or beef, seasoned with garlic, cumin, and coriander, and eaten with bread, salad, or rice.

Desserts & Sweets: In Egypt, no dinner would be complete without indulging in a variety of sweets and desserts, which are typically savored with a strong Arabic coffee or a cup of hot tea. Typical Egyptian confections consist of:

1. Basbousa: A rich, delicious semolina cake scented with orange blossom or rose water, sweetened with sugar syrup, and garnished with almond or coconut flakes.

2. Konafa: A rich pastry cooked till golden and crispy, composed of shredded phyllo dough covered with cheese or nuts and drenched in syrup.

3. Mahalabiya: A thickened cornstarch-based milk pudding scented with orange blossom or rose water, topped with almonds or pistachios.

You will come across a wealth of tastes, textures, and scents that are a reflection of Egypt's rich history, culture, and geography as you delve into its gastronomic delights. Egyptian food offers a wide variety of dishes to suit every taste and appetite, ranging from robust stews and savory pastries to delicate sweets and sweet delicacies. So take a seat, enjoy the tastes, and discover the gastronomic wonders of Egypt for yourself. Salutations!

- **Must-Try Egyptian Dishes and Street Fog hi**

Take a gastronomic tour of Egypt's busy streets and colorful marketplaces, where the perfume of spices and the sound of grilling food entices hungry tourists to experience a wide variety of mouthwatering street food treats. Here are some famous Egyptian dishes, ranging from savory staples to sweet confections, that you just have to try:

1. Koshari: A popular comfort food in Egypt, koshari is a filling and hearty dish made with layers of rice, lentils, pasta, and chickpeas, finished with crispy fried onions and a tart tomato sauce. This aromatic and substantial meal, which offers the ideal harmony of textures and tastes in each mouthful, is a mainstay of Egyptian street food vendors and neighborhood restaurants.

2. Ful Medames: Made from slow-cooked fava beans seasoned with garlic, lemon juice, and olive oil, Ful Medames is a simple yet fulfilling dish that is a classic Egyptian breakfast staple. Full madame, when served with warm pita or flatbread, hard-boiled eggs, and a sprinkling of fresh herbs, is a filling and delectable way to begin the day.

3. ta'ameya, also known as Egyptian falafel, is a common street food snack prepared from mashed fava beans or chickpeas combined with herbs and spices, shaped into balls or patties, and deep-fried until crispy and golden brown. It is similar to its Middle Eastern cousin. Ta'ameya is a tasty and filling vegetarian alternative that tastes great served hot and crispy with tahini sauce or tucked into warm pita bread.

4. Hawawshi: Made from minced beef or lamb seasoned with onions, garlic, and spices, hawawshi is a flavorful pastry filled with meat that is baked or grilled until it becomes crispy and golden. It is a popular and decadent street food item in Egypt. Hawaiian curry, when served hot and accompanied by pickled veggies and tahini sauce, is a filling and cozy dish.

5. Mahshi: With a long history, mahshi is a traditional Egyptian meal that is cooked in a tasty tomato sauce until the vegetables, such as grape leaves, eggplants, and bell peppers, are soft and aromatic. The filling is a savory blend of rice, herbs, and minced beef. Mahshi is a tasty and nourishing dish that highlights the abundance of Egypt's lush countryside. It is served hot and garnished with fresh herbs and a dollop of yogurt.

6. Baladi Bread: A typical Egyptian flatbread produced from whole wheat flour and cooked in a wood-fired oven until soft and fluffy, baladi bread is a must-have for any Egyptian dinner. Baladi bread, when served warm and straight out of the oven, is the ideal side dish for any dinner. It may also be eaten on its own as a quick and filling snack, dipped in olive oil, or used to mop up flavorful stews and dips.

Egypt's culinary scene is as colorful and varied as its rich history and culture, spanning from the busy streets of Cairo to the serene beaches of the Nile. Whether you're sating your sweet desire with rich sweets like konafa and basbousa or indulging in savory favorites like kosher and hawawshi, Egyptian cuisine provides a mouthwatering variety of tastes and textures to entice your taste buds and satiate your demands. Thus, take a seat at a street food vendor, sample some of these delectable delicacies, and discover the gastronomic enchantment of Egypt for yourself. Salutations!

- Dining Etiquette and Customs

In Egypt, dining is an experience that embodies the nation's rich cultural legacy and customs rather than merely a means of subsistence. From the value of hospitality to the practice of sharing food in groups, Here is a guide to Egyptian eating customs and etiquette:

1. Communal Dining: In Egypt, getting together around a table to share food and chat during meals is a common practice. It is typical for many meals to be served simultaneously so that patrons may experience a range of tastes and textures. It's customary to show kindness and hospitality by sharing food, so don't be shocked if your host insists on loading your plate high with an abundance of their favorite delicacies.

2. Wash Your Hands: It's normal to wash your hands well before sitting down to dine, especially if you plan to use your hands for food preparation. It's common for traditional restaurants and houses to lack utensils, thus patrons are expected to serve themselves from shared dishes or scoop food from communal platters with their right hand.

3. Appropriate Seating Arrangements: In more formal contexts, such as dining rooms or formal events, guests of honor may be seated at the head of the table or closest to the host in a hierarchical arrangement. When you enter a dining room, wait for the host or hostess to show you to your seat. Then, when it comes to seating and service order, do what they say.

4. Utilize Utensils Properly: If utensils are offered, utilize them properly, holding the knife in your right hand and the fork in your left. Feel free to use a slice of bread as a tool if necessary, because bread is frequently used in Egyptian cuisine to scoop up food or soak up sauces. After you've completed your meal, arrange your utensils on your plate such that they are parallel to one another.

5. Express Gratitude: It's traditional to thank your host or hostess for the great food and hospitality after the meal. Along with praises for the food and hospitality, a simple "shukran" or "jazakallah khair" (may God recompense you) is generally appreciated.

6. Leave Some Food on Your Plate: In Egyptian culture, leaving a tiny quantity of food on your plate signifies that you've finished eating and is considered courteous. If you finish everything on your plate, your host could think you're still hungry and give you more food even if you're already satisfied.

Indulging in the delectable tastes of Egyptian food, interacting with locals, and experiencing their rituals and traditions are all part of the dining experience in Egypt, which goes beyond simply sating one's appetite. You may respect your hosts, take in the camaraderie of Egyptian eating, and enjoy the delectable cuisine of this intriguing nation by adhering to these dining etiquette and customs. So take a seat, unwind, and savor the feast!

- ## Recommended Restaurants and Cafes in Major Cities

Every Egyptian city offers a different mix of modern cuisine, local specialties, and exciting dining experiences, making exploring the country's culinary scene an adventure in and of itself. Here are some suggested restaurants to check out in Egypt's largest cities, ranging from well-known eateries providing traditional Egyptian cuisine to hip cafés selling foreign food:

Cairo:

1. Khan El Khalili Restaurants: Situated in the center of the thriving Khan El Khalili market in Old Cairo, this neighborhood is home to several classic Egyptian eateries that serve regional delicacies including falafel, kosher, and grilled meats. Try the local cuisine at well-known restaurants like El Fishawy and the Naguib Mahfouz Cafe.

2. Sequoia: This restaurant, which is located by the banks of the Nile River, serves modern Mediterranean food with an Egyptian flair and provides breathtaking views of Cairo's skyline. In a trendy and contemporary atmosphere, savor meals like grilled fish, mezze platters, and specialty drinks.

3. Zooba: For a taste of contemporary Egyptian street cuisine, visit Zooba, a well-liked restaurant noted for its inventive takes on classic fare like kosher, grilled meats, and ta'ameya (Egyptian falafel). Located all around the city, Zooba provides a lively and informal eating experience.

Alexandria:

1. Balbaa Village: A well-known seafood restaurant providing fresh catches from the Mediterranean Sea, Balbaa Village is situated in El Raml Station's historic quarter. Savor grilled shrimp, calamari, and fish while taking in the vibrant environment and coastal views.

2. Fish Market: As the name suggests, this restaurant lets patrons choose from a selection of freshly caught seafood and have it prepared to order. Select from an assortment of fish, prawns, and crustaceans, and then have your dinner on the patio with a view of the port.

3. Mosaic: Housed in the Four Seasons Hotel Alexandria in San Stefano, Mosaic is a chic restaurant that serves contemporary Egyptian food. Savor delicacies like filled vine leaves, slow-cooked lamb, and fresh salads while taking in expansive vistas of the Mediterranean.

Luxor:

1. El Tarboush: This well-known eatery, which serves traditional Egyptian food in a laid-back setting, is close to the Luxor Temple. Sample the grilled meats, robust stews, and stuffed pigeons, along with freshly made bread and regional sweets.

2. Al Sahaby Lane: Nestled among the bustling bazaar district of Luxor, Al Sahaby Lane provides a delightful alfresco-eating experience within the city's historical environs. Savor traditional Egyptian fares such as falafel, kebabs, and kofta while taking in the vibrant ambiance of this busy street.

3. 1886 Restaurant: Located on the Sofitel Winter Palace Luxor's premises, 1886 Restaurant provides a classy eating experience reminiscent of the opulence of the Belle Époque period. Savor fine French and Egyptian cuisine while taking in the stunning surroundings of old buildings and verdant gardens.

Aswan:

1. Abu Ashara: Known for its mouthwatering falafel sandwiches, grilled meats, and Egyptian-style pizzas, Abu Ashara is a local favorite in Aswan. This relaxed restaurant, which is close to the Aswan Market, serves tasty food at reasonable prices in a lively setting.

2. Ferial Garden: Perched on the banks of the Nile, Ferial Garden provides a serene environment for al fresco eating with views of the neighboring islands and the river. on a laid-back and picturesque setting, indulge in classic mezze, seafood tagine, and grilled fish, among other Egyptian favorites.

3. Nubian Village: Visit the Nubian Village restaurant on Elephantine Island to get a sample of Nubian food and culture. Savor foods like vegetable tagines, kofta, and grilled Nile fish while taking in traditional Nubian dance and music performances.

Egypt provides a wide range of eating experiences to suit every appctitc and inclination, whether you're exploring the busy streets of Cairo, taking in the coastal ambiance of Alexandria, marveling at the ancient treasures of Luxor, or unwinding along the banks of the Nile in Aswan. These suggested restaurants will tantalize your taste buds and leave you yearning for more of Egypt's delectable cuisine. They range from elegant eateries providing modern cuisine with a twist to traditional eateries serving traditional Egyptian delicacies. So prepare to revel in the delicacies of this fascinating country by bringing a chair and coming hungry. Salutations!

Chapter 4. Nightlife and Entertainment

- ### Nightlife Hotspots: Bars, Clubs, and Live Music Venues

Discover the lively energy and throbbing beats of Egypt's nightlife, where a diverse array of pubs, clubs, and live music venues come to life on the streets after dark. Here's a list of the trendiest places in Egypt for nightlife, from subterranean clubs thumping with electronic sounds to hip rooftop pubs with expansive city views:

Cairo:

1. Cairo Jazz Club: One of the most well-known nightlife venues in the city, Cairo Jazz Club is a music lover's paradise for live performances of jazz, funk, blues, and other genres by both domestic and foreign performers. It's the ideal place to relax and take in wonderful music because of its warm ambiance and large drink selection.

2. Zigzag: Located in the center of downtown Cairo, Zigzag is a stylish rooftop lounge and bar with breathtaking views of Tahrir Square and the city skyline. Savor specialty drinks, a varied selection of music from resident DJs, and a vibrant ambiance that draws in a fashionable clientele of both foreigners and locals.

3. The Tap Maadi: Situated in the posh Maadi area, The Tap is a well-liked hangout that is well-known for its large assortment of specialty beers, laid-back atmosphere, and frequent live music events. The Tap has something to offer everyone, regardless matter whether they appreciate beer or music.

Alexandria:

1. La Bodega: A stylish bar and restaurant offering inventive cocktails, premium wines, and gourmet tapas-style fare, La Bodega is housed in a historic villa with a view of the Mediterranean Sea. It's a popular hangout for Alexandria's sophisticated demographic, including live music performances and an elegant atmosphere.

2. Pub 33: Nestled in the heart of Alexandria's busy downtown district, Pub 33 is a welcoming English-style bar with pool tables, a relaxed vibe, and a wide array of beers, spirits, and cocktails. Pub 33 provides everything you may want for a fun night out or a quiet drink.

3. Graffiti Lounge & Bar: This hip location in the historic Stanley Bridge district is well-known for its inventive concoctions, eye-catching paintings, and varied musical selection. Graffiti provides an unforgettable night in Alexandria, whether you're dancing to the rhythms of resident DJs or relaxing on the outdoor patio.

El Sheikh, Sharm:

1. Pacha Sharm El Sheikh: A member of the well-known worldwide Pacha nightclub network, Pacha Sharm El Sheikh provides an unparalleled nightlife experience with its top-notch DJs, cutting-edge sound system, and amazing themed parties. At this legendary club on the Red Sea, you may dance the night away beneath the stars.

2. Little Buddha: Located in the center of Naama Bay, Little Buddha is a glitzy lounge and nightclub renowned for its exotic drinks, lavish décor, and electrifying vibe. Partygoers in Sharm El Sheikh should check out Little Buddha, a must-visit location with a blend of Eastern mysticism and Western elegance.

3. Hard Rock Café Sharm El Sheikh: For a taste of glamorous rock 'n' roll, visit Hard Rock Café Sharm El Sheikh, where themed events, live music, and traditional American fare all come together in a lively setting. Hard Rock Café provides an unforgettable evening experience, whether you're rocking out to live bands or drinking drinks on the outdoor terrace.

Egypt's nightlife culture has something for every taste and preference, whether you're partying beneath the stars in Sharm El Sheikh, sipping drinks by the water in Alexandria, or dancing till dawn in Cairo. These locations for nightlife provide life-long experiences and memories, ranging from edgy rooftop bars and stylish lounges to energetic clubs and small live music venues. So grab your pals, get out on the town, and let Egypt's vibrant nightlife transport you to an exciting and adventurous realm.

- ## Cultural Performances and Traditional Shows

Experience the mesmerizing cultural performances and traditional acts that highlight Egypt's history, music, dance, and folklore, and lose yourself in the country's rich tapestry of culture and legacy. Here's how to enjoy the finest of Egypt's cultural entertainment, from captivating Sufi whirling dervishes to colorful folkloric performances:

1. Whirling dervishes of Sufis: Discover the fascinating spiritual practice of Sufi whirling dervishes, a mystical tradition that has been practiced for centuries. Observe as artists in flowing white robes spin elegantly in circles to the mesmerizing beats of classic Sufi music, signifying a transcendental and enlightening trip. Sufi performances are held in many locations in Egypt, such as cultural centers and old mosques.

2. Tanoura Shows: Originating in the Sufi tradition, tanoura shows include artists spinning and twirling in vibrant skirts embellished with sequins and lights, producing an enthralling display of movement and light. Tanoura dancers offer a visually stunning performance that enthralls audiences of all ages, accompanied by traditional music and percussion as they deftly swirl and twirl. Tanoura performances are a well-liked kind of entertainment at festivals, cultural gatherings, and tourist destinations all around Egypt.

3. Folkloric Dance Performances: Vibrant shows honoring Egypt's cultural legacy and regional customs will introduce you to the great range of Egyptian folkloric dance. Folkloric performances provide a vibrant window into the traditions and customs of Egypt's many populations, showcasing everything from the exuberant dances of Upper Egypt to the upbeat rhythms of Saidi music and the elegant moves of Nubian dance. Seek out chances to see traditional dance performances in resorts, cultural centers, and special events.

4. Sound and Light performances: At famous archaeological sites like the Pyramids of Giza, the Karnak Temple in Luxor, and the Philae Temple in Aswan, experience a trip back in time and see the ancient wonders of Egypt come to life with captivating sound and light performances. These multimedia performances use cutting-edge technology to tell stories of pharaohs, gods, and heroes while projecting pictures onto the stone walls of Egypt's ancient structures, illuminating its mythology and history.

5. classic Music Performances: Using real instruments like the oud (lute), qanun (zither), ney (flute), and tabla (drum), skilled performers will dazzle your senses with the melodies and rhythms of classic

Egyptian music. Arabic traditional music performances, which range from energetic folk melodies and upbeat shaabi (popular) songs to classical Arabic music, provide a vibrant and immersive cultural experience that appeals to audiences of all backgrounds.

6. Puppetry & Shadow Theater: Take in the artistic talent of Egyptian shadow theater and puppetry, a beloved custom that has been practiced for generations. See as talented puppeteers weave stories of mythology, everyday life, and folklore using magnificent sets and finely built puppets, bringing characters to life. The Arabic term "khayal al-zill" refers to shadow theater, which uses illumination and translucent screens to produce captivating illusions and silhouettes that enthrall both young and old audiences.

Egypt offers a compelling voyage through its rich history, music, and culture through its cultural performances and traditional acts, which range from the spiritual whirling of Sufi dervishes to the vibrant beats of folkloric dance. Whether you're taking in the vivid rhythms of traditional music and dance or seeing ancient treasures brought to life via light and sound, these cultural experiences are sure to make an enduring impact and increase your respect for Egypt's enduring legacy. Thus, take a seat back, unwind, and let the allure of Egyptian culture transport you to a realm of fascination and wonder.

- **Evening Cruises on the Nile River**

An evening cruise down the Nile River promises spectacular sights, an enticing environment, and unique experiences. Set out on a wonderful adventure over the fabled waters of the river. Here are some things to anticipate from a nighttime Nile cruise, whether you're drinking cocktails on an opulent dinner cruise or seeing the twinkling city lights from a classic felucca:

1. Beautiful Scenery: The Nile River turns into a sparkling ribbon of gold as the sun sets, illuminating the surrounding area in a captivating radiance. A nighttime cruise gives unmatched views of Egypt's most famous sites lit up against the dusk sky, from the imposing temples of Luxor and Karnak to the timeless beauty of Elephantine Island in Aswan.

2. Romantic Ambience: A Nile River cruise creates the ideal environment for romance and intimacy, whether you're commemorating a particular event or just spending a romantic evening with your significant other. Enjoy a romantic meal on the terrace, sip champagne beneath the stars, and let the soft sound of the flowing water lull you as you walk hand in hand down the riverbanks.

3. Cultural Entertainment: Take in Egypt's lively rhythms and customs with onboard cultural entertainment that vividly depicts the nation's rich past. A nighttime cruise offers a spectacular presentation of

Egyptian culture and craftsmanship, ranging from stunning dance shows comprising folkloric and belly dance performances to live music performances by outstanding musicians playing traditional instruments.

4. Gourmet Dining: Savor a delectable spread of gourmet food offered on classy dinner cruises that rival the best eateries on land. Dining aboard a Nile River cruise is a gastronomic experience not to be missed, with multi-course dinners produced by award-winning chefs and opulent buffets offering a delectable selection of worldwide and Egyptian favorites.

5. Famous Landmarks: Pass by some of Egypt's most famous sites and architectural marvels, such as the brightly lit temples of Luxor and Karnak, the elegant feluccas gliding down the river, and the busy promenades along the river in Cairo and Aswan. You'll learn about the background and significance of each location as you sail by, thanks to the informed comments of your friendly guides.

6. Relaxation and Serenity: Get away from the bustle of the city and rest in the quiet surroundings of the Nile River. Here, the mild breeze and the slow-moving water create a tranquil atmosphere. A nighttime cruise is the ideal way to unwind and revitalize, whether you're relaxing in a snug cabin with expansive views or enjoying a cool drink on the deck.

A nighttime cruise on the Nile River offers an amazing voyage into the heart of Egypt's timeless beauty and tradition, complete with romantic meals beneath the stars, vibrant cultural performances, and expansive views of the country's most famous structures. A Nile River cruise delivers an exquisite experience that will leave you enthralled and yearning for more, whether you're looking for romance, leisure, or cultural immersion. Now jump on board, set sail, and allow the Nile River's majesty to carry you away on a once-in-a-lifetime journey.

- **Tips for Enjoying Nightlife Safely**

It might be thrilling to spend a night out in a new city or nation but to make the experience memorable and pleasurable, safety and well-being should come first. Here are some crucial pointers for enjoying nightlife safety, whether you're relaxing on a tranquil nighttime cruise down the Nile River or experiencing the lively nightlife of Egypt's busy cities:

1. Make a plan in advance: Before leaving for the evening, spend some time learning about the place you'll be going, being acquainted with the rules and customs of the region, and organizing your schedule appropriately. Note down reliable places to go out at night, ways to get about, and emergency numbers. Then, let a family member or close friend know what you have planned.

2. Pay Attention to Your surroundings: When taking in the nightlife, always be alert and conscious of your surroundings. Watch out for your possessions, stay out of isolated or dark places, and follow your gut if anything doesn't feel right. When going on a nighttime stroll by yourself, stay in well-lit, busy locations and think about using a cab or ride-sharing service from a reliable source.

3. Drink Responsibly: If you decide to have alcohol while out at clubs, pubs, or restaurants, make sure you do it sensibly and sparingly. Drink in moderation, switch out alcoholic drinks for water, and don't take drinks from strangers or leave your drink alone. If you start to feel sick or drunk, know when to get help from a buddy you can trust or the venue personnel.

4. Travel in Groups: When visiting the nightlife scene, try to go with a group of friends or companions. By enabling you to assist one another and share memories throughout the evening, this not only increases safety and security but also improves the whole experience. Remain together, watch out for each other, and arrange a meeting place in case you end up apart.

5. Respect Local Laws and Customs: When enjoying Egypt's nightlife, especially in conservative or religiously significant locations, keep in mind local customs and rules. Wear proper clothing, abstain from actions that may be seen as impolite or insulting, and abide by local regulations governing curfews, public conduct, and alcohol usage.

6. Trust Your Instincts: Above anything else, follow your gut and put your safety and well-being first. Never be afraid to leave the area and ask for help from authorities or other reliable people if you feel intimidated or uneasy in any scenario. To secure your safety at all times, follow your instincts and be proactive.

You may make the most of your nighttime excursions in Egypt while lowering dangers and guaranteeing a pleasant and unforgettable experience according to these guidelines for enjoying nightlife safely. It is possible to truly enjoy the thrill and attraction of Egypt's thriving nightlife scene by putting safety and mindfulness first, whether you're sailing along the serene banks of the Nile River, exploring the busy streets of Cairo, or dancing the night away in a hip nightclub. So go forth, have fun, and create lifelong memories while maintaining your safety and security.

5. Top Attractions

- **Exploring Cairo: The Heart of Egypt**

Tucked down on the banks of the magnificent Nile River, Cairo is a bustling metropolis where the contemporary world and old history collide. Cairo, the capital of Egypt, is a vibrant metropolis that captivates tourists with its unique combination of ancient sites, cultural riches, and lively marketplaces. This is your guide to traveling across the center of Egypt:

1. Iconic Landmarks: Start your exploration of Cairo with a visit to some of its most famous sites, such as the mysterious Sphinx, the magnificent Pyramids of Giza, and the Egyptian Museum, which houses priceless artifacts from antiquity. Admire the architectural wonders of Islamic Cairo, including the magnificent Muhammad Ali Mosque and the ancient Citadel of Saladin, and meander through the maze-like lanes of Khan El Khalili, the city's most active and oldest market.

2. Cultural Immersion: Discover Cairo's many districts, each with its distinct charm and personality, and fully immerse yourself in the city's rich cultural tapestry. Wander through the old alleyways of Coptic Cairo, where historic churches and synagogues serve as reminders of Egypt's religious past, or stroll through the creative haven of Zamalek, which is home to galleries, shops, and riverfront cafés.

3. Culinary Delights: As you explore Cairo's vibrant culinary scene, treat your senses to the mouthwatering flavors of Egyptian cuisine. Savor regional vendors' specialties, such as kosher, falafel, and ta'ameya, or treat yourself to a fine meal at one of the city's well-known eateries, where you can have regional specialties like ful medames, grilled meats, and fragrant tagines.

4. Exuberant Nightlife: Cairo offers a plethora of pubs, clubs, and live music venues that come alive after dark. Take advantage of this active nightlife environment. Savor refreshing drinks at rooftop bars with breathtaking views of the Nile, party hard at hip Zamalek or Mohandiseen nightclubs, or take in traditional Egyptian dancing and music at cultural centers like El Sawy Culturewheel.

5. Hidden jewels: If you want to get away from the throng and find hidden treasures, check out Cairo's off-the-beaten-path attractions and hidden jewels. Discover the charmingly maintained medieval houses and artisan workshops that line the ancient Al-Muizz Street, or visit Al-Azhar Park, a serene haven with gorgeous vistas and lush gardens that offer a respite from the bustle of the city.

6. Useful Advice: Wear modest clothing when touring Cairo, particularly when you're in religious or conservative districts.

Make use of trustworthy modes of transportation, such as ride-sharing or taxis, and haggle over prices beforehand.

Particularly in the sweltering summer months, drink plenty of water and shield your skin from the heat by wearing a hat and sunscreen.

In busy places, remain on the lookout for pickpockets and make sure your possessions are safe at all times.

Respect regional traditions and customs by getting consent before snapping pictures of individuals or places of worship.

Cairo provides an enthralling fusion of ancient history and contemporary charm that will keep you enthralled, from its recognizable landmarks and cultural treasures to its exciting nightlife and gastronomic pleasures. Cairo offers a tour into the heart of Egypt that will not soon be forgotten, whether you want to see the magnificent Pyramids of Giza, indulge in the delicacies of Egyptian cuisine, or simply immerse yourself in the bustling city culture. Thus, prepare for an incredible journey through Cairo's mystique by packing your luggage, embracing the unknown, and letting the city's history enchant you.

- **Iconic Landmarks: Pyramids of Giza, Sphinx, and Egyptian Museum**

Take a trip back in time to ancient Egypt and be amazed by three of the most recognizable sites on earth, each of which attests to the majesty and glory of one of the greatest civilizations in history. These iconic locations, which include the majestic Pyramids of Giza, the mysterious Sphinx, and the vast collection of artifacts kept at the Egyptian Museum, bear witness to Egypt's ongoing past and ageless appeal.

1. The Pyramids of Giza: The Pyramids of Giza are a magnificent example of the Egyptians' architectural talent and inventiveness, rising magnificently from the desert sands. Constructed more than 4,500 years ago as the last resting places of the pharaohs Khufu, Khafre, and Menkaure, these enormous constructions still astonish and amaze people to this day. The greatest of the three pyramids, the Great Pyramid of Khufu, is a sight to behold. Marvel at its sheer grandeur and consider the mysteries surrounding its construction and potential secrets.

2. Sphinx: The Great Sphinx of Giza, guardian of the Pyramids, is arguably the most mysterious and recognizable relic from ancient Egypt. This amazing monument, which is said to symbolize the pharaoh Khafre, is carved from a single limestone block and represents a legendary monster with the body of a lion and the head of a human. The Sphinx, which is 73 meters long and more than 20 meters tall, never ceases to astound tourists with its enigmatic grin and ageless stare, arousing curiosity and conjecture regarding its real function and importance.

3. Egyptian Museum: The Egyptian Museum in Cairo is home to the largest collection of Egyptian antiquities in the world. Explore this treasure trove of historic relics and rare finds. Discover galleries brimming with lavishly adorned sarcophagi, jewelry, and sculptures that provide a window into the everyday lives and artistic output of ancient Egypt. Highlights include the magnificent objects unearthed from Queen Hatshepsut's tomb, the golden riches of King Tutankhamun, and the royal mummies of Egypt's pharaohs.

From the eternal grandeur of the Giza Pyramids to the mysterious charm of the Sphinx and the unrivaled wealth of the Egyptian Museum, these famous sites serve as everlasting reminders of Egypt's rich past and rich cultural legacy. A visit to these iconic locations guarantees an amazing voyage through time, whether you're admiring the architectural marvels of the pyramids, contemplating the secrets of the Sphinx, or exploring the intriguing world of ancient relics at the museum. Come, set out on a journey of exploration, and see the wonders of ancient Egypt materialize before your very eyes.

- **Luxor: The World's Largest Open-Air Museum**

Luxor, which is perched on the banks of the magnificent Nile River, is a tribute to the majesty and splendor of ancient Egypt. Known as the "World's Largest Open-Air Museum," this ancient city is home to an unmatched concentration of archeological treasures, ranging from imposing tombs and stately temples to breathtaking structures spanning thousands of years in the making. Here's a guide to help you discover Luxor's treasures:

1.Temple Complexes: Enter a different era as you discover Luxor's breathtaking temple complexes, all of which are devoted to the gods and pharaohs of old Egypt. Set out on your adventure in the Karnak Temple Complex, where imposing obelisks, finely carved reliefs, and towering columns testify to the might and majesty of the New Kingdom pharaohs. Proceed with your investigation at the magnificent Luxor Temple, which is decorated with enormous sculptures, tall pylons, and exquisitely preserved hieroglyphics. It is a magnificent example of ancient Egyptian architecture.

QDive deep into the desert to explore this place where the pharaohs of the New Kingdom were buried in ornate tombs decorated with beautiful murals and hieroglyphic inscriptions As you tour these fascinating archaeological sites, marvel at the exquisitely adorned chambers of famous tombs like those of Tutankhamun, Ramses II, and Seti I. You'll also learn more about the mystery surrounding ancient Egyptian burial customs.

3. Valley of the Queens: This area, which is next to the Valley of the Kings, is home to elaborately designed tombs that were formerly used to entomb queens, princesses, and high-ranking officials. Investigate the exquisitely painted chambers of tombs, such as the one belonging to Queen Nefertari, Ramses II's adored wife, and behold the vivid hues and fine details that grace the walls, portraying scenes from the afterlife and the soul's journey.

4. Colossi of Memnon: Gaze in wonder at the imposing Colossi of Memnon, two enormous sculptures that formerly stood watch above the entrance to Amenhotep III's funeral temple. Admire the enormous size and grandeur of these commanding statues, which are more than 18 meters tall and have been watching over the Nile for more than 3,000 years. The sculptures are said to have an enigmatic "singing" sound that they make at dawn, which adds to their charm and mystery.

5. Luxor Museum: The Luxor Museum, which has an amazing collection of antiques and antiquities spanning thousands of years of Egyptian history, is a wonderful place to learn about the history of Luxor and the surrounding area. Learn about ancient Egypt's culture, religion, and way of life by visiting displays that feature sculptures, reliefs, and other objects found in its temples, tombs, and monuments.

Luxor is deserving of its moniker as the "World's Largest Open-Air Museum," given its unrivaled abundance of ancient treasures. Luxor is an enthralling trip into the past of Egypt, whether you're touring the majestic temples of Karnak and Luxor, deciphering the mysteries of the Valley of the Kings and Queens, or just taking in the enormous sculptures of Memnon. Come see the ageless beauties of Luxor and lose yourself in history; each stone reveals a tale of a civilization that has captivated the attention of people for ages.

- **Aswan: Gateway to Nubian Culture and Nile Cruises**

Aswan, which is tucked away on the banks of the magnificent Nile River, entices visitors with its serene beauty, energetic culture, and extensive history. This charming city provides a compelling combination of historical antiquities, traditional hospitality, and beautiful natural scenery. It serves as the entryway to Nubian culture and the beginning point for spectacular Nile cruises. Here is a guide to help you explore Aswan:

1. Nubian Culture: Wander about Aswan's colorful districts and take in the beautiful tapestry of Nubian culture, where typical Nubian houses painted in bright hues line the streets. Discover the traditions, crafts, and music of this ancient culture by visiting the Nubian Village on Elephantine Island. You may also enjoy traditional cuisine and get true Nubian hospitality.

2. Nile Cruises: From Aswan, go on an opulent voyage of exploration to discover the ageless splendor of Egypt's most famous river. Travel south toward Luxor, passing by charming towns, lush islands, and old temples. You'll stop at places of historical significance along the road, such as Edfu Temple, Philae Temple, and Kom Ombo Temple. A Nile cruise guarantees an amazing experience, whether you're seeing ancient monuments, dining outside beneath the stars, or just relaxing on the sundeck.

3. Philae Temple: Take in the splendor and majesty of one of Egypt's most cherished and gorgeous historical landmarks, Philae Temple. Philae Temple, devoted to the goddess Isis, was moved to the neighboring island of Agilkia Island during the building of the Aswan High Dam to protect it from inundation. Stroll around the temple's hallowed halls and courtyards and marvel at the magnificent reliefs, soaring columns, and serene environs.

4. Aswan High Dam: Visit the Aswan High Dam, a remarkable engineering achievement that regulates the Nile River's flow and provides Egypt with hydroelectric power, to get an understanding of contemporary engineering wonders. From the dam's viewing sites, take in expansive views of Lake Nasser and the surrounding countryside while learning about the dam's construction, importance, and effects.

5. Elephantine Island: Take a break from the bustle of the city and visit Elephantine Island, a quiet haven with beautiful gardens, historic ruins, and breathtaking views. Discover the history of the island by visiting the Aswan Museum, seeing archeological sites like the ruins of the ancient village of Yebu, or just unwinding under a palm tree's shade and taking in the scenery.

6. classic Felucca Rides: Take a classic felucca ride along the Nile River, sailing a wooden sailboat as the sun sets. This is a wonderful way to take in the everlasting beauty of the river. As you set off on a tranquil and remarkable ride, float down the river's moderate currents, feel the breeze in your hair, and take in expansive views of Aswan's cityscape and the surrounding desert environment.

With its vivacious Nubian culture, tranquil Nile cruises, and historical attractions, Aswan provides an enthralling window into Egypt's essence. The timeless beauty and legacy of Egypt's southern gateway are waiting for you at Aswan, where you can immerse yourself in the rich traditions of Nubian hospitality, explore old temples, or take a leisurely cruise down the beautiful Nile. Come experience Aswan's beauty and go on an unforgettable he w journey that will leave you wanting more.

- **Alexandria: A Mediterranean Gem with a Rich History**

Alexandria tucked away along the glittering Mediterranean Sea coast, entices visitors with an alluring blend of sophisticated urbanism, ancient history, and spectacular coastal beauty. Alexandria, the second-biggest city in Egypt and a historically significant hub of study and culture enthralls tourists with its colorful history, intriguing present, and ageless charm. Here's how to discover this treasure of the Mediterranean.

1. Ancient History: Travel back in time and see Alexandria's rich historical tapestry, where the enduring influence of famous characters like Julius Caesar, Cleopatra, and Alexander the Great is evident. Explore the mysterious remains of the Library of Alexandria, which was once the world's greatest library, and take in the imposing columns of the Roman Amphitheater, the scene of gladiatorial combat and wild cheering from onlookers.

2. Architectural Marvels: Explore Alexandria's architectural gems, which include elaborate Islamic monuments, regal Greco Roman sites, and tasteful neoclassical structures. Admire the elegant curves and elaborate decorations of the Qaitbay Citadel, a medieval stronghold constructed on the site of the ancient Pharos Lighthouse, and explore the magnificent Catacombs of Kom El Shoqafa, a Roman necropolis.

3. Cultural Heritage: Take in Alexandria's thriving literary, artistic, and musical scenes against the stunning backdrop of the sea and historic ruins. Explore the colorful street art culture that covers walls and alleyways around the city as you stroll through the city's varied districts, which are home to galleries, theaters, and cafés that are humming with creativity and innovation.

4. Coastal Beauty: Take in the serene beauty of Alexandria's breathtaking coastline, which features immaculate beaches, quaint promenades by the sea, and lovely marinas that provide the ideal setting for leisure and enjoyment. Take a leisurely boat ride to discover secret coves and isolated islands, wander along the picturesque Corniche shoreline, or soak up the Mediterranean sun on Stanley Beach's golden beaches.

5. Culinary Delights: Indulge in the pleasures of Alexandria's thriving food scene, where mouthwatering fish, flavorful spices, and authentic Egyptian cuisine entice the senses. Indulge in world cuisine in sophisticated restaurants with views of the sea, or sample local specialties like grilled fish, filled vine leaves, and creamy hummus at cafés and restaurants by the water.

6. nautical Heritage: Discover the rich nautical history of Alexandria at the Alexandria National Maritime Museum, which features displays that chart the history of the city's seafaring people from prehistoric times to the present. Discover the history of Alexandria's old harbor, the fabled Pharos Lighthouse, and the city's significance as a cross-cultural hub for trade and travel.

Travelers from all over the world will be enthralled and inspired by Alexandria's intriguing combination of past and present, which is highlighted by its rich history, architectural wonders, cultural legacy, and breathtaking coastline scenery. Alexandria promises an amazing voyage through the heart and soul of this Mediterranean treasure, whether you're visiting ancient ruins, meandering along the beachfront promenade, or relishing the delicacies of Egyptian cuisine. Come experience Alexandria's enchantment and go on an unforgettable journey that will leave you wanting more.

6. Day Trips and Excursions

• Day Trip to Saqqara and Memphis: Step Back in Time

Take a day excursion to Saqqara and Memphis to see the wonders of ancient Egypt, where wonders dating back thousands of years await discovery. These archeological sites, which include the famous Step Pyramid of Djoser and the ruins of Egypt's first city, provide insight into the pharaohs' rich past and ongoing impact. Here's how to travel back in time using this guide:

1. Saqqara: Start your day excursion in Saqqara, a large necropolis south of Cairo that is the site of some of Egypt's oldest and most remarkable pyramids. Admire the magnificent Step Pyramid of Djoser, the oldest stone pyramid in the world and a marvel of prehistoric architecture. Discover more than 4,500-year-old pyramids, tombs, and temples inside the expansive Saqqara complex, including the Pyramid of Teti and the Tomb of Ptahhotep.

2. Imhotep Museum: Learn more about Saqqara's past at this museum honoring the illustrious Egyptian polymath and architect Imhotep, who created the Step Pyramid of Djoser. Discover the architectural styles, religious doctrines, and everyday life of ancient Egypt by visiting displays including antiquities, sculptures, and reliefs found at Saqqara.

3. Memphis: Proceed to Memphis, the UNESCO World Heritage Site situated south of Saqqara. Memphis was the ancient Egyptian capital. Discover the remnants of this formerly magnificent metropolis, where pharaohs reigned and colossal sculptures of gods and monarchs embellished the terrain. Admire the enormous statue of Ramses II, which was sculpted from a single limestone block, and explore the outdoor museum that displays sphinxes, sculptures, and stelae among other objects that have been unearthed from the site.

4. Dahshur: If you have time, think about adding a visit to Dahshur, another historic necropolis south of Saqqara, to your day trip itinerary. Explore the Red Pyramid and the Bent Pyramid here. These two lesser-known but no less spectacular pyramids in Egypt are renowned for their distinctive architectural characteristics and well-preserved interiors.

5. Useful Advice: Dress comfortably and wear shoes that are appropriate for walking and touring ancient sites.
To shield yourself from the sun's rays, carry a hat, lots of water, and sunscreen.
Refrain from climbing on monuments or touching historic items out of respect for cultural heritage and archeological sites.
Take a guided tour or hire an informed guide to learn more about the background and significance of Memphis and Saqqara.

When visiting the sites, be aware of the desert's topography and potential dangers such as loose rocks and uneven ground.

You may experience a fascinating journey through Egypt's ancient history and discover the remarkable accomplishments of ancient civilization by taking a day excursion to Saqqara and Memphis. These archeological sites offer a glimpse into the past and a chance to be in awe of the continuing heritage of Egypt's ancient wonders, from the famous Step Pyramid of Djoser to the ruins of the ancient city of Memphis. Come, travel back in time, and set off on a once-in-a-lifetime experience in the land of the pharaohs.

Exploring the Valley of the Kings and Queens

Take a voyage of discovery through the revered necropolises in the Valley of the Kings and Queens, the magnificent and revered last resting places of the ancient pharaohs and queens. These eternal burial sites, which are close to Luxor on the west bank of the Nile, provide insight into the customs, beliefs, and creative accomplishments of ancient Egypt. Here is a guide to help you navigate these impressive locations:

1. Valley of the Kings: Enter the huge necropolis that was the last resting place for the pharaohs of the New Kingdom and immerse yourself in the heart of ancient Egypt. Admire the utter magnificence of the valley's rock-cut tombs, which are all embellished with elaborate murals, hieroglyphic writing, and treasure-filled burial chambers. Discover famous tombs like the one belonging to the young king Tutankhamun, whose remains were found almost entirely in 1922 and which have a wealth of artifacts and information about ancient Egyptian burial customs.

2. Valley of the Queens: This area, which is next to the Valley of the Kings, is home to ornate tombs with colorful paintings and inscriptions that are meant to entomb royal consorts, princesses, and high-ranking officials. Explore tombs like the one belonging to Queen Nefertari, the adored wife of Ramses II, which is well-known for its stunning decorations and vibrant colors that have remained amazingly well-preserved over the years. Learn about the beauty and elegance of these lesser-known burial sites.

3.The architectural wonders and creative triumphs of the tombs in both valleys are a sight to behold. Skilled artists and craftsmen worked tirelessly to build ornate burial chambers that befit royalty. Appreciate the elaborate reliefs, vibrant paintings, and minute vignettes that portray the gods, goddesses, and legendary animals who followed the pharaoh on his everlasting trip.

4. Conservation Efforts: Find out about the continuous conservation initiatives aimed at safeguarding the Valley of the Kings and Queens tombs for the next generations. Learn how scientific methods and contemporary technology are being utilized to counteract the impacts of humidity, erosion, and tourism on these priceless ancient artifacts to keep them preserved and accessible for many years to come.

5. Useful Advice: Put on shoes that are appropriate for walking and exploring rugged terrain, and dress comfortably.
To shield yourself from the sun's rays, carry a hat, lots of water, and sunscreen.
Avoid touching or resting on the old walls and decorations to preserve the sacredness of the burial sites.

Take a guided tour or hire an experienced guide to learn more about the meaning, symbolism, and history of the tombs.

To maintain the integrity of the historic artwork and inscriptions, be aware of photographic limits and adhere to standards.

Discovering the Valley of the Kings and Queens is a voyage into the center of ancient Egypt, bringing to life in stunning detail the pharaohs' magnificence and the secrets of the afterlife. These hallowed locations provide an insight into the values, customs, and creative accomplishments of one of the greatest civilizations in history, from the majesty of the royal tombs to the exquisiteness of the painted murals. Come experience the everlasting wonders of the Valley of the Kings and Queens, where the heritage of ancient Egypt is waiting to be explored and appreciated. Travel back in time.

- **Felucca Sailing on the Nile: A Serene Escape**

A felucca sailing trip is a peaceful and remarkable way to take in the everlasting beauty and serenity of the Nile River, providing an exclusive look at Egypt's historic waterway. A felucca voyage promises to take you to a peaceful and tranquil place, whether you're floating with the calm currents, gliding by famous sites, or soaking in the golden light of the sunset. Here's how to make the most of this magical experience:

1. Timeless Tradition: Travel back in time by boarding a classic felucca, an elegant wooden sailboat that has been cruising the Nile for generations. Set sail aboard this renowned warship, whose construction and design haven't altered much since the era of the pharaohs, and embrace the spirit of ancient Egypt. As you go through time, experience the sensation of the river beneath you, the wind in your hair, and the sun on your skin.

2. Enchanting vistas: As you travel down the Nile, unwind and enjoy the expansive vistas of the surrounding countryside and the riverbanks. Admire the enduring beauty of the arid dunes, the verdant riverbanks, and the imposing monuments—ancient temples, mosques, and palaces—that border the coastlines. Whether you're taking in the serene Upper Egyptian countryside or the busy cityscape of Cairo, every moment spent on a felucca presents a fresh and enthralling sight to witness.

3. Sunset cruise: Take a sunset felucca cruise to truly capture the allure of the Nile at nightfall, when the setting sun creates a golden glow over the river and the sky bursts into a riot of color. Take in the breathtaking view of the river being painted in shades of orange, pink, and purple as the sun sets. As you give in to the beauty of the moment, you'll feel calm and tranquility flood over you. A sunset cruise on the Nile is an experience that will stick with you long after the sun goes down, whether you're enjoying it with loved ones or just enjoying the quiet.

4. Cultural Immersion: Get involved with the customs and culture of the area as you converse with your felucca's crew, who are frequently eager to give tales, anecdotes, and insights into life on the Nile. Discover the background of felucca sailing, the river's cultural significance in Egypt, and the everyday routines of life on the water. Use this chance to speak Arabic, ask questions, or even try your hand at navigating the boat with the help of more seasoned sailors.

5. Relaxation and Reflection: Give yourself to the tranquil sounds of the river and the gentle sway of the felucca as you allow yourself to decompress and unplug from the stress of everyday life. Spend some time thinking back on your voyage, appreciating the beauty of your surroundings, and embracing the calm and serenity that come with being on the ocean. A felucca voyage on the Nile provides the ideal chance to discover comfort, inspiration, or just a moment of peaceful reflection.

A felucca sailing trip down the Nile is more than simply a boat ride; it's an immersive experience that satisfies the senses, replenishes the spirit, and makes lifelong memories. A felucca voyage gives a singular and fascinating viewpoint on Egypt's ageless river, whether you're enjoying the historic sites of Aswan, the ancient marvels of Luxor, or the busy districts of Cairo. Come, go on a voyage of tranquility, exploration, and amazement as you set sail down the Nile and allow the beat of the water to carry you away.

- **Desert Adventures: Oasis Towns and Bedouin Camps**

With a desert adventure, you may take an exciting trip into the heart of the desert and visit Bedouin camps and oasis villages, where you can experience their old customs, breathtaking scenery, and kind hospitality. These desert tours guarantee an amazing experience that will leave you with lifelong memories, from the dazzling dunes of the Sahara to the untamed beauty of the Sinai Peninsula. Here's your adventure handbook for the desert:

1. Oasis settlements: Travel to oasis settlements tucked away amid the desolate surroundings to uncover the undiscovered beauties of the desert. Admire the verdant vegetation, palm groves, and glistening springs that adorn the desert landscape, offering a refreshing diversion from the parched surroundings. Discover historic settlements like Siwa Oasis, which is tucked away in the western desert close to the Libyan border. Here, mud-brick homes, old ruins, and traditional marketplaces provide a window into the rich history and culture of the oasis' residents.

2. Bedouin Camps: Spend a night in a Bedouin camp in the desert and immerse yourself in the ageless customs and warmth of the Bedouin tribe. Take in the warmth of Bedouin hospitality as you are greeted with open arms, served traditional meals, and encouraged to gather around the campfire to enjoy music and storytelling. Stay the night in a traditional Bedouin tent while admiring the limitless night sky and the sounds of the desert.

3. Desert Safari: Climb into a tough 4x4 car and set out on an exciting safari journey to explore the wide and constantly shifting desert landscapes. Discover a secret oasis, nomadic towns, and spectacular panoramas as you travel further into the desert. Traverse towering dunes, steep valleys, and old caravan routes. A desert safari guarantees an exhilarating experience unlike any other, whether you're racing across the dunes, camel trekking across the desert, or just taking in the peace of the desert.

4. Stargazing: Marvel at the majesty and beauty of the universe while taking in the charm of the night sky above the desert. The desert provides unmatched chances for stargazing, with a pure, black sky that highlights the Milky Way, constellations, and shooting stars in all their grandeur. It is the perfect place to be away from city lights and pollution. In the stillness and seclusion of the desert, take an astronomy tour with a guide or just recline on a blanket and look up at the stars, allowing the majesty of the universe to envelop you.

5. Cultural Immersion: Get involved with the neighborhood and discover the habits, values, and manner of life of the people who live in the desert by immersing yourself in their environment. Take part in customary pursuits like weaving, bread-making, and camel herding, or go on a guided tour of the desert with experienced Bedouin guides who can impart wisdom about the region's nature, history, and mythology.

A trip through the desert to Bedouin camps and oasis villages is a special chance to engage with the environment, history, and culture in one of the most famous settings on earth. Whether you choose to go on an exciting safari adventure, explore lush oasis towns, or camp out beneath the stars in the desert, the desert promises an incredible journey that will satiate your senses, uplift your spirit, and leave you deeply appreciating the resilience and beauty of the desert environment. Come, take a break from the bustle of the city, and set off on an adventure that will take you across the sands of time to a realm of wonder and discovery.

7. Museums and Galleries

- Egyptian Museum in Cairo: Treasures of Ancient Egypt

Explore the Egyptian Museum in Cairo to uncover a world of wonder and discovery. This museum is a treasure trove of antiquated items, royal jewels, and precious relics that provide a window into the rich history and civilization of Egypt. Situated in the center of Cairo, this renowned museum holds the largest collection of ancient Egyptian antiquities in the world, encompassing more than 5,000 years of history. Here is a guide to help you discover the Egyptian Museum's hidden gems:

1. History and Architecture: As you enter the Egyptian Museum's majestic entryway, which is filled with imposing sculptures and elaborate reliefs, you may immerse yourself in the museum's rich history and architectural design. Learn the intriguing history of the museum's establishment in 1902 by French Egyptologist Auguste Mariette, as well as about the building's later growth and renovations. Admire the museum's magnificent halls, lofty ceilings, and neoclassical façade, which serve as the ideal setting for the thousands of treasures kept within.

2. Treasures of Tutankhamun: Take a tour around the fabled riches of the young king, whose tomb in the Valley of the Kings produced one of the most important archeological finds ever made. Admire the stunning items unearthed inside his tomb, such as the famous death mask made of gold, the finely carved sarcophagi, and the priceless jewels that had been on his mummified body. Discover the mystery surrounding Tutankhamun's life, death, and legacy by perusing the galleries devoted to his reign.

3. Royal Mummies: Visit the museum's display of royal mummies, which includes the skeletal remains of pharaohs, queens, and other royal family members, to pay your respects to Egypt's past rulers. Observe the melancholy beauty of these antiquated figures as they lie in state, their wrappings covered with ornate burial inscriptions, their features fixed in time. Discover the ins and outs of the afterlife, the mummification process, and the customs and rites that surrounded the interment of Egypt's nobility.

4. Thematic Galleries: Take a tour of the museum's thematic galleries, which feature items from the Old Kingdom, Middle Kingdom, New Kingdom, and Late Period of ancient Egyptian history. Admire the magnificent sculptures of gods and goddesses, ornately carved reliefs, burial relics, and commonplace items that provide insights into ancient Egyptian culture, religion, art, and daily life. Highlights include the Amarna Gallery, the Royal Jewelry Collection, and the Rosetta Stone, which offered the solution for decoding hieroglyphic writing in ancient Egypt.

5. Conservation & Preservation: Find out about the continuing initiatives to save the museum's irreplaceable objects for the next generations. Learn the methods and tools used by conservation specialists to shield delicate items from light, moisture, and pollution, and acquire an understanding of the difficulties and complexity involved in maintaining Egypt's cultural legacy in the face of contemporary dangers.

More than just a storehouse of antiquated items, Cairo's Egyptian Museum is a window into Egypt's spirit and a living example of the inventiveness, inventiveness, and tenacity of one of the greatest civilizations in history. Whether you're admiring Tutankhamun's riches, honoring the royal mummies, or visiting the themed galleries, the museum provides an immersive experience that will transport you to the marvels of ancient Egypt and inspire you. Come, enter the past, and take a journey through the centuries among the Egyptian Museum's treasures.

- **Luxor Museum: A Window into Pharaonic History**

The Luxor Museum, which provides visitors with an enthralling look into the rich history and culture of the pharaohs, is situated on the banks of the magnificent Nile River and serves as a tribute to the majesty and magnificence of ancient Egypt. Located in the center of Luxor, this top-notch museum offers an exceptional chance to delve into the intriguing heritage of one of the greatest civilizations in history. It displays an amazing collection of items spanning thousands of years. Here is a guide to help you explore the delights of the Museum of Luxor:

1. History and Architecture: As you pass through the Luxor Museum's contemporary front, which is embellished with soaring columns and exquisite reliefs, you will be fully submerged in the museum's history and architectural design. The museum's modern architecture, which was created by Egyptian architect Mahmoud El-Hakim, contrasts dramatically with its historic surroundings. Discover how the museum was established in 1975 and how its later renovations and expansions made it a premier organization committed to presenting and conserving Egypt's cultural legacy.

2. Masterpieces of Ancient Art: Admire the museum's magnificent collection of ancient art items, which includes sarcophagi, sculptures, reliefs, and pharaonic artifacts. The magnificent statue of the goddess Hathor, the imposing granite head of Amenhotep III, and the exquisitely preserved reliefs from the Hatshepsut temple at Deir el-Bahari are among the collection's highlights. Every relic offers a glimpse into the world of ancient Egypt by narrating the tale of the pharaohs, their gods, their accomplishments, and their enduring legacy.

3. Royal Mummies: Take a look at the museum's well-known collection of royal mummies, which includes the likes of Ahmose I, Seti I, and Ramses II, three of Egypt's most well-known and powerful pharaohs. Experience the majestic elegance of these antiquated statues as they lie in state, their characteristics maintained for all time, providing a unique chance to interact with the pharaohs of old. Discover the ins and outs of the afterlife, the mummification process, and the customs and rites that surrounded the interment of Egypt's nobility.

4. theme Galleries: The museum's theme galleries go further into the era of ancient Egypt by examining many facets of pharaonic history, religion, and daily life. Discover galleries devoted to the secrets of the afterlife, the worship of the sun god Ra, and the cult of the deity Amun. There, items like tomb decorations, religious artifacts, and funerary goods provide insights into the beliefs and customs of the ancient Egyptians. Explore the galleries and be in awe of the objects' exquisite craftsmanship, poignant meanings, and ageless beauty.

5. Educational Programs: Take part in the museum's educational programs and events, such as seminars, lectures, and guided tours, to deepen your knowledge and appreciation of the history and culture of ancient Egypt. Talk with informed tour leaders and specialists who can shed light on the significance of the museum's exhibits, the methods ancient artisans employed, and the most recent findings and investigations in the area of Egyptology.

The Luxor Museum invites tourists to take a trip through time and discover the treasures of ancient Egypt, serving as a beacon of knowledge and enlightenment. The museum offers an engrossing and immersive experience that will deepen your appreciation for the lasting legacy of one of the greatest civilizations in history, whether you're marveling at ancient art masterpieces, paying respect to the royal mummies, or exploring the mysteries of the pharaonic era. Come discover the mysteries of the Luxor Museum, where historical artifacts from ancient Egypt bring history to life.

- **Modern Art Galleries and Cultural Institutions**

Modern art galleries and cultural institutions are bright spots of creativity, innovation, and expression in Egypt's rich cultural environment. They provide artists with a dynamic platform to present their work and interact with global audiences. These organizations, which provide anything from interactive cultural events to exhibits of modern art, are essential in influencing the conversation about the arts and encouraging a greater appreciation of Egypt's rich cultural legacy. Here is a guide to helping you discover Egypt's modern art galleries and cultural institutions:

1. Contemporary Art exhibits: Take in the innovative exhibits showcasing the work of up-and-coming and established artists who are pushing the frontiers of expression and creativity to fully immerse yourself in the vibrant and diverse world of contemporary art. These galleries are located throughout Egypt's modern art districts. These exhibitions provide a window into the changing terrain of Egyptian art and culture, reflecting the social, political, and cultural currents of the modern world. These range from painting and sculpture to multimedia works and performance art.

2. Artist Residencies and Workshops: Modern art galleries and cultural organizations all across Egypt provide artist residencies and workshops that allow you to get hands-on experience with the creative process.

Take part in hands-on workshops conducted by regional and global artists, where you may pick up new skills, try out various media, and develop your creative vision with the help of knowledgeable mentors. These immersive events provide a singular chance to engage with the local art community and broaden your creative horizons, regardless of your level of expertise.

3. Cultural Events and Festivals: Throughout the year, modern art galleries and cultural organizations offer a calendar of events and festivals that honor Egypt's cultural scene's richness and vitality. These events promote cross-cultural communication and exchange while showcasing the abilities of Egyptian artists and performers, ranging from poetry readings and dance recitals to film screenings and music performances. Whether you're going to a live concert, book launch, or gallery opening, these cultural events provide a diverse range of experiences that honor Egypt's creative spirit.

4. Art Education and Outreach Programs: Through art education and outreach initiatives provided by contemporary art galleries and cultural institutions around Egypt, you may empower the future generation of artists and art fans. These activities, which range from artist lectures and lecture series to school field trips and community workshops, provide children, students, and adults alike priceless chances to interact with art, discover artistic traditions and methods, and consider the function of art in society. These programs support the advancement of creative quality and the enrichment of Egypt's cultural legacy by encouraging creativity, critical thinking, and cultural awareness.

5. Digital Platforms and Virtual Exhibits: Take advantage of the digital era by embracing contemporary art galleries and cultural organizations that provide audiences with the opportunity to view art from the comfort of their own homes through online platforms and virtual exhibits. These digital projects offer access to art and culture in fresh and inventive ways, bridging geographical divides and uniting audiences worldwide, whether you're perusing digital galleries, taking virtual tours, or taking part in online workshops and conversations.

Contemporary art galleries and cultural establishments serve as more than simply places to see art; they are thriving centers of innovation, creativity, and cross-cultural interchange that improve the quality of life for both people and communities. These organizations provide a multitude of possibilities to interact with art, make connections with people, and celebrate the variety of Egypt's cultural history, whether you're looking to explore contemporary art exhibits, take part in artist residencies, or attend cultural events and festivals. Come explore Egypt's dynamic artistic environment and the world of modern art and culture. You'll be amazed by the endless opportunities it presents.

8. Technology and Travel

- **Travel Apps and Online Resources for Exploring Egypt**

Traveling to Egypt has never been simpler in the modern era of technology, with a wealth of travel applications and online resources available to provide visitors with essential support, knowledge, and ease. These digital tools offer a smooth and fascinating travel experience, enabling you to make the most of your trip through the land of the pharaohs, from seeing ancient monuments to finding hidden jewels. This is your guide to the best travel apps and websites for learning about Egypt:

1. Navigation and Maps: Use navigation applications like Google Maps, Waze, and Maps. me to stay on track and easily traverse Egypt's busy streets and ancient monuments. These applications offer precise, real-time navigation, directions, and traffic updates to ensure a hassle-free trip—whether you're traveling through the narrow lanes of Cairo's historic district, over the wide Sahara Desert, or down the meandering Nile River.

2. Language and Translation: Use programs like Google Translate, Duolingo, and iTranslate to translate text and overcome language hurdles to connect with locals efficiently. These applications offer quick translation and language learning tools to help you manage discussions and encounters with confidence and ease, whether you're asking for directions from a bystander, haggling prices at a market, or placing an order at your favorite local restaurant.

3. Accommodation and Booking: Use applications like Booking.com, Airbnb, and Hotels.com to find the ideal spot to stay in Egypt. These applications provide a broad range of alternatives to fit any traveler's budget, inclination, and style, whether they are seeking a traditional Bedouin tent in the desert, a luxurious resort overlooking the Red Sea, or a quiet guesthouse nestled among Luxor's old alleyways.

4. Local Tours and Guides: Use GetYourGuide, Viator, and TourScanner, among other local tour booking apps, to find Egypt's off-the-beaten-path jewels and hidden treasures. These apps provide a range of guided tours and activities selected by local experts to improve your trip experience, whether you're taking a guided tour of the Giza pyramids, touring the Luxor temples with an Egyptologist, or sailing the Nile on a classic felucca.

5. Cultural and Historical Information: Use instructive and insightful applications like Egypt Travel Guide, Ancient Egypt, and Egyptology to fully immerse yourself in Egypt's rich history and culture. These apps offer insightful analyses, articles, and multimedia content to enhance your knowledge and appreciation of Egypt's rich cultural legacy, whether you're studying the pharaohs and pyramids, touring historic temples and tombs, or learning about the country's contemporary traditions and customs.

6. Travel Safety and Alerts: Use apps and alerts like Safeture, STEP (Smart Traveler Enrollment Program), and TravelSafe to be informed and travel securely in Egypt. Whether you're keeping track of health advisories, security warnings, or local safety advice, these apps offer invaluable data and tools to keep you informed and ready when traveling in Egypt.

It has never been easier, more convenient, or more rewarding to explore Egypt thanks to travel applications and internet tools. Whether you're exploring the streets of Cairo, making hotel reservations in Luxor, or learning about the customs and heritage of ancient Egypt, these technological tools enable you to get the most out of your trip and generate priceless memories along the way. So grab your preferred travel applications, save your favorite websites, and set out on a once-in-a-lifetime journey to the land of the pharaohs.

- **Tips for Using Technology While Traveling**

The digital era of today has made technology an essential travel companion, providing a plethora of tools and resources to improve every part of the trip. Tech can make traveling easier and offer priceless support along the road, from figuring out new streets to keeping in touch with family and friends back home. Here are some pointers for making efficient use of technology when traveling:

1. Research and Planning: Make use of technology to prepare and conduct research on your itinerary before leaving on your trip. To learn more about your destination—including its restaurants, hotels, sights, and customs—use travel blogs, forums, and websites. To ensure a seamless and stress-free vacation experience, make reservations for hotels, excursions, flights, and transportation in advance by using online booking sites.

2. Navigation and Maps: Use navigation applications and digital maps to stay on track and find your way around new areas. Use applications like Google Maps or Maps. me to get offline maps of your location so you can access instructions and sites of interest even when you're not online. Utilize GPS tracking to locate yourself precisely, locate neighboring sites of interest, and unearth undiscovered treasures off the usual route.

3. Language and Translation: Use language and translation tools to overcome communication gaps and interact with locals efficiently. To enhance your ability to navigate foreign language menus, read signs, and comprehend conversations, download offline dictionaries or translation software like Google Translate. To improve your relationships and demonstrate respect for the local way of life, learn some simple words and greetings in the language.

4. Travel Documentation: Store digital versions of your most important travel papers on your tablet or smartphone to keep them easily accessible and organized. Travel insurance, passports, visas, and other critical papers may all be scanned or photographed and safely stored in cloud storage or a password-protected app. This makes simple access possible when needed and guarantees that you have backup copies in case of loss or theft.

5. Safety and Security: Use technology to keep informed and organized when traveling, making safety and security a top priority. Use travel safety apps and official websites to investigate potential health and safety problems. Sign up for travel advisories and alerts via initiatives like STEP (Smart Traveler Enrollment Program) to get up-to-date information on crises and security issues in your location. For loved ones back home, use monitoring applications or share your itinerary with reliable contacts to keep in touch and ensure peace of mind.

6. Entertainment and Communication: Use entertainment and communication applications to keep yourself occupied and connected on lengthy drives or during downtime. Download movies, podcasts, or e-books to pass the time on planes or trains. No matter where you are in the globe, you can remain in touch with your loved ones and share your trip experiences by using video calls, social media, or messaging applications.

Travelers may improve their trips, expedite their experiences, and maximize every minute spent on the road by utilizing technology. Technology provides a multitude of tools and resources to assist and enhance the travel experience, from planning and navigation to communication and safety. So embrace the digital age, make use of the newest innovations, and set out on your next journey with comfort and confidence.

- **Internet and Connectivity Options in Egypt**

For many travelers to navigate, interact, and share their experiences in today's hyperconnected world, keeping online is imperative. A variety of internet and connection alternatives are available in Egypt to guarantee that you maintain connectivity during your trip. Here is a guide to Egypt's internet and connection options:

1. Mobile Data and SIM Cards: Using mobile data and getting a local SIM card is one of the easiest methods to remain connected in Egypt. Numerous significant mobile network operators, such as Etisalat, Vodafone, and Orange, are available in Egypt and provide prepaid SIM cards with different data bundles. SIM cards are readily available for purchase at kiosks located in shopping centers, airports, and mobile phone retailers around the nation. Once enabled, you may use your smartphone or other devices to access the internet by topping up your data plan as needed.

2. Wi-Fi Hotspots: In Egypt's main cities and popular tourist locations, Wi-Fi is extensively offered in hotels, eateries, cafés, and other establishments. While many lodging establishments provide free Wi-Fi to their visitors, some could charge a small price or demand that visitors buy food or beverages to use the internet. Public parks, libraries, and transit hubs all include Wi-Fi hotspots that provide travelers with on-the-go handy connectivity alternatives.

98

3. Internet Cafes: In Egypt, internet cafes are a practical choice if you need dependable internet connectivity for extended periods or if you need access to a computer. For a modest cost, these cafés provide high-speed internet access, printing, scanning, and other services. Internet cafés are a useful choice for tourists who need to catch up on work, interact with loved ones, or access online resources. They may be found in tourist destinations, business districts, and university campuses.

4. Hotel Connectivity: Wi-Fi and wired internet connectivity are provided to visitors by the majority of hotels and lodgings in Egypt. Check the hotel's facilities before making your reservation to find out if an internet connection is provided, and find out if there are any additional costs or limitations. While some hotels could charge a daily fee or only provide internet access in certain locations, others might offer free Wi-Fi in public areas or guest rooms.

5. Roaming and International Plans: Find out whether your mobile network carrier offers international roaming or travel packages if you would rather stick to your current plan while visiting Egypt. For a set daily or monthly charge, these programs can let you use your phone and data overseas with seamless connectivity—all without the need for a local SIM card. But keep in mind that overseas roaming costs can be high, so before you go, make sure you understand the terms and conditions of your plan.

6. Satellite Internet: If a visitor is going to be visiting more isolated or off-the-grid parts of Egypt, satellite internet can be their sole means of communication. You can access the internet almost anywhere, even in remote locations with limited or nonexistent traditional internet infrastructure, such as mountains, deserts, and rural regions, thanks to satellite internet providers' portable satellite dishes and modems. Remember that compared to typical choices, satellite internet services could be more expensive and slower, so make appropriate plans.

With so many internet and connectivity alternatives available, keeping connected in Egypt is now simpler than ever, whether you're seeing the ancient ruins of Luxor, taking a cruise down the Nile, or just lounging on the beaches of Sharm El Sheikh. There are several options to stay online and connected when traveling, ranging from internet cafés and hotel connectivity to mobile data and Wi-Fi hotspots. So as you discover the wonders of the land of the Pharaohs, load up your gadgets, keep your SIM card close at hand, and enjoy uninterrupted access.

Chapter 9. Beyond the Tourist Trail

- Off-the-Beaten-Path Destinations and Hidden Gems

Egypt is known for its famous pyramids, historic temples, and vibrant cities, but it also has a lot of off-the-beaten-path locations and undiscovered treasures that are just waiting to be explored. These lesser-known gems, which range from isolated islands in the Red Sea to lonely oases in the desert, provide a window into Egypt's varied topography, fascinating history, and lively culture. Here's how to discover Egypt's most well-kept secrets:

1. Siwa Oasis: Nestled in the center of the Western Desert, Siwa Oasis is a peaceful sanctuary renowned for its distinctive culture, historic ruins, and natural beauty. Discover this oasis surrounded by palm trees, where salt lakes and freshwater springs offer a cool respite from the scorching desert sun. Explore Siwa's rich history by visiting the Temple of the Oracle, where Alexander the Great is renowned for having asked the gods for guidance, and by meandering through the ancient town's winding lanes, where mud-brick homes and traditional marketplaces await you.

2. Ras Muhammad National Park: Located at the southernmost point of the Sinai Peninsula, Ras Muhammad National Park is a great place to get away from the throng and take in the natural beauty. Discover beautiful coral reefs, immaculate beaches, and glistening marine-life-filled waterways. Dive or snorkel among vibrant coral gardens, exotic fish, and occasionally even sea turtles or dolphins. Take a hike along the coastline paths, which provide stunning views of the Red Sea and beyond from their craggy cliffs and expansive panoramas.

3. Dendera Temple Complex: Head off the beaten route and see the Dendera Temple Complex, which is close to the Upper Egyptian town of Qena. This ancient temple complex, which is dedicated to the goddess Hathor, is nearly 2,000 years old and has beautiful paintings, an astronomical roof, and well-preserved reliefs. Admire the finely carved columns, evocative statues, and hallowed chambers as you discover this little-known treasure of Egyptian spirituality and architecture.

4. White Desert: Situated in the Farafra Depression in the Western Desert, the White Desert is a bizarre sight straight out of a dream. Discover a huge area of chalk-white rock formations that have been shaped into strange patterns and sculptures by the wind and sand. In this bizarre setting, where white rock contrasts sharply with azure skies, camp beneath the stars for an unforgettable and enthralling experience.

5. Aswan Nubian hamlet: Visit a typical Nubian hamlet close to Aswan to learn about the colorful customs and lively culture of the Nubian people. Travel to the settlement via traditional felucca boat, sailing down the Nile River past verdant palm trees and historic temples. Discover the labyrinthine alleyways, which are embellished with elaborate paintings, colorfully painted homes, and traditional handicrafts. Experience genuine Nubian food, converse with amiable residents and discover the rich legacy and history of this historic society.

6. Fayoum Oasis: Southwest of Cairo, the Fayoum Oasis is a secret haven of peace and scenic beauty. Discover the peaceful lakes, verdant fields, and the old archeological ruins that dot the oasis. Explore the ruins of the Greco-Roman city of Karanis, pay a visit to the Temple of Crocodile God Sobek at Kom Ombo, or just take time to rest and enjoy the breathtaking surroundings of this lesser-known jewel of Egypt's desert terrain.

Egypt offers an abundance of options for adventure, discovery, and cultural immersion in its off-the-beaten-path locations and hidden jewels, ranging from remote oasis and immaculate beaches to ancient monuments and strange landscapes. These undiscovered gems provide life-long experiences and memories, whether you're looking for seclusion in the desert, scuba diving in the Red Sea, or seeing historic sites off the beaten path. So gather your courage, go off the usual route, and set out on a quest to see Egypt's lesser-known attractions.

- **Community-Based Tourism Initiatives**

Community-based tourism programs have gained significant momentum in recent times, providing tourists with exceptional chances to interact with local people, endorse sustainable development, and partake in genuine cultural exchanges. These grassroots efforts enable communities, whether they are in rural villages or urban neighborhoods, to take control of local tourist resources, protect their cultural legacy, and enhance their economic opportunities. This is a guide to Egypt's community-based tourism initiatives:

1. Cultural Immersion Experiences: Through community-based tourism projects, visitors to Egypt may get a firsthand look at the vibrant local cultures and customs. Through engaging in customary cooking workshops, acquiring traditional goods from local artists, or attending cultural events and festivals, tourists may obtain firsthand knowledge of the beliefs, customs, and lifestyles of Egypt's different groups.

2. Homestays and Guesthouses: To experience true hospitality and help local tourist projects, stay with local families, or in guesthouses managed by the community. By giving guests the chance to interact with local hosts, share meals, and swap tales, these lodgings promote meaningful cross-cultural exchanges and help visitors make lifelong memories. Travelers immediately support sustainable tourism practices and the economic health of the town by lodging in locally owned facilities.

3. Ecotourism and Nature Conservation: By taking part in ecotourism events run by regional groups, you may take in Egypt's breathtaking natural splendor while also helping to fund conservation efforts. These programs provide visitors with the opportunity to discover Egypt's many ecosystems while learning about environmental conservation and sustainable resource management techniques. Activities range from guided walks in desert oases to birding expeditions in wetland environments.

4. Community-Led Tours and Experiences: Go off on guided tours with locals to find off-the-beaten-path sights and hidden gems. These trips provide special insights into the natural and cultural legacy of Egypt's communities, whether you choose to explore ancient districts, go to local markets, or learn about traditional agricultural methods. Travelers may directly support local guides and craftspeople while encouraging ethical tourism practices by supporting community-led projects.

5. Volunteering and Cultural Exchange Programs: Take advantage of the volunteer and cultural exchange opportunities that local tourist organizations arrange. Volunteers may make a difference while learning important lessons about the way of life and culture in the area by helping with community development projects, teaching English in rural schools, or taking part in conservation measures. These initiatives promote understanding, communication, and deep linkages between visiting groups and the host communities.

6. Sustainable Development and Empowerment: In Egypt, community-based tourism projects are motivated by the ideas of social inclusion, sustainable development, and community empowerment. These efforts serve to enhance livelihoods, decrease poverty, and develop resilience in vulnerable areas by supporting cultural preservation, reinvesting tourism profits into community projects, and incorporating local stakeholders in decision-making processes. Travelers may help with these initiatives and contribute to favorable social and environmental results by engaging in responsible tourism behaviors.

In Egypt, community-based tourism programs give visitors the chance to interact meaningfully and transformatively with local populations outside of the typical tourist route. Travelers may discover varied cultures and customs, feel the warmth of Egyptian hospitality, and support sustainable development initiatives that benefit locals and tourists alike by lending their support to grassroots initiatives. Travelers may thus make a difference while making priceless memories in the land of the Pharaohs, whether they want to engage in ecotourism activities, stay in a guesthouse operated by the community, or start a cultural exchange program.

- **Sustainable Travel Practices in Egypt**

It is our duty as tourists to reduce our environmental effects, help out the community where we are visiting, and protect the area's natural and cultural assets. Traveling sustainably is essential to preserving Egypt's famous sites, varied ecosystems, and energetic local populations for future generations. While taking in Egypt's beauty, tourists may contribute positively by embracing sustainable travel habits. This is your guide to eco-friendly travel methods in Egypt:

1. Respect Cultural Legacy: Before you visit, familiarize yourself with the customs, traditions, and etiquette of the area to show respect for Egypt's rich cultural legacy. Respect religious places, archeological sites, and historical monuments by abiding by the established standards, keeping your distance from flimsy buildings, and not engaging in disruptive activity that might jeopardize the integrity of the site or the surrounding community.

2. Encourage Local Communities: By encouraging locally owned companies, artists, and tour guides, you can strengthen the local economy and give communities more influence. Select lodging, dining establishments, and retail establishments that have an emphasis on fair labor practices, sustainability, and community involvement. Look for homestays, cultural exchanges, and community-based tourism programs that provide genuine experiences and immediate benefits to the local population.

3. Reduce Plastic trash: Use fewer single-use plastics and assist Egypt's efforts to cut down on plastic trash. Refill your reusable water bottle from huge containers supplied by lodging and dining establishments or from filtered water kiosks. Steer clear of plastic straws, bags, and cutlery wherever you can, and use environmentally friendly substitutes instead. Engage in beach clean-up events and lend your support to groups who are battling plastic pollution in Egypt's coastal regions.

4. Conserve Water and Energy: During your visit to Egypt, try to save water and energy by turning off lights and air conditioning when not in use, taking shorter showers, and reusing towels and sheets to cut down on washing. Select lodgings that provide an emphasis on renewable energy sources, such as solar or wind turbines, water conservation, and energy efficiency. Encourage programs that protect the environment and advance sustainable resource management in Egypt's natural areas.

5. Respect for Wildlife and Marine Life: When participating in outdoor activities like diving, snorkeling, and wildlife viewing, please respect Egypt's varied ecosystems and species according to local laws and rules. Do not feed, touch, or chase wild animals; instead, leave nesting birds, coral reefs, and marine life alone. Select ethical tour companies and guides who place a high value on protecting habitats, conserving species, and having moral relationships with animals.

6. Use Responsible Travel Photography: When taking pictures of individuals in public areas, especially, remember to respect their privacy and dignity to preserve the memories of your vacation to Egypt. Before shooting pictures of people, religious places, or cultural events, get permission. You should also be aware of local photography norms and sensitivities. Steer clear of being obtrusive or rude, and don't take advantage of weaker or underprivileged populations only to get a good picture.

To save Egypt's natural resources, maintain the country's cultural legacy, and promote the welfare of the local populace, sustainable travel practices are imperative. Travelers may experience Egypt's warmth and natural beauty while also having a beneficial influence by supporting sustainable projects and adopting responsible practices. Therefore, let's step carefully, leave a good impact, and make sure that Egypt continues to be a popular travel destination for future generations—whether we're diving in the Red Sea, touring ancient sites, or taking a Nile River cruise.

Conclusion

We have memories that will last a lifetime in our hearts and minds as we draw to a conclusion about our adventure through the legendary kingdom of Egypt. Egypt has enthralled us with its rich history, varied culture, and unending hospitality. From the timeless charm of the pyramids to the busy streets of Cairo, from the serene serenity of the Nile to the vivid colors of the souks, Egypt has it all.

We have marveled at the architectural achievements of historic societies, gasped at the sight of soaring examples of human ingenuity, and followed in the footsteps of kings and pharaohs over the sands of time on our journeys. We have experienced exploring maze-like passageways, sailing under the stars in feluccas, and relishing the tastes of Egyptian cuisine; all of these activities have deepened and expanded our knowledge of this amazing nation.

Beyond the well-known sites and prominent landmarks, Egypt has also shown itself to us in unexpected ways, such as via chats with kind strangers, periods of quiet meditation in remote oases, and experiences with local artists. We have seen the tenacity of underdog villages, the kindness of strangers who became friends, and the steadfast spirit of a country that has withstood the test of time.

Let us take with us the knowledge gained, the moments treasured, and the relationships formed as we say Egypt farewell. Recall the significance of conscientious travel, safeguarding cultural legacy, and assisting local communities in their endeavors to flourish. And wherever our travels may lead us, let us bring the spirit of Egypt—its resiliency, beauty, and wonder—with us.

Egypt is a voyage of wonder and discovery, a treasure trove of experiences ready to be shared, and a tapestry of stories just wanting to be told. It is more than simply a place to visit. So let's keep in mind as we flip the last page of this travel guide: Egypt, with its ageless charm and limitless secrets, will always call us back, urging us to explore, discover, and unearth the treasures that lie beyond the horizon. So let's remember that the adventure never really ends.

I hope your journey is full of inspiration, adventure, and magical experiences. And may Egypt always have a particular place in your heart because of its everlasting beauty and unending hospitality.

Safe travels, and Ma'a as-Salama (dieu) and Maa al-Salama (farewell) till we cross paths again on the banks of the Nile.

Steyne's \

A Jewish Journey

David H Stone

To my good friend Mike — you have been an inspiration on this journey. Warm wishes & Happy Birthday from David

This is a work of narrative non-fiction based largely on events that occurred in the course of my life. I have changed many (but not all) names and a few other sensitive details in order to maximise privacy.

Copyright © 2020 David H Stone
All rights reserved.
ISBN: 9798674792178

DEDICATION

For Harry, Sofia, Leo, Clara, Diego, Amelie and Lavi – and all who follow after them.

ACKNOWLEDGEMENT

I couldn't have completed this book without the wise and skilled editorial assistance of my daughter Natalie, whose eye for detail and emotional intelligence improved the finished product beyond recognition.

OVERVIEW

This is the life story of Daniel Steyne, a Scottish Jew who finds himself, from an early age, caught up in the maelstrom of the Arab-Israeli conflict.

Part 1

Daniel is whisked off to Jerusalem at the age of nine months by his idealistic parents who, after five years, abandon their struggle to survive in the reborn Jewish state. The family returns to Glasgow, Scotland where the young Daniel is horrified to discover a grey, brutally hostile society that drives him to near despair.

Part 2

Following a bumpy but ultimately successful trajectory through school and university, Daniel makes *Aliyah* (immigration) to Israel, this time with a wife and children in tow. After a gruelling five years, including military service that takes him into the madhouse that is Israel's First Lebanon War, the Steyne family return to Scotland and our hero tries to relegate Israel to the back burner. Henceforth, he strives to devote his energies to medical research, teaching and career building. Family history has repeated itself. Or so it seems.

Part 3

Over time, the political environment on the campus of Glasgow University becomes gradually transformed from hostility to Israel and Zionism into something much deadlier: barely disguised antisemitism. In alarm, Steyne resigns from his post and takes early retirement from academe to focus on what he now understands is his prime responsibility – to complete the circle of his life that had begun in Jerusalem in the early 1950s.

Part 4

Relocating to London to be closer to his children and grandchildren, Steyne seeks to reinvent himself as a writer, speaker and educator. He is determined to preserve his family's legacy and help ensure that the darkest chapter of Jewish history of the twentieth century is not repeated. That involves dedicating his remaining years to fighting for the future safety of his family, the community and the still-precarious Jewish State.

Article 1, Chapter 1 of United Nations Charter 1945

The Purposes of the United Nations are:

1. To maintain international peace and security, and to that end: to take effective collective measures for the prevention and removal of threats to the peace, and for the suppression of acts of aggression or other breaches of the peace, and to bring about by peaceful means, and in conformity with the principles of justice and international law, adjustment or settlement of international disputes or situations which might lead to a breach of the peace;

2. To develop friendly relations among nations based on respect for the principle of equal rights and self-determination of peoples, and to take other appropriate measures to strengthen universal peace;

3. To achieve international co-operation in solving international problems of an economic, social, cultural, or humanitarian character, and in promoting and encouraging respect for human rights and for fundamental freedoms for all without distinction as to race, sex, language, or religion; and

4. To be a centre for harmonizing the actions of nations in the attainment of these common ends.

Note: The UN was created after the horrors of World War Two and the Third Reich. It was intended to prevent such phenomena ever blighting humankind again. Not only has the UN failed to fulfil its lofty ideals, as described in the UN Charter, it has become a sick parody of itself – particularly in its relationship to the world's only Jewish state.

Prologue

Permit me to take you back, briefly, to a time not so long before ours, to the final two decades of the nineteenth century and the early years of the twentieth. The events of that era are crucial to the later unfolding of this story, not least because they set in train an unprecedented historical earthquake, the aftershocks of which are still reverberating today.

Helga and Edwin Steyne (rhymes with pine) were a handsome, intelligent, Scottish-Jewish couple who hailed from lower middle-class families of Lithuanian, Latvian, Polish and German origin. The Baltic component of the family had arrived in the mid-1880s by boat at Leith, the port of Edinburgh, where they had disembarked in the belief — according to unverifiable family legend — that they had arrived in the New World. Their reasons for undertaking what must have been an uncomfortable and expensive journey are lost in the mists of time but were likely to have been connected to the growing antisemitism in the Czarist empire in the late nineteenth century following the assassination of Alexander the Second in 1881.

After a brief sojourn in the Scottish capital, about which we know nothing, the impecunious immigrants crossed the central belt of Scotland to the more welcoming West coast where a tiny Jewish community had already been established, perhaps in the expectation of a forward journey to the United States. That didn't happen so they, along with many of their Yiddish speaking contemporaries, planted roots in Glasgow, the Second City of the Empire, and henceforth became enthusiastic and loyal Scots.

*

My mother, Helga (how she loathed that name), was a primary schoolteacher, and an extremely beautiful one at that, with high cheekbones, brown eyes and a good figure. She was born to Daniel and Tessa Esher in modest circumstances. Her elder sister, Beulah, was a striking redhead who married a dapper furniture salesman, Ralph Winston. The Eshers had settled in Glasgow's notorious

Gorbals, a slum-ridden magnet for new immigrants where most of Scotland's Jewish community set up home. They ran a moderately successful army surplus store that I visited many times as a child, though the only solid memories I've retained of it are mountains of heavy-duty green socks and a substantial collection of gleaming British military medals.

My maternal grandfather, Daniel Esher (after whom I was presumably named), was of Latvian origin and died shortly before I was born leaving his widow, Tessa, in charge of the business over which she ruled highly effectively, over several decades, with an iron rod. I used to observe her chain smoking while computing the day's takings at the huge cash register in the shop's office. It was an awesome sight. Everyone adhered to one overriding mantra in that place – *don't mess with Tess*. Apparently her marriage had not been an ecstatically happy one – Daniel had had a roving eye and sharp temper – but my mother spoke of him so rarely that I have no way of validating that judgement. One of the few reminiscences she did let slip was that, unlikely as it sounds, Daniel had played cards with the young Stan Laurel (in his pre-Hollywood days) at a Glasgow bridge club.

I know frustratingly little of my maternal great-grandparents other than their names – Jacob Fisher and Sarah Cohen.

Helga Esher was unusually gifted at both English literature and maths. In the early 1940s Helga had been shortlisted for the wartime code-breaking team at Bletchley Park; apparently her aspiring career there was snuffed out before it had started by her disapproving parents. Instead, she studied an arts degree at Glasgow University followed, after graduation, by a year of teacher training.

Helga's husband Edwin (whom everyone called Ed), my father, was the elder son of Emanuel (Manny) Lowe, originally Lowenstein, and Evie Mars, born Marzitsky (from Berlin, also of Polish origin). Manny's father (my father's grandfather and my paternal great-grandfather), Sholem Daniel Lowenstein, hailed from Poland, although some family accounts suggest he was born in Lithuania. (In those days there was much movement across borders to avoid pogroms and other hazards). Sholem Daniel was a rabbi and a strictly observant one at that. (I may also have been named after him). He will feature, albeit in a minor role, later in this tale. Here's his entry in a popular genealogical website:

Born in Wladyslavov, Poland on/about 1863 to Aaron Rubenstein and Reska

Bellinger. Sholem Hoppenstein married Sophia Wurttemberg and had 9 children. He passed away on 1944 in Glasgow, Scotland.

The website provides no further information on Aaron and Reska, my paternal great-grandparents. They presumably belonged to large families whose fate is lost in the fog of forgotten memories – and, in all likelihood, in the killing fields of Eastern Europe.

Manny (my paternal grandfather) had harboured ambitions to become a doctor but was compelled to abandon his studies prematurely to earn an income for the struggling family. He switched to a career in optics combined with pharmacy and plied his trade from a chemist shop in London Road, Bridgeton, a poverty-stricken district in the East End of Glasgow. He became a stalwart of the nominally orthodox Garnethill *shul* (synagogue) located in the more genteel west end of the city, close to where they lived. I well remember his silk top hat bobbing in the box in which sat the *parnes*, or president. Despite having been coached in Judaism by his strictly orthodox rabbinical father, Manny was a religious moderate.

Two of Manny's three children, Edwin (my father) and his younger sister Esther (who suffered a lifelong psychosis, probably schizophrenia, and died young), followed the path of traditional mainstream Judaism while his third, Astor, embraced a more rigorous form of the faith that included strict kashrut (observance of dietary laws) and *shabbat* (sabbath) observance. I liked my grandparents and saw a good deal of them. Grandma Evie was a diminutive, homely soul who was perpetually boiling kettles on the gas stove as a prelude to serving tea and biscuits. My grandfather, Manny, was a pleasant if remote figure who got along well with everyone. He must have been delighted when his elder son, Edwin, announced that he wanted to study medicine.

Ed went on to become an extremely distinguished clinician – initially a paediatrician and later a child psychiatrist – but he could just as easily have been a professional jazz pianist and was offered a such a post in cruise-ship dance band in 1939 (I never discovered which one). He met Helga while they were students at Glasgow University and both were instantly smitten. They married at the end of the war under the auspices of Garnethill *shul*, though I gather that the actual ceremony, conducted by the eccentric dog-collar-wearing minister Dr Cosgrave, took place in a Victorian pile called the Pollokshields Burgh halls on the south side of the city.

At that point (or shortly thereafter) I enter this story.

PART 1

1

I've always been sceptical of the notion that under hypnosis we can regress to a time that predates self-awareness, perhaps even to the day we gasped our first breath. Can the moment of our birth be recalled? The question is, of course, self-evidently absurd. While I struggle with the concept of intra-parturitional recollections, a surprising number of people claim to harbour them. As a child, I was convinced I was among this select minority. Even now, I am reluctant to dismiss the idea out of hand.

I cling to the unshakeable belief that I remember something, a flickering image, a transient vision: a distant pinpoint of light, brightening, tumescing slowly but inexorably into its pitch-black surroundings. This tiny spot enlarges into a perfectly delineated saucer of whiteness, its brilliance intensifying and so blinding that I can no longer look. I am now bathed in its blinding luminescence and am becoming aware of an accompanying sound, a low rumble of thunder perhaps. This is punctuated by something more disturbing, even violent. The *son-et-lumière* crescendo builds – and finally ends, melting into a cacophonic void.

I have recounted this episode rarely, knowing that it would be bound to attract ridicule and disbelief. Naturally its authenticity is questionable. I am the first to acknowledge that. Yet the memory (or perhaps a memory of a memory) is there, however distorted or reinterpreted, whatever it signifies, and I refuse to disown it.

Later, at around the age of three, I encountered a version of this hypothetical assault on my immature senses in another guise. This took the form of a recurrent nightmare. The dream started with a flashing bright light accompanied by the rhythmic thumping of what could have been a bass drum. The noise would grow in volume as the tempo accelerated, reaching an ear-shattering and terrifying climax. Its origins were never clear. The phenomenon seemed to coalesce around a distinct memory of the troubling impact of – ludicrous as it sounds – a faulty central heating system in our newly-built Jerusalem flat that we rented in the 1950s. (In recent years, I've formed an alternative hypothesis: that the frantic crescendo of bumps and thumps was actually the disturbing sound of amorous activity seeping through the paper-thin wall that divided my bedroom from the salon where my parents slept in a pull-down bed).

Whatever their underlying cause, the nightmares became increasingly troublesome. They were terrifying phenomena in themselves, but they also provoked an even more alarming psychosomatic sequel in the form of prolonged asthmatic attacks that accompanied me throughout my early childhood and, to my consternation, caused me to miss out on several fun-filled days of kindergarten in Jerusalem.

When I was around seven, and back in my native Scotland, my psychiatrist father arranged for a motherly psychotherapist colleague to interview me in his clinic in Oakfield Avenue on the Glasgow University campus. Her name was Dr Harris. I remember her thrusting a few Rorschach ink-blots in front of my face and demanding that I describe to her what I saw. I have no recollection of my answers, or whether these were discussed with me or my parents in detail.

Strangely – and of this singular fact I am almost certain – that consultation was beneficial and I never suffered the dreams again. But I am equally convinced that some residue of fear lingered for many years. That childish conflation of searing brightness against a menacing, pulsating backdrop would accompany me throughout my youth and well into maturity.

A lightbulb moment occurred to me later about this logically implausible duo: the endlessly competing forces of light and darkness, and their unbreakable interconnectedness in my mind, is simply a metaphor for my encounter with humanity in all its facets.

2

Many visitors to Jerusalem have described it as a special place, a luminescent city. It always glows. During the Mandate, the British decreed, in their colonial wisdom, that all construction must employ local Jerusalem limestone. *Jerusalem of Gold* is not just a popular song by Israeli composer Naomi Shemer.

My hyper-alert three-year old imagination was ignited by this extravagantly romantic cityscape. The buildings glowed an iridescent pink, yellow-white or tawny, and for most of the year the city beamed its gloriously variegated hues to the world. Exploring the alleyways around our apartment block, I loved to touch the alluring surfaces, my fingers caressing the dapples as if I were stroking an animal hide. The heat enveloped me like a good friend as I immersed myself in its calming embrace. There were sounds in the air too – birdsong, rumbles of thunder, traffic, sirens and other disturbances of which I understood little. I took it all in my stride. Somehow it made perfect sense. The city and my developing persona were inseparable and mutually nourishing.

*

How did this small, pale-skinned, Scottish child end up in the Holy Land? Perhaps a more pertinent question is this one: how did this small Jewish child end up in Scotland? Well, the answer to both is interconnected and complicated; I'll spare you the long version though I feel obliged to recount (briefly) the contextually relevant three millennia of Jewish history in the Levant.

In the year 1003 BCE, after conquering Jerusalem from the Jebusites (a Canaanite tribe), King David anointed the city as Israel's capital of the United Kingdom of Israel (in the north) and Judah, later known as Judea (in the south) whose residents were the ancestors of all today's Jews. David's tenth son and heir, Solomon, built a Temple in the heart of the city; that magnificent structure was destroyed twice, most recently in 70 CE by the Romans who expelled most of the surviving Jewish population. These refugees then endured a long and anguished journey across space and time. The Jewish Diaspora, as they became known, set off more-or-less simultaneously in multiple directions, the north-easterly one of which carved out the geographical trail that became synonymous with the great European branch of Jewry known as the Ashkenazim, while the southern migration headed for Spain where the other great branch, the Sephardim, was born.

Modern political Zionism, motivated by the abject failure of the Enlightenment to protect Jews from antisemitism and given powerful voice by the prophetic Theodor Herzl, inspired many Jews of the late nineteenth and early twentieth century to return to their homeland and re-establish full Jewish sovereignty.

Among those who undertook this journey (*Aliyah*) were my idealistic parents. They undoubtedly saw themselves as returning home, metaphorically and literally. In 1950, they took their first-born infant son with them.

*

1953. We were just a group of Israeli kids on a picnic, a favourite national pastime then as now. I was the youngest in the party and needed help to clamber across the rocky wastes adjoining our estate next to no man's land between Israel and Jordan. A teenage girl – I think her name was Jill – was the self-appointed leader of the pack. She kept a proprietorial eye on me, ensuring I got my share of roasted potato that our designated chefs had prepared over a bonfire. I loved everything about that jaunt: the adventure, the camaraderie, the attention, the food.

The hazy afternoon drifted into dusk and we were soon confronting that unique blackness that shrouds Jerusalem in the late autumn. We lost our bearings on the return hike and it felt like midnight before we arrived home. There we were greeted at the foot of our apartment building by a cluster of agitated parents who were loudly haranguing each other. Kidnappings and child murders were a frequent *fedayeen* (terrorist) tactic at the time so their fear was probably well-founded. I knew next to nothing of any of that though I sensed the adults' extreme relief mixed with anger at our alleged delinquency. No punishment was delivered or even implied, yet the episode was imprinted on my toddler's psyche as a peculiarly disturbing one.

3

Just before my third birthday, my sister arrived. By a strange quirk of memory, I recall my mother's white and red patterned dressing gown as she greeted my father and me at the gate of the Hadassah maternity hospital to introduce us. Julie, known to me at that point as Yael, was a new, baffling and complicating presence in my life. I was greatly enamoured by her tiny, fragile frame but less so, I suspect, by the extraordinary attention that she demanded round the clock from my mother. Helga, too, struggled with this immensely exhausting additional parenting demand and it took a toll on her mental health almost immediately.

*

In those days, I was a staunch believer in a supreme being. Why? Because I had a conversation with God. (You too would believe in Him – or rather Her – in such special circumstances, I promise). It happened one day as I was gazing across the dusty landscape from our second-floor balcony in the district of Katamon on the edge of the Rechavia neighbourhood. The exchange was brief and to the point. I will recount every word that passed between us exactly as I recall them.

"Daniel" said a disembodied voice, a woman's. I looked upwards and saw nothing.

"Daniel?" A question this time.

"I am here. Who is that?"

"Who do you think I am?" said The Voice. I looked up again. Nothing. I reflected briefly and took the plunge.

"Are you God?"

She paused for a moment longer than I would have wished.

"Do you think I am God?"

"Yes I think so," I replied, a little too softly.

"What did you say, Daniel?"

"I think you are God. Yes, you are. Why not?"

"If you say so," replied The Voice.

Later, I excitedly recounted this curious paranormal incident to my parents, as young children do. They smiled knowingly. This was the Holy City after all.

I have gone out of my way to revisit Jerusalem on innumerable occasions since those kindergarten years. It always feels like a homecoming. The sights and scents of the city have been imprinted on my memory with such clarity that they are like old friends when I rediscover them: the velvety texture of the brickwork, the multicoloured flora, the minty scent of hyssop, the honeyed fragrancy of acacia blossom, and the taste of damp dust in the winter.

Then there is something more, something elusive and nameless, a kind of mystical ectoplasm that envelopes the city, its inhabitants and even tourists. If you have been there, you'll know this to be true. Perhaps it is the sheer weight of history, the overpowering sense of the historic events that have taken place there, and threaten to do so again. That's a logical and rational but wholly inadequate explanation.

Jews, Arabs, Muslims, Christians, believers, atheists, agnostics – we are all attracted to Jerusalem and driven close to madness by her. Jerusalem Syndrome – if it exists – is described as a quasi-psychotic state that affects both residents and tourists and turns militant atheists into messianic prophets predicting the end of days. Something very odd regularly happens to visitors who are exposed to the peculiar atmosphere of the place. Some see inspiring visions; others hear angelic voices. In short, it causes normally sane people to lose their minds at least for a week or two, often changing lives for ever. Not a few commit horrendous, unprovoked acts of violence and end up permanently incarcerated in penal or psychiatric facilities. What is the cause of the disorder? No-one knows for sure. It is as if an intangible presence in the ether grips the soul. History, landscape, language, culture, faith, literature, architecture, politics – all of those, and more, are interwoven into an array of stimuli that simultaneously assail all five senses. Added to that is the emotional maelstrom of aspiration, joy, jealousy, reverence, fear, despair and hope. No wonder so many are continually drawn to the city's unparalleled beauty and moved to tears by its unfathomable essence.

4

Without a point of comparison, it is hard to assess the relative happiness or otherwise of one's childhood. My pre-school years in the Middle East were, as I recall them, blissful. I adored *gan chova* (compulsory kindergarten). The teachers (with whom we children were all on first name terms) were extraordinarily warm, patient and caring. Zipporah, my first non-parental authority figure, was a sweet, perpetually smiling lady with whom I instantly fell in love. I acquired a wide circle of three-year old friends who would visit me when I was housebound due to recurring attacks of asthma (an affliction that remained with me until I was ten). My closest friend and soulmate was a neighbour, Nechama Rothman, who is today an ENT surgeon in Tel Aviv. We were inseparable. *Nechamale* (as I called her) was my first serious girlfriend after my mother.

Those were long, untroubled and eventful days for me. I honestly don't recall a single disagreeable incident (apart perhaps from vaccination day) or any of the debilitating *Sturm und Drang* that was to characterise my later school years. The Jewish festivals were celebrated with gusto at the *gan* and even the routine *Shabatot* (Sabbaths), spent largely at home, were invariably pleasurable. (For readers who may be confused, these occasions were imbued with minimal religious content in the mainstream secular educational system into which the Jewish state had consciously incorporated all of these celebrations as part of the routine ethos of national life). Best of all were the special kindergarten trips. These treats were usually timed to coincide with national holidays.

One scented late spring morning, on Independence Day, we were led as a group to the local park where a police band was playing, resplendently arrayed atop a makeshift bandstand. I gazed longingly at the musicians decked out in their full-dress regalia, epaulettes glistening in the strong sunshine. I was immediately captivated by this theatrical sight, but that was the least of it; my ears were drawn irresistibly towards the mellow tones and glorious resonance of harmonising brass and woodwind. I studied with interest the more exotic instruments, especially to the bass drum and glockenspiel tucked in behind the clarinets and trumpets. This was my first encounter with live music and its clever trick of filling my head with wondrous, sensuous, pleasing sounds. So entranced was I by this audio-visual delight that they had to drag me away, physically, or I would be lingering in that park still.

As the *Pesach* (Passover) holiday approached, our class visited a local *matzah* (unleavened bread) factory. It was an intimidating place for visitors of any age yet they seemed well used to parties of children. On all sides, we were dwarfed by high metallic cliffs of stacking shelves, giant crates, and other noisily clanking equipment. At a certain point in the proceedings, I became unwittingly separated from my friends and wandered along an aisle on my own. Turning a corner, I found myself face-to-face with a fearsomely blazing open furnace, its bright glare stinging my face with a blast of radiant heat, and its huge gaping jaws daring me to approach the dancing yellow flames within. I stopped, held my ground, stared at the spectacle and waited. The roar of the fire was simultaneously terrifying and exhilarating. I stood there, paralysed with awe and wonder, for several seconds that felt like half a lifetime.

When I finally managed to edge away from the iron monster, my classmates were nowhere to be seen. I took a few ginger steps along a gloomy corridor before the realisation dawned that I was lost. Without panic, I started walking casually through the factory, as if I were merely taking my usual morning constitutional. After a minute or two, an aproned worker spotted me, took me by the hand and led me back to the pack who, to my irritation, had remained quite oblivious to my temporary disappearance.

5

Idyllic day merged into paradisal month. I am not being hyperbolic, that is how I remember those early years. The heady scents and brilliant colours of Jerusalem permeated every cell of my rapidly growing body. My circle of friends was steadily expanding and I seemed destined for a glorious, stimulating and fulfilling (if hazardous) childhood. It was not to be.

Inasmuch as I was aware of the nature of their relationship at all, I sensed a certain tension between my parents. My father was a largely mythical figure, increasingly consumed by a busy and exacting medical career at the prestigious Hadassah teaching hospital. He had been recruited as a paediatrician but was soon diverted to the fledgling specialty of child psychiatry that was grappling with a growing burden of childhood mental illness and psychological disturbance. He worked long and exhausting hours with minimal support. His main role, I gathered later, was fire-fighting – identifying and treating, as best he could, the most emotionally damaged and acutely endangered children – while simultaneously battling an inflexible and unsympathetic bureaucracy.

The country was attempting to absorb tens of thousands of traumatised children (including large numbers of orphans) of all ages who had arrived from the DP camps of Europe, many of them wretched remnants of the Holocaust. These were soon followed by another influx from Arab and North African countries that had turned viciously on their ancient Jewish communities in the wake of the establishment of Israel in 1948. (Palestinians never fail to remind us of their *Naqba*, when around 700,000 Arabs fled or were expelled from their homes during the first Arab-Israeli war in 1948. By contrast, the even greater Jewish *Naqba*, in which 850,000 Jews were ethnically cleansed from the region in spiteful revenge for Israel's creation, has been scandalously erased from history).

My mother, already struggling with an unforgiving confluence of Levantine culture, language, and environment, fell pregnant and, following the birth of my sister Julie, succumbed to what I now presume was a prolonged bout of post-natal depression. To my untutored eyes, she was in a frightening near-catatonic state, languishing for long periods in a state of unresponsive lethargy. This was punctuated by angry outbursts of frustration, some of which were directed at me. In retrospect, I realise that she must have been deeply miserable. All I knew at the time was that I had to tread on eggshells to avoid incurring maternal displeasure, fury or worse.

The wider environment was equally unpropitious. The nature of regional geopolitics was, of course, beyond me but I sensed the chronic adult anxiety arising from the ongoing security crisis. Jerusalem at that point was under unremitting threat from hostile Arabs who surrounded the city. Danger was perpetually in the air, with *fedayeen* snipers picking off random civilians, adults and children, at all hours of the day and night. A renewal of full-scale warfare between Israel and her neighbours was more of a probability than a possibility so the atmosphere was permanently strained.

Money for state-building was tight – prime minister David Ben Gurion regularly appropriated government-funded salaries for the defence budget – and fresh food was scarce or non-existent. The only way to get hold of fruit and vegetables was to smuggle it in from generous relatives who lived in nearby moshavim or kibbutzim where decent quality produce was still available. My parents later recounted how, on returning to the capital in their jalopy (a clapped-out Ford Prefect), they hid sacks of apples, oranges, pears and olives under my baby sister's carry-cot in the back seat to distract the brusque but soft-hearted policemen who might otherwise have launched a more exhaustive search of the vehicle.

Because our fragile nutritional status, as young children, was prioritised, our parents suffered severely in this era of *Tzenu* (austerity). (Jerusalem at that time was subjected to a real siege, in striking contrast to the *faux-siege* of Gaza so beloved of the anti-Israel propagandists half-a century later). My father contracted two serious diseases – infectious hepatitis and sandfly fever – either of which could have killed him. When my mother's eyesight was threatened by a malnutrition-induced corneal ulcer, they decided enough was enough: we would return to the UK. It all happened at lightning speed. Everything was sold, the keys of the flat were handed to neighbours and we were off. We travelled by sea (from Haifa to Marseilles) on the Israeli steamship *Negba*, then by propeller plane to London, and finally by train to Scotland, ending up in a cold, damp, grimy and alien city.

We might as well have arrived on another planet.

6

After the initial settling-in phase – an intrinsically exciting process for any small child – I quickly became disillusioned. At first, I was slightly confused, uneasy and restless. Before long, I grew to nurse a visceral hatred for the place that was allegedly my new home.

I just couldn't get my head around this place people called Glasgow in those first weeks. Once the Second City of the British Empire (a descriptor that must now be a source of embarrassment to its citizens in these "woke" times), its shipyards and factories had been bombed mercilessly during the blitz and had entered a post-war economic slump from which it never fully recovered. Like the rest of the UK in the fifties, Scotland was a colourless place where the populace had forgotten how to smile. Life was hard and the only way to get through it was to grit your teeth, pull your collar up and lower your head against the chill headwinds.

I was naturally unaware of the wider socio-economic context. All I could see was the monotonous suburban street, Carleton Drive in middle-class Giffnock, where we lived temporarily with my maternal grandmother, Tessa. My new home offered no redeeming features whatsoever. Everything about that baffling location – the grey sky, the incessant rain, the all-enveloping gloom, the smoking chimneys, the early winter frost – coalesced into an unbearable burden of disappointment that threatened to crush me. My bright Israeli balcony had been rudely exchanged for draughty bay windows through which I could see – well, almost nothing. Pressing my face against the cool panes, I would trace the slithering streaks of rainwater with my forefinger. My life had been turned upside down and I didn't appreciate the view.

This unwelcome upheaval cast a baleful psychological shadow over pretty well everything and provoked a pronounced change in my mood. I withdrew into myself, responding to adult entreaties only when absolutely necessary. I gradually filled the void left by my beloved Jerusalem with a substitute environment in the form of a rich private fantasy world. My parents must have noticed this transformation though presumably felt helpless to remedy it. Did they try? I have no way of knowing and it's too late to ask them.

I recoiled from virtually all forms of interaction, physical and verbal, with my fellow human beings. Well-meaning relatives must have been exasperated. I recall at least one grandparent – in effect a complete stranger to me at that time – complaining loudly about my introversion and even sullenness. *What a strange little boy – why does he never talk to me?* I suspect I was aware that the impact my growing antisocial behaviour was having on the cast of unattractive characters populating my new existence. In my book, they fully deserved the cold-shoulder I offered them.

While doting family members were just about tolerable, if tiresome, intruders into my universe, the other adults who sought to engage with me were, in general, beyond the pale. Their demeanour was, more often than not, cold and humourless. Stern expressions contorted horribly into ugly, inexplicable rage at a moment's notice, and bore down upon me with unmistakeable malice. In contrast to their Israeli counterparts, those drawn Scottish faces radiated minimal warmth, little affection, and no joy. What kind of a country was this where children were treated as troublesome creatures, barely a notch above vermin? These ill-tempered people regarded us juniors with contempt; we were wild and dangerous animals to be herded, ordered and bullied into submission. (I hold them responsible for my lifelong tendency to misanthropy).

I responded in kind to this mass sociopathy in authentic Israeli fashion, with lip-curling defiance, and then found myself blamed for graceless ingratitude. Life had, in the blink of an eye, become all but intolerable. I knew I would have to summon all my inner resources to survive though I never for a moment doubted that I would.

It transpired that my optimism was entirely misplaced. There was worse, much worse, to come.

PART 2

7

I am prepared to concede, reluctantly, that the weeks and months following my return to Scotland weren't all doom and gloom. I caused considerable amusement with my pidgin English: my grandmother Tessa never tired of recounting, with a chuckle, how I asked her, having consumed a banana, what to do with the skin – *Grandma, into de fire I should throw it?* – using a syntax that was a direct translation from the Hebrew.

I spent a few relatively contented weeks at Giffnock primary school – the calm before the storm – prior to our removal to Pollokshields, a middle-class suburb closer to the city centre that was to become my home for the next twelve years. My parents had purchased a vast sandstone villa in an elegant district known as "The Avenues" for next to nothing; in those days few people could contemplate the expense involved in maintaining and heating such a property. I was transferred to a local preparatory school, St Ronan's, that had a reputation among ambitious parents for propelling its pupils to stardom when the time came to apply for the prestigious Glasgow secondary schools. The first day at my new school should have been a joyful one. After all, I had just turned five. The reality was different.

Whatever the calendar said, this was still a pre-twentieth century world. The Glasgow buildings that had survived the war hadn't changed in decades. The streets of Pollokshields were gravel-surfaced until around 1955 – I remember the exciting smell and acrid taste of the newly laid hot tar fumes to this day. At night, the streets were illuminated by gas lamps; I watched the friendly gaslighter doing his evening rounds with his magic, yellow-tipped wand every dusk.

We had electricity but in many respects our home was an archetypal nineteenth century one. Clothes were washed in a large porcelain sink in the scullery and squeezed through a ringer before being suspended from the kitchen ceiling on a pulley. Water was heated via a wood-burning iron stove. Coal was delivered to a rear cellar (where, *in extremis*, I would hide despite the tell-tale dirt) by grime-covered men splendidly decked out in full-body leather aprons. Their bulging sacks were hauled off horse-drawn carts that rumbled along the relatively empty roads once a week. And then there were the trams – identical in appearance whether examined from front or rear. These bone-shaking contraptions ferried us to and from school. Ah, school. I'd rather not linger on that subject but I suppose I must. A little.

Picture the scene. It is mid-August 1954. Rows of restless, animated children, barely out of infancy, were excited to meet the headmistress, Mrs Kermit, a middle aged, lanky, beak-nosed but otherwise unremarkable looking woman except that she was peculiarly garbed in a long black cloak. Her initial demeanour was fairly relaxed, almost ostentatiously festive. Then, in a microsecond, the atmosphere changed.

We were ordered out of our seats and meticulously arrayed in a single straight line at the front of the classroom. Out of one of the deep pockets of her gown, the creature (for I am loath to dignify her with a human appellation) withdrew a long, thick black leather strap with two or possibly three fronds. I had never seen such an implement before and had absolutely no clue as to its purpose. Nor did my classmates. We were about to be enlightened.

With a leering smile (or perhaps a grimace), she instructed all of us to raise our extended hands, one nestled in the other, to chest height. We were bemused and even mildly amused. Was this some kind of game? As the swishing tawse crashed down on successive innocent palms, as the singeing pain throbbed and surged along our tender arms, as each child's face crumpled in surprise, disbelief and sobs, the full horror of our situation dawned. We were being beaten: heartlessly, sadistically, pointlessly. Why? The explanation came at the end of the brutal initiation ceremony.

"Children," grinned The Beast, baring a double set of crooked, yellowing teeth, "you have done nothing wrong, but now you know what the strap feels like. Do as you are told and you won't taste its sting again. Disobey me at any time during your schooling here and I will strap you many, many times until you beg for mercy. Is that understood? Now go to your seats."

What had just happened to us was completely beyond our comprehension. By now Mrs Kermit had been joined by another, taller woman whom we would learn to address as Mrs Forrest (the headmistress's sister). In one hand, she dangled a long yellow leather strap that she lovingly caressed with the fingertips of the other. At the sight of this second instrument of torture, we all visibly trembled. You could almost hear the collective chattering of milk teeth.

Through the blurred vale of tears, I remember studying the faces of our tormentors with a clinical intensity. The details are etched on my memory to this day. I suppose they both must have been aged around forty though they could have been younger. Both had cold, blue-grey eyes that were framed by crow's feet. Their expressions, while animated, radiated what I perceived to be a boundless capacity for cruelty. I was right.

Mrs K used her favourite thick black leather strap to "thrash" (her word) the children under her care regularly, on a near-daily basis. She was a real enthusiast for the task, throwing her whole body into each strike, while lifting one leg (the left, or contralateral one to the active arm) a few inches off the ground as the blow resounded. With each downward stroke, she emitted a high-pitched squeal of the type associated with certain contemporary women tennis players.

Mrs F was more restrained but had an equally deadly aim. Her favourite ploy was to hang her hateful prop across the top of the blackboard as an ominous reminder of the fate that awaited us should we step out of line. In its own terms, the strategy worked. The threat of chastisement hung permanently in the air, all day and every day, and we did everything in our power to avert the lash.

I must stress to the incredulous reader that this sort of scenario was considered a normal part of schooling in Scotland until the 1970s (or even later in some benighted corners), one of the many remnants of the Victorian era to which certain right-wing politicians seem to have an inexplicable attachment. It is hard to fathom nowadays but in the fifties and sixties it was perfectly acceptable, and in some quarters thought highly praiseworthy, for teachers and parents to beat small children to a pulp. Snitching wasn't an option. Nor was refusing to accept the punishment. I witnessed one boy protesting and being instantly expelled for his trouble. (For some reason, we all feared the shame of expulsion even more than the pain of the belt).

I do acknowledge, albeit grudgingly, that I received a decent education in the spaces between the spasms of violence that were rarely directed at me personally. I suppose I was strapped no more than a couple of times a year, usually receiving one or two strokes at a time. Others were far less fortunate. A handful of children were picked on disproportionately. The rest of us could do nothing to help them. But we were all – pupils and teachers alike – obliged to share their deliberately contrived, agonising humiliation.

8

The beatings were usually public affairs. This was a deliberate strategy designed to terrorise the entire school. When a hapless victim was summoned to the headmistress's office for punishment, all classroom doors were opened so that the loud whacks of leather on flesh could be clearly heard – along with the accompanying cries and sobs of the child – as they resonated throughout the building. Routine teaching ceased, as if on a pre-ordained command, and we silently counted the strokes; these usually ceased at six (the decreed upper limit in state-funded schools, a restriction from which the private sector was unaccountably exempted) but, on occasions of particularly heightened drama, ten, fifteen or even twenty were administered. (I used to lose count but someone always kept the precise score). When the appalling ritual ended, the doors were all closed in unison and a semblance of normality was restored throughout the school. Until the next time (usually within a day or two).

We children were being brainwashed, of course; we were forced to swallow an educational principle, presumably of Victorian or perhaps Medieval Christian origin, that stern discipline enhanced academic performance. A related lesson was that we should learn to display the British stiff upper lip in all circumstances, however trying. But those terrible sounds of a schoolmate's anguish left permanent scars, haunting us all for hours, days, decades. I was determined to escape, as best as I could, from the torment of this endless nightmare and instead to plumb the more comforting depths of my imagination in the hope of conjuring better times out of the inner ether. They came, eventually, but not before I had jumped – or been thrown – through some further fiery hoops.

On one searingly unforgettable occasion I was summoned to the dreaded Kermit study – for what reason I knew not – and was soon reduced to a petrified, cowering wretch. Nothing untoward happened but the fear of a vicious walloping at the hands of my nemesis was enough to immobilise me. I recall Mrs K asking me some inane questions, including "Are you feeling all right?" Receiving no reply, she telephoned my mother at home to tell her that I looked unwell and that she was sending me home.

Why didn't I alert my parents to the abuse? They must surely have known. I try not to judge them too harshly. Their concern for our welfare was unquestionably sincere enough. It just didn't extend to the disciplinary methods employed by our teachers since, in those not-so-far-off days, these were widely regarded as an unavoidable if regrettable part of growing up. In any case, I intuited that they might not have taken my side of the argument.

I often ask myself this question: how did I endure four long years in that pitiless institution? As a matter of necessity, I invented survival strategies through trial and error. I became highly creative and stumbled upon tactics that, when carefully executed, invariably proved effective. One was to perform well academically – that was easily achievable as I was a bright child, most of the learning was by rote and I had a decent memory. Another was to ingratiate myself with the class teachers, an altogether riskier path, but I soon learned that a combination of transient eye contact and enthusiastic, sycophantic head-nodding seemed to do the trick.

Away from the terrors of school, I lived for the moment. I sought companionship with my younger sister, Julie, with whom I got on reasonably well at that point, and with an antisocial black cat, a stray we named Susie, whom nobody else in the family could abide. But my best ruse of all was a psychological one.

By focusing all the mental energy I could summon, I discovered that I could stretch time at will so that evenings and weekends spent in the relative bliss of home edged ever closer to infinity. Radio (or *the wireless* as we called it in those pre-television days) played an indispensable role in filling my "off duty" hours (extended via the days when I could avoid school through illness, real or feigned) – *Housewives Choice Children's Favourites, Take It From Here, the Goon Show, Movie-Go-Round* and many more. I was determined to savour every precious second of freedom before the dreaded journey back to Strapland shattered my short-lived peace of mind. In the process, I constructed an inner universe that was filled with an endless array of heady, unfathomable delights comprising music, books, theatre and (unbelievably) the fairer sex.

9

Does an eight-year-old boy have a sex life? Sigmund Freud's answer was unequivocal. In the 1950s, so was Britain's – the very notion was regarded as ludicrous by the psychology establishment.

I'm with Freud. (I've always had a soft spot for the Austrian-Jewish psychoanalyst, probably because my father was trained in a Freudian school of psychotherapy. His theories have been partially or wholly discredited but the bearded sage did make the breakthrough discovery of the existence of the unconscious mind). My fantasies were not in any way overtly sexual but their erotic content was unmistakable. Cupid's arrow would strike unannounced anywhere, any time. I exulted in the thrill and despair of falling in love before ever hearing that phrase. Most of the objects of my affection inhabited the artefactual worlds of cinema (Debbie Reynolds sensually crooning *Tammy*) or theatre (Julia Lockwood playing a coquettish Wendy alongside her mother Margaret in *Peter Pan* at Glasgow's famous Theatre Royal – how Sigmund would have appreciated that one) or were simply conjured up from the hazy depths of precocious daydreams.

These fetching (though generally androgynous) heroines were not merely aesthetically satisfying hallucinations with which I adorned my prepubescent mind. To me, they were wholly real, passionate, living creatures to whom I could relate emotionally and perhaps quasi-sexually, and with whom I became utterly obsessed for protracted periods. I didn't just love my women; I was *in love* with them. I paid the usual price that comes with this territory: pain and joy were inextricably conjoined, like Siamese twins, not necessarily in equal measure.

I initiated absurdly expansive, elaborate virtual conversations with these goddesses and they never failed to respond to my advances with affection and kindness. Lying each night in bed in the dark, I would confess my devotion in carefully crafted soliloquies and would coax invented, yet somehow authentic, responses from the mouths of my illusory confidantes. I was an ardent but fickle lover. One day, the young woman of interest would be the athletic trapeze girl at the local circus, the next a buxom shop assistant with luminous green eyes.

I threw myself with unfettered abandon into these phantom

relationships and they fed my immature, voracious heart with emotional calories for years. Nevertheless, my boyish aspirations to consummation were repeatedly and infuriatingly frustrated. I soon discovered, with deep dismay, that those idealised women were invariably located just beyond my physical reach, a pattern that was to become a familiar if unwelcome feature of much of my subsequent adolescence. This is one of the great, experiential lessons of growing up: what is in essence unreal remains so, however hard one would wish otherwise. One by one, I loosened my amorous grip on these dear companions until none remained, bar a fading memory. I was leaving early childhood, with all its sorrows and wonders, behind.

*

The birth of a baby brother, Melvyn, provided a brief but, to my eye, less than noteworthy distraction from my inner preoccupations. One mewling and puking infant was much like another, as far as I could see, and I remained largely indifferent to the cooing and cawing soundtrack that accompanied his much-heralded arrival from the maternity ward. He, like my sister Julie, would nevertheless later become an important teenage co-conspirator as we three battled, with minimal success, to throw off what we all regarded, albeit for different reasons, as the unnecessarily restrictive shackles of family life.

*

My hyperactive imagination was reignited by one particularly bizarre and singularly terrifying episode. One evening, while our parents were entertaining friends, Julie and I encountered what I can only describe as a paranormal phenomenon – in short, we (nearly) met a ghost. That was the only conceivable explanation we could concoct for the night visitor who, having audibly ascended the staircase, padded around the well-lit landing outside our rooms while casting no shadow. Julie called out "Who's there?" and I strained to hear an answer. None came. We had heard gently creaking floorboards as The Thing approached and then again as It descended the staircase. No open doors or windows were identified, and neither of our parents' guests had, we were emphatically assured, left the living room even briefly.

I strongly suspect that Julie assumed that I had perpetrated the deception as a brotherly jape designed to frighten her but in fact I was terrified out of my mind. My retrospective theory is that an intruder entered the house (perhaps having noticed that the front door had been left inadvertently ajar) and, finding no jewellery, cash or anything else worth pilfering, abandoned his quest and fled. It was one of those tantalising childhood mysteries that will never be solved.

My relationship with Julie survived our ghostly ordeal but was probably affected by it. Like all siblings, we had our ups and downs but the former outweighed the latter. Still, I couldn't help pondering whether that strange and disturbing incident had for evermore undermined my younger sister's trust in me.

10

Secondary school – the prestigious Glasgow High School – offered new opportunities and freedoms, as well as a few unanticipated hazards. It was an all-male state-subsidised grammar school that set a high academic standard and I generally responded well to its teaching methods. After the unmitigated horror of St Ronan's, I felt I was embarking on a fresh start that was infinitely more appealing.

Nevertheless, corporal punishment was deployed regularly and with relish; on one occasion, I was hit so hard without the usual protective covering on my wrist that blood oozed from a ruptured vein just above the base of my palm. But the unbridled savagery of my previous school was generally absent. Occasional outbursts of casual sadism were a fact of life – we all knew which teachers to treat warily – but these became steadily rarer as I progressed through the school. I never witnessed Miss Barrie, my first primary school teacher, use the belt and I wanted to hug her for it. The only time she chided me was for performing badly in a history test: *I thought all Jewish boys were good at history*. This was my first experience of being stereotyped as a Jew, albeit rather benignly in this instance.

A year later, a charismatic primary six teacher, the dashing Mr Merryweather, entertained us with jaw-dropping stories of his exploits as a Second World War fighter pilot in the Royal Air Force. The most memorable of these was his account of how a careless trainee colleague was ripped in half, on the runway, by an aircraft's propeller. The more bloodthirsty the content, the more we lapped up his anecdotes of heroism and derring-do. He was a shrewd operator; he knew exactly how to command the attention and respect of his class of ten-year old boys.

Merryweather was so effective that our entire class leap-frogged over our contemporaries straight into secondary school. We were effectively used as guinea pigs in an educational experiment that gave us a year's advantage all the way through to sixth form. The school's forbidding headmaster, or Rector as he was known in the school's arcane vocabulary, was a cold fish called Douglas Letts who (implausibly) partnered my Grandma Tessa occasionally at her bridge club.

Overall, I'm fairly sure the High School was good for me. As well as performing more-or-less competently academically, I formed close and lasting friendships, embarked on life-changing violin lessons, and dabbled, with some success, in rowing (in preference to the aromatic and muddy discomforts of the rugby field). I was even awarded a special jersey denoting that I had won half-colours in sport. All of these achievements, each of which was modest, exerted a cumulatively positive effect on my self-esteem that had been fractured by the traumas of my early years. It also instilled in me a growing tough-mindedness that never overpowered my innate gentleness of spirit. I would later have to draw on that inner strength many more times in my life than I would have wished.

By now I was a fully acculturated Scot while never entirely renouncing the tiny pearl of inner identity as an Israeli, albeit a lapsed one. Some years later, Judaism – or rather Jewishness – became the ethno-cultural vehicle for bridging those parallel nationalities. Around ten per cent of the school populace was Jewish, whether by chance or quota, and we were solidly, if at times awkwardly, integrated into the mainstream. (I don't think there were any Catholic pupils, so religiously segregated was the educational system in Scotland at that time). Jewish prayers, held in a large examination hall, was a noisy and invariably shambolic affair where the sacred never stood much chance in its daily clash with the profane. The services were run by a select band of unbadged Jewish prefects to whose number I was eventually appointed in my senior years.

Racism was endemic in that school (as it was in broader Scottish and British society) and a handful of bullies roamed the playgrounds expressing their disdain for all minorities both verbally and physically. But their most lethal venom was reserved for Jews. I kept well clear of these thugs and was mostly untroubled by their occasional verbal swipes ("the one that Eichmann missed" being a favourite epithet). One of the more notorious practitioners of "Jew-baiting," as the Rector inelegantly characterised their violent pastime, rose to the rank of school captain. This sent a powerful symbolic message to the school community that disastrously undermined the official disavowals of religious and ethnic bigotry. Though I was oblivious to it at the time, those early encounters with both the positive and negative dimensions of my fragile Jewish identity forged within me a gritty defiance in the face of prejudice on which I would come to rely heavily many decades later.

11

Antisemitism on an altogether different scale played its part in moulding my growing Jewish self-awareness. In the early sixties, mass circulation paperbacks about the Holocaust began to be published. The sheer scale of the Nazi murder of Europe's Jews, and the calculated savagery with which it was carried out, emerged fully into public consciousness for the first time. This occurred, in part, as a result of the publicity generated by the trial in Jerusalem of the captured architect of the Final Solution, Adolf Eichmann.

One of my classmates had got hold of a paperback that was filled with photographs of the death camps taken by liberating troops in 1945. Today we are familiar with the images of mountains of corpses, skeletal survivors, mounds of shoes and hair, and all the other grisly manifestations of genocide that the Allies confronted when they entered Bergen Belsen, Auschwitz-Birkenau and the rest. For young teenagers, these scenes were peculiarly compelling.

Surprisingly, we Jewish kids were as ignorant of these mind-numbing obscenities as our gentile peers. Were we appalled? I hope so, but honesty requires me to reveal that my abiding memory is of a huddle of schoolboys purring with prurient fascination over the gory details, much as we did with the sex scenes in Lady Chatterley's Lover that had been published around the same time. I didn't consciously connect the horrors of the Holocaust with my own situation though I came to reflect on the issue in depth when I moved away from the safe confines of home and encountered evidence of ugly and potentially lethal antisemitism at almost every turn.

I must make mention of an area of aesthetics that was to have a seminal influence on my cultural education. At home, we had a succession of record players including a classic, bright red *Dansette* model that must have been unbelievably robust so often was it played. I was inseparably attached to some old shellac records (Frankie Lane's *Rose, Rose, I Love You* was one that I had played incessantly since my Israeli days) and somehow acquired an extensive collection of popular hits of the day including scratchy pressings of Perry Como's *Catch a Falling Star*, Doris Day's *Black Hills of Dakota*, Frank Sinatra's *Love and Marriage*, Charles Trenet's *La Mer*, and Jean Sablon's *Sur Le Pont D'Avignon* and *Je Tire Ma Révérence*.

I also explored the fabulous treasures contained in vinyl LPs of classical warhorses such as Sibelius's *Karelia Suite*, Bizet's *L'Arlésienne Suite*, Schubert's *Unfinished Symphony*, Mendelssohn's *violin concerto* and Dvorak's *New World Symphony*. Occasionally, more demanding works would come my way – Stravinsky's jazzy *Ebony Concerto* performed by the Woody Herman orchestra was one I latched on to with delight. These treats were mainly delivered by post from a mail order firm called the World Record Club to which my father had presciently signed me up.

Pop music, epitomised by the mop-headed *Beatles* and all their works, was the cultural phenomenon that defined a generation of rebellious teenagers in the early sixties. It certainly grabbed my attention, channelled largely by "pirate" radio stations such as Radio Caroline as they broadcast the ever-changing hit parade to millions of newly invented transistor radios, surreptitiously secreted under the pillows of young fans around the country.

Let's rewind to 1958. My first music master, Mr Mulligan, was an eccentric, avuncular figure with a penchant for madrigals and Crusader-era folk songs (*Sir Eglamore was a valiant knight, fa-la-lanky-down-dilly*). His forays into early English musical byways were met with little enthusiasm by his nine-year old charges. As conductor of the school's first orchestra, by contrast, he revealed a surprising talent for coaxing maximum musicality out of minimal resources.

Filing with my classmates one memorable morning into a packed assembly hall – it must have been a formal gathering in honour of Founders' Day or perhaps some religious festival – my young ears were assailed by the sounds of a full symphony orchestra for the first time. This was the school's senior orchestra in top form and it was a life-changing moment. I luxuriated in the ear-splitting waves of sound that may have subliminally resonated with the revelation at the Jerusalem bandstand five years earlier.

However debatable the quality of the playing, the youthful musicians' vigorous exposition of Mendelssohn's *Ruy Blas* overture was powerful enough to trigger within me a psychic earthquake the reverberations of which would continue throughout the succeeding decades. Around that time, I heard (and sometimes participated in) creditable school performances of several masterpieces including the famous march from Verdi's *Aida*, movements from the Bruch and Mendelssohn violin concertos (played to an excellent standard by soloists Donald Goskirk and Eric Levin respectively), Handel's *Zadok the Priest*, and Rossini's *La Danza*.

The assistant music head was a new arrival called James Belling. Initially I liked him as he was in the habit of playing, as we trooped into his classroom, a medley of Gershwin or Porter in the Art Tatum style of stride piano playing reminiscent of my father's. Superficially charming, Belling turned out to be capable of extreme cruelty. One day, at a class change-over, he took exception to the somewhat exuberant manner in which one of the boys (an amiable pal of mine called Donald – we shared the same birthday) swayed his hips in time with the rhythmic music emanating from the piano as we headed for our desks. Belling suddenly slammed down the piano lid and shouted, "You boy – get out here at once!" The startled Donald pointed at himself quizzically. "Yes you, cheeky scoundrel. I will not tolerate that sort of behaviour in my class." He opened a desk drawer and withdrew a medium sized leather belt. "What age are you, son?"

"Thirteen, sir" came the nervous reply.

"Right, in that case you're ready for Big Brother." Out came a second, much more fearsome instrument – in fact one of the largest and heaviest of its type that we'd ever seen. Then followed the usual preliminaries – hands carefully placed one on top of the other and a yellow duster arranged meticulously on top of the wrists to protect the underlying blood vessels. The unfortunate child sustained two powerful lashes, each administered with the full force of the teacher's upper body, in the process generating a deafening crash as the leather fronds struck human tissue. Donald's face collapsed into tearful defeat as he tottered unsteadily back to his seat.

That episode killed any atmosphere of jollity or enjoyment that we associated with music lessons, as well as Belling's credibility in my eyes henceforth. We maintained cordial relations, especially after I was appointed leader of the school orchestra that he conducted, but I was permanently wary of his dark side and I think he sensed my ambivalence. Many years later, I encountered him again at the home of my parents' friends, the Mansons. The thought struck me that he was having an affair with Isla Manson, a histrionic woman and ex-professional pianist, whom my father once described to me as "a moral criminal." If her husband knew, his attitude seemed one of amused indifference or possibly even approval.

12

Despite the atrocious behaviour of James Belling, music would continue to play a prominent role in my life. Both my parents were musical (though Helga had abandoned her piano playing after she married, apparently in deference to – or perhaps resentment at – her husband's more prodigious keyboard skills) and Ed was at his happiest when tinkling the ivories. He was an extremely gifted pianist, a natural jazz improviser with an uncanny feel for harmonic progression even when the piece was unfamiliar to him. (On several occasions, I appealed to him to explain to me the secret of this musical trickery, but he never would – or could). His playing was credited with inspiring my first cousin Eric Wolf to become a professional musician, and a highly successful one at that: the Alan Preston Project, the rock band Eric co-founded, had several big worldwide hits in the 1970s and 1980s.

I had inherited a modest degree of talent for instrumental playing though its initial manifestations were obscure. At school, I was offered tuition in any orchestral instrument of my choice but had always nursed an affinity for the violin and it seemed to me the only serious option. (I may have been primed by hearing my father play duos with a violinist colleague in Jerusalem when I was aged around three). Miss Moran, my first violin teacher, was a small, pear-shaped Irishwoman with an unconcealed loathing for small boys. Her methods included pointing the tip of a violin bow at various wayward parts of our anatomy and swinging the said implement with a resounding whack across our calves. I provoked her ire due, I think, to my supposed physical resemblance to the young Jascha Heifetz; to her consternation, there the comparison ended. Progress was (literally) painfully slow and my parents decided, to my eternal gratitude, to relieve Miss Moran of further responsibility for my musical education and soon found me a new teacher.

He was an elderly Italian who lived in an old, dank terrace house in Cecil Street in Glasgow's West End. Signor Salvatore Secchi had once been a child prodigy, becoming a famous virtuoso in his native Florence. This wasn't an invented fantasy – I saw the original dog-eared programmes complete with sepia photographs of the boy wonder holding his violin under his arm. He could trace his violinistic lineage back through many great musicians, from near-contemporary giants such as Heifetz (that name again), Flesch and Ysaÿe all the way to Viotti, Corelli and Vivaldi. Somehow Salvatore had ended up in Scotland with an English wife and several unruly children. By the time I became his student, he was a tiny, bespectacled, bald-headed figure of indeterminate (but indubitably advanced) age. A chain smoker to his dying day, he was wracked by chronic bronchitis and my lessons were invariably accompanied by bouts of convulsive coughing, each ending with the expulsion of a large globule of sputum directly into a silver cup that perched precariously at the edge of his desk.

His first task was to reset my technique fundamentally as everything Miss Moran had taught me he condemned as misguided. In effect, I started to learn to play the violin from scratch. He loved the fact that I was Jewish: "The Jewish people are the brainiest people in the world," he insisted. I was doubtful about the veracity of this dogmatic pronouncement but was happy enough to accept the compliment.

My response to this development was positive. I sensed I was privileged to be studying violin with a musician who had emerged from the European tradition of great violin playing. The contrast with the abominable Miss Moran was startling. He was always a gentleman, never raising his voice other than to shout a rasping *Bravo* and interspersed his wise technical advice with delightful anecdotes about the great violinists of the past and present, sprinkled with withering criticisms of several contemporary superstars (including, to my dismay, David Oistrakh, for whom he had little time).

For the first time, I was thoroughly enjoying the instrument and motivated to practise daily. I discovered that violin playing was more than merely pleasurable; it offered an outlet for dissipating my frequent bouts of mental restlessness – a state of mind that has blighted me for as long as I can remember – when other activities just didn't cut the mustard. Within a couple of years, I was honing my technique on Kreutzer and Wohlfahrt studies and was able to tackle some of the more accessible classics, including sonatas by Haydn, Mozart, Beethoven and Brahms, with recognisable if hardly electrifying effect. Had he lived just a few years longer, he might have hauled me up into the more rarefied and exciting heights of virtuosic violinism. Still, those hours spent in the Hillhead garret provided me with a foundation for a long and enjoyable amateur career in orchestras and chamber music groups. If I could meet maestro Secchi now, I would shake him by the hand and thank him profusely for giving me such a priceless gift.

13

My first close encounter with death, or rather the dying, was when Manny, my paternal grandfather, developed bladder cancer and was admitted to hospital. He was a gentle, kindly man who seemed to have a soft spot for me though for some reason we never grew especially close. I was taken along to visit him on the ward right at the end of his life. He knew I was there but by that stage he presented a truly pitiful sight — pale, cachectic and barely able to speak let alone converse.

Mortality was not a concept to which I had devoted much thought. When I first overhead adult discussions on the subject when I was about five, I adamantly refused to acknowledge let alone internalise its existence. Now there was no escaping its inevitability as my grandpa had died. He was sixty-eight. "That's not so terribly old," muttered my grieving father.

Around that time, with my approaching thirteenth birthday, I had to prepare for a seminal event in my Jewish life, my *Bar Mitzvah*. I accompanied, without much prompting, my father to the synagogue every Shabbat to hear him recite *Kaddish* (the Jewish prayer for the dead) during the traditional year of mourning. My grandmother, Evie, certainly approved of my transient religiosity: "Your grandpa would have been very proud of you." The logical absurdity of this use of the conditional tense was baffling but I was in position or mood to argue. She always showed an interest in my progress at school and encouraged me to keep practising the violin – she was quite a music buff. So I was somewhat taken aback when my father, towards the end of his life, revealed that she (unlike her husband) had a troubling tendency to resort to (unspecified) corporal punishment during his childhood.

I looked forward to my big day. In those days, a British *Bar Mitzvah* was (and probably still is) a formulaic, stilted affair. The main benefit for the child was the privilege of becoming the total centre of attention for a defined period in an otherwise indifferent or (more usually) antipathetic adult world. The snag was that you had to learn to read, or rather sing, a section of the *Torah* and the associated Prophetic passage in the synagogue. For several months before the event, I attended weekly preparatory classes at the home of the synagogue *chazan* (cantor), an amiable cleric called Reverend

Segal. That was a tiresome chore, only made tolerable by his wife's excellent sponge cake that she presented on a tea tray at the end of each lesson. At least I turned up for the lesson – in contrast to the mid-week *cheder* (religious education) classes held in draughty classrooms in Woodside Academy.

My parents used to drive me and my cousin Richard every Tuesday and Thursday to Shields Road subway station from where we were supposed to travel to the West End to assuage our spiritual hunger. We had other ideas, and other appetites. For months at a time, we evaded this fate by simply remaining on the train – it moved in perpetual circular motion – reading comics, consuming chocolate and drinking *Irn Bru* for a couple of hours. My parents were eventually alerted to our non-attendance by the indignant teacher, Dr Cosgrave, but I don't recall their being surprised or even angry. Maybe they secretly admired our ingenious ruse.

Within the pubescent Jewish sub-culture I inhabited, there was only one pressing *Bar Mitzvah* question – what presents will you get? In my case, the answer was a curious mixture of the sensible (ties, a fountain pen, a desk), the humdrum (book tokens, travelling clocks), the exotic (an ivory-handled shaving brush, a Lazy Susan), and the downright bizarre (a catalogue of all the Gilbert and Sullivan operettas staged by the *D'Oyly Carte* company). On the appointed *Shabbat*, I performed competently enough in the synagogue but remember little of the formal lunch after the service, except that I had to make a speech, largely written, I presume, by my parents. I do recall Dr Cosgrave cracking a lame joke that I enjoyed: "Ed and I are old friends. There's isn't anything we wouldn't do for each other – he wouldn't do anything for me, and I wouldn't do anything for him."

It's often said that this Jewish religious milestone is a critical developmental moment that determines the trajectory of the child towards spiritualism or secularism. My course was unstoppably set upon the latter. Like Ed, I was never hostile to religion (unlike Helga who was openly scornful of "all that mumbo jumbo" until her dying day) but I was incapable of internalising its basic supernatural premise. And so I was content to let it accompany me, like an entertaining but troublesome pet, throughout life while always holding it at a safe distance in a state of constant wariness.

*

About three months after my *Bar Mitzvah*, something terrifying and incomprehensible occurred. The world nearly came to an end. At least that's what we discovered long after the event.

The Cuban missile crisis hardly impinged at all on our lives in any direct sense at the time though we followed the news avidly as though we were watching a TV drama serial. For us Scots, the threat of nuclear war was especially discomfiting as the UK's Polaris nuclear missile base – a prime NATO target of the Soviet Union – was located at Faslane in the Firth of Clyde, about a half hour drive from our front door.

Had the worst happened, I shudder to contemplate the hand that fate would have dealt my generation. Even the most sober of commentators suggest that we, the hapless residents of the densely populated west central Scotland, would likely all have been incinerated in the initial exchanges that, we were promised, was predicated on the dubious strategy of MAD – Mutually Assured Destruction – that constituted the military orthodoxy of the day. Because you are reading this (if you are), you may assume that the apocalypse didn't happen but all of us, religious or not, who lived through the crisis carry with us to this day a small, silent prayer of gratitude for our survival.

14

As I was growing up, girls were an absolute no-go area for what felt like decades. Barring kindergarten and primary school, and my sister (who didn't really count), I had no interaction with them of any kind, other than within the recesses of my fantasy world. My first real close-up glimpse of the fairer sex as a teenager was at ballroom dancing classes (bizarrely endorsed by my all-boys' school) to which I signed up with alacrity. These were run by the Warren School of Dancing and held in the mirror-lined basement of Glasgow's famous art deco Albert ballroom almost next door to my school.

I have no memory of the fine detail but I can just about recall the unfamiliar and heady sense of sophistication – or perhaps it was just the whiff of cheap perfume – as a comely young woman rested her blonde locks against my shoulder. How I coped with even that rudimentary level of female proximity is beyond my understanding. Fourteen-year-old boys are, in general, staggeringly inept at social interaction with anyone; the idea of taking a young woman in their arms and guiding her around a dance floor would, in most cases, generate more than anxiety – it would cause an instant emotional meltdown.

We understood only too well that we were no exception to that rule. Yet somehow we overcame our excruciating, heart-stopping embarrassment and acquired, to the accompaniment of a crackly Victor Silvester EP, passable skills in the waltz and quickstep, along with the basic etiquette of adolescent romantic synergy. I suppose we were motivated by the intoxicating prospect of further glittering (if indefinable) prizes lying in wait for us at the end of this sequin-lined road. Our instructors suggested that we test out our prowess at special early-evening "teenage dances" that the ballroom regularly hosted, no doubt highly profitably, for their adventure-seeking students.

We didn't need a second invitation – trust me. Surprisingly, my normally puritanical parents didn't object. Perhaps the branding of the activity as *educational* – however dubious the moniker – was sufficient to mollify them. The Warren dances were undoubtedly rites of passage for my cohort, throwing open a hitherto locked door into an exciting future of girls, relationships and sex. These hormonally super-charged evenings soon acquired, within our teen subculture, a near-mythical reputation for unbridled hedonism and debauchery.

The reality was, naturally, far more prosaic. No alcohol was on sale but we didn't need any. I revelled in the permissive ethos of these occasions, when much clumsy touching, groping and Hollywood-style kissing were *de rigueur*. Much of this inept conjoining was quite public, often during set-pieces that were vaguely related to Scottish country dances such as the *Gay Gordons* and *The Dashing White Sergeant*.

The routine was always the same. Early in the evening, I would try to identify an appealing young lady and then seek to impose my presence on her for half an hour or so. Most declined (teaching me an important if unsettling lesson in itself) – but some obliged, perhaps due to a marginal advantage conferred by my considerable height for my age. I vividly recall the seductive smile of a brown-eyed redhead to whom I had taken a fancy, and I think the interest was mutual though nothing whatever came of the flirtation.

I wasn't quite sure what these unfamiliar feelings signified, except that at times they threatened to overwhelm me. The next day's schoolroom chatter focused exclusively on the events of the previous evening, and especially on who had "got off" with whom. Clearly this was a highly competitive topic. Tales of unbelievable conquest were recycled endlessly – not that my peer group was a reliable source of information. My impression was that even where genuine liaisons were established, they were fleeting in the extreme and I doubt whether they contributed anything of lasting value to our generation's emotional or sexual maturation.

I was reared in a familial atmosphere that may diplomatically be described as sheltered and it did me no favours whatsoever. As a consequence, I've probably been overcompensating ever since. I had always assumed that my two younger siblings fared better in this regard though our conversations in adulthood suggested otherwise; it transpired that their experience was only minimally more satisfactory. Nevertheless, I suspect that Elder Child Syndrome placed me in the front line of parental experimentation and, more often than not, outright blundering, in the accident-prone world of child rearing.

By around my mid-teens, I became consumed by what I can only describe as an obsessive fascination with the fairer sex. I would do anything to glimpse a female pouting lip or shapely calf even to the point of attending synagogue on otherwise dreary high festivals. All my efforts to gravitate closer to these mysteriously elusive beings, whether at social gatherings, summer camps or private parties, were summarily blocked by unyielding parental disapproval.

Why my parents were so obtusely resistant to the idea that their teenage son might harbour romantic aspirations I can only speculate. I hesitate to depict them as Victorian prudes as that would be unfair. Nevertheless, they had a blind spot about this. Though open displays of affection either for each other or for their children were beyond their capability, they were far from unfeeling and I was never deprived of their emotional warmth for long. But my growing sense of exasperation at the sheer paucity of opportunities for meeting girls made no impression on them; if they were aware of my frustration, they were loath to acknowledge it.

I comforted myself with the thought that nothing – not even enforced adolescent celibacy – lasts for ever and looked forward to the day when my desperate shyness would dissolve into a distant if painful memory.

15

R & R. My two closest childhood friends in Glasgow were both called Richard. One was my first cousin, Richard Winston, who was a near neighbour in Hamilton Avenue. The other was Richard Manson, the son of my parents' close friends, Irene and Jack (to whom I have introduced the reader previously). Irene had once been an accomplished concert pianist whose career had stalled due her inability to overcome crippling stage fright. She channelled her frustrated musical ambitions into her elder son who would become, she predicted, the world-renowned soloist that she might have been.

Richard M was indeed a wonderful cellist, a fine musician who had first studied with Joan Dickson, a competent if uninspiring Scottish teacher. After a few years, Dickson issued the usual proclamation about child prodigies: *I've taught him all I know*. So at the age of thirteen, Richard was spirited off to Paris to study at the Conservatoire under the great French maestro Paul Tortelier. I met this fabled character, with his distinctive shock of unruly white hair and piercing blue eyes, several times. He spoke English well but with an almost comically exaggerated French accent. I had absolutely no doubt that this larger-than-life figure would ensure a stellar career for Richard, who was, I gathered, one of his most promising pupils.

Unfortunately for my friend, he faced serious competition in that cello class of '62. It took the form of a shy and gawky English teenager who seemed to possess an exceptional if indefinable talent that was evident every time she grasped a cello between her knees. It transpired that Tortelier, whether by design or otherwise, focused his musical (and perhaps other) energies on this young woman with highly productive results. On one occasion when Tortelier was playing in London, Richard asked me if I'd like to meet the great man. We went backstage where the English starlet happened to be lingering too. There we were formally introduced – her name was Jacqueline Du Pre.

*

In passing, I should mention another great musical encounter that occurred in, I think, my early teens. My father took me to a concert at the Usher Hall during an Edinburgh Festival. The start attraction was the famous cellist Mstislav Rostropovich who was performing a new work by a contemporary Russian composer. The piece was the Shostakovich first cello concerto. I recall little about the music (though I came to know it well later) but the highlight of the evening occurred when the composer himself was beckoned by the conductor (Colin Davis?) onto the stage. A small, bespectacled, grey-haired man crept up onto the podium and shyly squinted up into the spotlights as though deeply puzzled as to why he was there. I didn't realise at the time that this unimpressive figure was one of the greatest composers of the twentieth century.

*

My nebulous recollection of my middle to late teens is that they were largely uneventful. I fulfilled my academic duties efficiently but felt stifled emotionally and under-appreciated in general. I sensed that I would become trapped in a permanent state of *ennui* unless I did something dramatic about it. But what? The violin offered one escape route and I practised a good deal if perhaps not quite enough. School work was uninspiring. I was mediocre at sport. My social life was severely restricted, with a few exceptions.

One of these was a trip that Richard M and I undertook to the Casals Festival in Prades in south west France. After a long and uncomfortable journey on a *couchette* train from Paris to Perpignan, during which we were attacked voraciously by bed bugs, we hired a taxi to the picturesque little village near the Spanish border. There we saw and heard some superstar musicians – pianist Wilhelm Kempff stands out in my memory – and it was a thrill to attend a live concert given by the legendary cellist Pablo Casals himself. But those pleasurable recollections are somewhat overshadowed by one desperately embarrassing one.

We were staying in a tiny, dirt-cheap *pension* and had eaten an unidentifiable dish (possibly cow's brain – the menu was in Catalan) just before heading off for the evening's concert in the local church. It was given by the *Wiener Solisten*, a youthful collection of (mainly) blond, blue-eyed, uber-Aryan string players. During the first movement of their opening piece, an early Mozart symphony, I was suddenly gripped by severe, colicky abdominal pain. I realised with horror that I was about to throw up and hurriedly pushed my way past the crowded row of irritated music lovers, treading on a dozen toes in the process. I didn't even make it to the door before physiology dictated events. Somehow I managed to direct my projectile vomit into a crypt just out of view of the main auditorium. This could not have been well received either by the audience or the church authorities as the foul stench must have quickly penetrated the entire hall. I didn't wait to evaluate their reaction. Within ten minutes I was back in the hotel room feeling distinctly the worse for wear.

Twenty minutes later, lying supine on my hotel bed in an attempt to recover some composure, the door opened gingerly and in staggered Richard. His clothes were covered in yellowish streaks. "Exactly the same," he announced. He had felt perfectly well until my dramatic exit but within minutes was overcome by the same impulse to empty his stomach contents as a matter of urgency. He was somewhat sketchy about the details, but I gathered that his neighbours in the audience, already deeply disgruntled by my distasteful interruption of their enjoyment, were even less forgiving when it happened a second time.

Richard never gave me a full account of his ordeal which is perhaps just as well. This episode occurred towards the end of our visit to the festival so we were spared the ignominy of having to show our faces at that concert venue again. I suspect that, had we done so, we would have been instantly lynched.

16

During my sixth and final year of secondary school, in early 1966, I attended a large international conference on child psychiatry in Edinburgh as a family delegate – a category that my father, as secretary general of the organisation, probably invented. It was a high-profile event (in the world of child psychiatry) with a star-studded line-up of famous speakers including John Bowlby and Serge Lebovici. My parents entertained some of these luminaries in their home. I was introduced to a few of them, including an American psychologist with film-star looks who was said to have been an advisor to President Kennedy.

Two incidents at the conference stand out in my memory. One was a long snog in a taxi with a teenage American girl with whom I had struck up a friendship. I hesitate to call it more than that. The daughter of a distinguished psychiatrist, she was a shy, sweet girl from Baton Rouge, a town I had never heard of. There was no real prospect of that relationship taking off though we corresponded dutifully for a few weeks. In her final letter, she congratulated me on England winning the soccer world cup; I don't suppose the teaching of British geography is a strong point of the Louisiana educational system. The other recollection related to an altogether more troubling occurrence.

On one of the many pre-conference social outings, I had been spouting hard-left political convictions to anyone who would listen. One did rather too intently. A blond German youth aged about twenty persuaded me to take a short boat trip with him into the Firth of Forth as he wanted to discuss *an important matter* with me out of earshot of bystanders. He turned out to be a recruiting agent for a radical student movement that was establishing an international network of supporters. Its purpose was to campaign to change the world and ultimately, having seized power, to overthrow the established order. (That sounded pretty reasonable to me as such organisations were ten-a-penny in the sixties. In my first year of medical school, I co-founded one myself that we called *The Red Cell*. At its zenith, it attracted all of three members). Then the conversation took a much darker turn. My new German friend hinted that the group might have to resort, *in extremis*, to violence. Would I, he asked, be able to cope with that?

Being a politically aware seventeen-year-old, I was flattered. I also sensed danger. Here we were virtually alone, bar the skipper, on a small boat in the middle of a choppy bay. I gave a non-committal answer and asked for time to have a think about it. He handed me a sheet of paper that listed named contacts across Europe, circling in red ink one that I should regard as the organisation's leader. Why he trusted me with this highly sensitive information I have no idea. Though I have no proof, I suspect that I was being sounded out as a potential recruit to an embryonic terrorist group such as the *Baader-Meinhof Gang* (later the Red Army Faction that killed dozens of civilians in the seventies). In my innocence, I was flattered to have been approached for such a weighty role but had the sense to realise that I should try to keep my distance from these people. Back on dry land, we shook hands and I never saw nor heard from him again.

*

September 1966. The day finally came when I was to leave the family home and head for the fleshpots of Edinburgh and its prestigious university. As my father loaded the boot of the car with my luggage, my mother wept – this was clearly as great a wrench for her as it was an adventure for me. I was about to embark on my medical career.

Was I pushed in that direction or did I jump? Originally, I had decided that I would be a molecular biologist. I had no real clue as to what that involved – the phrase rolled so beautifully off the tongue that it didn't seem to matter. I was sure that one fine day I would don a white coat and make ground-breaking discoveries that would benefit humanity. I had been converted to this view by a BBC television series presented by Nobel prize-winner Jacques Monod. His visual aids were crude – giant jigsaw pieces – but he was sufficiently compelling to persuade me that his exploration of the hidden world of enzymes and genes held the key to the future. I was completely enchanted.

That must have rung loud alarm bells with my parents as unsolicited career advice started pouring in from relatives and colleagues of Ed. The thrust of this was that I should be wary of seeking a science qualification without a medical one in tandem. In the end, it came down to future earning potential, a line of argument that struck me as mercenary and bourgeois. Reluctantly, I agreed on a compromise – to study medicine alongside an intercalated science degree. That plan was frustrated largely through my unanticipated ineptitude at science, and I found myself, almost by accident, on the road to becoming a doctor without fully understanding why. No matter, I told myself, I will have time to solve the puzzle further down the line. I was soon caught up in the hurly-burly of student life and pushed such weighty dilemmas to the back of my mind.

In contrast to the dour, staid nature of its self-satisfied host city, Edinburgh University in the mid-sixties was a lively place, awash with student rebelliousness that took the form of political radicalism, rallies against the Vietnam war, anti-Apartheid torchlight processions, "occupations" of university offices, and a proclivity to general mayhem. At freshers' week I encountered a handful of youthful and highly ambitious politicos – Malcolm Rifkind, Gordon Brown and George Foulkes among them – as well as a tiny student Jewish Society from which I pointedly distanced myself with a flourish of open disdain (of which more later).

An elderly contrarian journalist, Malcolm Muggeridge, had just been inexplicably elected Rector by the student body but he underwent some sort of religious transformation around that time, becoming a deeply moralistic Christian. Inevitably, he soon clashed with his student constituents, led by a charismatic Glaswegian, Steve Morrison (later the CEO of Granada Television) and his blonde bombshell girlfriend Anna Coote (who was destined to become a distinguished economist). These self-appointed student leaders contrived to generate publicity for themselves via press coverage of their antics that comprised, in Muggeridge's words, incessant demands for "pot and pills". Eventually, an exasperated MM resigned. Whether he stepped down or was pushed I never knew but his departure was widely hailed (or condemned) as a stunning victory for "student power."

17

I observed these campus shenanigans from a safe distance, as if I were viewing a slightly risqué cabaret through a keyhole. After the tedium of secondary school, the whole performance struck me as stupendously glamorous yet fundamentally unreal. There was a good reason for that perception. Medical students were somewhat detached, to my deep regret, from the rest of the student body. I was certainly disconnected from the maelstrom of socialising that was swirling around me.

Living in the university's newly-opened Pollock Halls of Residence was mind-boggling for many reasons – the freedom, the camaraderie, the friendships, and, above all, the sex. Or, more precisely, the lack of it. I was surrounded by countless beautiful women, all of whom, without exception, were out of reach. It was as if I were being subjected to a cruel anthropological experiment. I must have been young for my age – 17 going on 12 – and just couldn't absorb let alone participate, biologically or socially, in the endless parade of pairing, coupling and other unfathomable consequences of a mixed gender environment. I felt imprisoned by my own inadequacy. The (uncertain) knowledge that my time would eventually come was cold comfort.

Away from the Halls, the early stages of medical education offered a weird cocktail of stimulation and dreariness. The former involved jumping through a series jaw-dropping hoops – the introductory sessions in the human anatomy dissecting room, and our first clumsy attempts at performing venepuncture (on each other) being among the more memorable. The latter was just a fact of life; we had to study hard or we would be out on our ears. We were consequently determined to exploit our limited leisure time to the full. That usually included the deliberate misuse of alcohol (the marijuana and LSD culture having seemingly bypassed the medical school entirely).

Having *a good night out* was code for indulging in one of the infamous Edinburgh pub crawls. These involved knocking back a dozen or more pints of beer in the course of three or four hours in the numerous hostelries of The Royal Mile or Rose Street. Unsurprisingly, by the end of the evening we could barely walk and were more than once ejected physically from our final watering hole by an angry landlord. The following morning, we would try to recall the highlights of the previous evening's escapades but few would come to mind. The only remaining trace of our nocturnal frolicking was the faint aroma of vomit that permeated every inch of our cramped living quarters. With the aid of my retrospectoscope, I can't begin to comprehend the attraction of such a pursuit. We were chronically impecunious students yet the beer must have been cheap enough for us to squander our meagre resources so irresponsibly and, frankly, joylessly.

The first year of medical studies had nothing ostensibly to do with medicine at all, being dominated by the basic sciences of physics, chemistry and biology. The first two left me completely cold while the last was rescued by an eccentric and charismatic lecturer, Dr Aubrey Manning. He was a self-described "eco-nut" who somehow persuaded a succession of distinguished medical personalities (usually psychiatrists) to address our enormous first year biology class.

The ones I recall with especial awe were celebrity psychiatrist and professional troublemaker RD Laing, a high-flying psycho-anthropologist (and BBC Reith lecturer) called Morris Carstairs, and child psychoanalyst Anna Freud, daughter of the great Sigmund. These and other leading lights of the day, many of whom my father professed to know personally, shared fascinating anecdotes, reminiscences and nuggets of wisdom with their star-struck young audience.

All of this was great fun but the looming exam season scared me to the point where I confined my extra-curricular pursuits to a bit of sport (rowing), some music-making (in the university orchestra and the occasional string quartet) and intermittent dating. All three were conducted with only mild enthusiasm combined with a remarkably consistent degree of incompetence.

Nevertheless, life was generally interesting, challenging and full. I gave little thought to my future career or to anything else other than my immediate academic and social surroundings. I had plenty of time, I felt, to decide what I really want to do with my life. My top priority was to pass my exams, which I did, just. I was the epitome of the single-minded, boring medical student. Then in the summer of 1967, everything changed.

*

My teenage Jewish identity was fragile at best. There had been, as I have mentioned, a fanatically orthodox Polish-Lithuanian rabbi in my family history (my father's grandfather, Zvi Daniel) who was, by all accounts, an extremely gloomy, uncompromising and altogether unattractive presence in my Ed's early years. According to the family folklore, so mistrustful was he of anyone else's adherence to *kashrut* (the Jewish dietary laws) that he carried a boiled egg and a teaspoon with him at all times, producing these items out of his coat pocket just as the meal was being served. The only beverage he would consume when away from his own home was a glass of water.

During my childhood, we marked (though didn't strictly observe) the main Jewish holidays, attended the services of a vaguely liberal (if nominally orthodox) synagogue a few times a year, and my mother would occasionally light the ceremonial candles prior to *Kiddush* (blessings for the arrival of the Sabbath) over a poppyseed *challah* loaf and sweet wine on a Friday night. Though our home wasn't really kosher, there was never a trace of forbidden foodstuffs such as pork or shellfish in the larder.

There was, however, one curious aberration: on a family summer holiday in Cornwall, we children were *instructed* to eat bacon for breakfast so that – according to my father – we wouldn't hold superstitious views about the dietary laws. Later, that struck me as absurd for two reasons. First, most Jews who keep the dietary laws don't do so for superstitious reasons but rather out of either religious commitment or cultural tradition (or both). Second, the strange holiday ritual merely baffled rather than educated us. But that singular episode was atypical.

It would be misleading to suggest that we in the Steyne family were heading for total assimilation. Both my siblings displayed intense if transient enthusiasm for aspects of their heritage at various times. On one occasion, I recall Melvyn railing with fury against my parents for bringing non-kosher meat into the home; this spasm of religiosity was short-lived. Julie, though generally secular in outlook, was a regular attender at the synagogue choir, an activity about which she frequently reminisced affectionately as an adult.

Yet I detected a subtle ambivalence in our family's complex relationship to Judaism and even an unspoken awkwardness about all things Jewish. I've never understood why this happened. Both parents had participated in Jewish organisations and had joined *Habonim*, a left-wing Zionist youth movement, even making *Aliyah* (immigration) to Israel in 1950, just a couple of years after the rebirth of the Jewish state. Their return to Scotland as *yordim* (emigrants) may have been guilt-laden as there was, in those days, a considerable stigma attached to those Jews who left the beleaguered homeland.

Throughout my childhood, the crucial subject of Israel rarely surfaced around the family dining table, a phenomenon that later caused me retrospective puzzlement, irritation and even anger. I had no issue at all with their lukewarm attitude to Judaism as a religion, but Israel was another matter. Had my parents renounced their Zionist ideology altogether, and, if so, why? Were they protecting their children from the dangers of associating with what was, in some circles, a virtual pariah state, or were they shielding us from the very real risk of military conscription?

Whatever their motivation, they appeared to me to have reneged, to an extent at least, on issue of fundamental importance to our Jewish identity. That just didn't add up. It was a conundrum I would revisit periodically throughout my life and one that I would never fully solve.

18

None of these ethnicity-related issues exercised me greatly at the time. I was a committed universalist and determined to fulfil my moral responsibilities to humanity as a citizen of the world, unencumbered by religious, ethnic or national tribalism. Life was difficult enough without being hindered by voluntary handcuffs. I just couldn't see the purpose of any of it. Particularism of any stripe, it seemed to me, led to unnecessary division and that produced, in turn, endless conflict and suffering. Judaism, Jewishness and Zionism all struck me as particularism *par excellence.*

I wasn't in any way antisemitic (I insisted) and had spent relatively little time working out a coherent intellectual argument to justify my position. I just didn't get it. Being Jewish was an inescapable fact of life but it had brought me and my community nothing but trouble over many centuries. Did I really want to inflict that fate on my children, should I have any? The answer was clear – that would not be my path.

In any case, none of my university friends was Jewish, I was barely aware of the Jewish calendar, and the only remnant of my Judaism was my circumcised penis to which I retained a fond attachment; that was an essentially anatomical rather than ethno-religious fact of life. Being a non-Jewish Jew didn't feel dishonest or uncomfortable. It suited me well. I was hell-bent on assimilation and regarded those who disagreed with me as bone-headed reactionaries. Such is the arrogance – and innocence – of youth.

Then, out of a clear blue sky, the world was transformed for ever. And I had to follow suit.

In the spring of 1967, towards the end of my first year of studies, tension started to rise between Israel and Syria, not for the first time. There were regular dogfights between Israeli Mirage jets and Syrian MIGs in the vicinity of the Golan Heights. Simultaneously, President Nasser of Egypt embarked on a series of openly bellicose acts culminating in the expulsion of UN peacekeeping forces from Sinai and the amassing of large troop concentrations on the border with Israel. These provocations (partly cynically engineered by the Soviet Union) were accompanied by escalating rhetoric that promised to obliterate the despised "Zionist entity" once and for all and to push its (Jewish) inhabitants into the sea. Nasser reiterated this ambition shamelessly. "Our basic objective will be the destruction of Israel," he informed the world in May 1967; in response, the world yawned.

British pro-Arabists queued up to explain to the BBC and anyone else who would listen that these bloodcurdling threats were "mere Arab rhetoric" and not to be taken literally. (Hypocritically, these same experts were quick to denounce hyperbolic Israeli statements with which they disagreed; they invariably took these as indicative of the sinister nature of Zionism). Israel's leaders were understandably unconvinced by these emollient assurances. A mere thirty years earlier, similar projections of Hitler's openly proclaimed intentions had proved disastrously wrong. The Israelis were not about to permit that catastrophic mistake to be repeated.

I have no recollection of the precise moment that I became aware of these ominous political and military tremors in the Eastern Mediterranean, nor when I concluded that they should concern me personally. Eventually I had no choice. Media interest was growing in intensity in the few weeks prior to the start of the full-scale war on the sixth of June 1967. That cataclysmic event – the Six Day War – politicised me almost overnight.

Living away from home, I had acquired a group of around six friends, all non-Jews, who gingerly began to probe my attitude to the unfolding drama. What did I feel about it, did I have relatives there, will another Holocaust occur? I had no answers, other than a dismissive shrug of the shoulders that expressed my detachment from the crisis. I found their approach melodramatic and was puzzled by their attempts to entangle me, personally, in a remote foreign stramash with which I had no connection. As their annoying prodding intensified, I responded with ever more truculent outrage, expressing my absolute disdain for any suggestion that the incidental (accidental?) fact of my Jewish birth should determine either my political posture or emotional attitude towards the Jewish state.

To my astonishment, my coolness provoked their criticism and, ultimately, outrage. *How can you, a Jew, be so indifferent? Your country is being threatened with destruction and another Jewish disaster is looming. Wake up! Whether you like it or not, you're involved. Can't you see that?*

19

No, I saw nothing, heard nothing and (initially) said nothing, and deeply resented their full-frontal assault on my world view. "Give me a break, guys," I protested, bristling with righteous indignation. "Why should I be more agitated by Israel's fate than that of, say, Iceland? As a citizen of the world, I care for everyone regardless of race or creed or nationality. Don't I have a moral obligation to all human beings equally? Naturally I don't rejoice in the threat to Israel's existence but I can't do anything about it, any more than I can intervene in, say, Eastern Nigeria. In any case, who are you to tell me what to think and how to feel? In case you haven't noticed, you are not me. I have autonomy and I will exercise it as I see fit."

These near-daily rants appalled my friends. To their credit (and my eventual gratitude), they persisted. They accused me of being in denial, of burying my head in the sand, and of turning my back on my own people. They were right on all three counts. Yet for many weeks I fought them off as though my life depended on it. Gradually, their entreaties started to hit the target. Then they posed a question that proved unanswerable: *Won't you at least pay attention to the news broadcasts so that you are minimally informed about what is going on over there?*

I didn't take kindly to this continuous hectoring but I could hardly refuse to become better acquainted with current events. And I didn't want to lose my friends. So I capitulated, ungraciously. That miniscule concession would lead to a radical overturning of almost everything I had believed about the world (and indeed myself) up to that point. People can and do change.

One evening, I joined the huddle of students lolling in front of the black and white TV in the student common room just as Israel's newly appointed and, at that time, totally unknown Defence Minister, Moshe Dayan, was about to embark on his famous press conference in early June just before the outbreak of the war. Something about the occasion grabbed me by the throat and compelled my full attention. As the global media flapped and flashed around him, Dayan's handsome face and authoritative manner somehow calmed the jangling nerves of Israelis and Jewish communities around the world. He seemed to embody the iron resolve of his tiny beleaguered state to confront whatever challenges lay ahead.

A foreign journalist asked, "General Dayan, are you looking to the West to provide military assistance to Israel in its hour of need?"

Fixing his one-eyed gaze on the questioner – the black eye patch would become his trade-mark feature – he made this devastating statement (and I paraphrase): "We appreciate your concern, but we don't want a single American or British boy to die for Israel. We will defend ourselves."

In the pause that followed that remark, the enormity of Israel's predicament struck me like a thunderbolt. Demographically and militarily, the odds were heavily stacked against her. In the ensuing days, as the Israel Defence Forces called up the reserves on which they were almost entirely dependent, I became a voracious consumer of the news and followed every intricate move by all the parties to that short-lived conflagration.

The Egyptians then closed the Straits of Tiran to all Israeli shipping – an unambiguous *casus belli* in international law – and sent the UN peacekeeping forces in the Sinai packing, all the while amassing d huge numbers of troops on the border with Israel. These aggressive acts forced Israel to act. A full-scale shooting war was underway. When it became apparent, after a mere couple of days, that Israel had won the war with her pre-emptive strikes against the Arab air forces – first reported by the BBC's Michael Elkins in the face of deep scepticism from his employers – the relief among Israelis, Jews and Israel's numerous supporters across the world (ah, happy days!), was almost palpable. I shared in the euphoria with my student friends. Although my memory is patchy, I hope I found the words to thank them for my belated awakening from a fool's slumber.

President Nasser railed against the Americans who had, he falsely claimed, joined battle with the Israelis. The entire Arab world was shocked into a state of frozen, silent incredulity. When the truth dawned on them, the Arab League formulated their intransigent response to Israel's peace offer in the context of UN Security Council Resolution 242 – *no peace, no recognition, no negotiations*. That has remained the formal posture of large parts of the Arab and Islamic world to the present day, with tragic consequences.

20

I didn't quite realise that I had become a fully committed Zionist until several weeks deeper into that fateful summer of 1967. Israel had appealed for volunteers from the Jewish Diaspora to help them rebuild the country after a war that had been ruinously expensive despite its brevity. A few brave young souls from the British Jewish community had actually signed up for military duty though few (if any) saw action.

For the first time in my life to that point, and somewhat to my amazement, my parents floated the idea of my flying out there with my cousin, Richard W, to show solidarity with their various Israeli friends and relatives. Perhaps the war had politicised them too? By this point, I needed little persuasion. I suspected that Richard's parents were subjected to a degree of arm-twisting as they never (in my presence) displayed the remotest interest in Israel either before or after these tumultuous events.

Arrangements were quickly made and flights booked. By late June we were on our way. Squinting into the darkness through the window of a specially chartered *El Al* propeller plane, I reacted viscerally to the expanding panorama of twinkling lights of Tel Aviv below: the Jewish State that Herzl had envisaged was real (despite the best efforts of her many foes) and I was about to (re)enter it. As the aircraft banked into its final descent to Lod (subsequently renamed Ben Gurion) airport, the tannoys blared a popular Israeli song *Hevenu shalom aleichem* (*We have brought you peace*) to which all the young passengers added their patriotic voices. In the midst of that raucous chorus, I genuinely felt I was coming home. It was a spine-tingling moment of epiphany.

Although we knew that the war had been short and sharp, we understood little else about it. We half-expected to see a country devastated by conflict, her people in need of humanitarian aid, serious and widespread damage and disruption to infrastructure, and a shattered economy. Instead we found, superficially at least, normality and tranquillity at every turn. That was an illusion. In our encounters with Israeli relatives and friends, it soon became obvious that something very abnormal was happening. The citizenry was grateful and even surprised to be alive. Israelis couldn't stop talking about the war and their overwhelming relief at having evaded the ravenous, snapping jaws of the predatory monster that was Arab annihilationism. Cinemas were running solemn black-and-white documentaries – there was virtually no television in the country at that time – describing the timeline and notable milestones of a conflict that was already entering the history books as one of the greatest military victories of all time.

The whole populace contributed to the national effort – with two important exceptions: (most) Arabs, who were exempt from military service partly because of their ambivalence (and sometimes fierce hostility) to Zionism and partly to avoid a scenario in which brother might be fighting brother; and the *Charedim* or ultra-Orthodox Jews, who refused to recognise the state on religious grounds and were often avowedly pacifist to boot.

Unsurprisingly, the army was feted in an outpouring of public gratitude for having passed its greatest test since 1948. Israelis, young and old, were revelling in their great escape. Who could blame them? (As it turned out, many did precisely that; the world was used to Jews acting out their predetermined role as eternal passive victims and was uncomfortable about their donning the mantle of victory, so sympathy for the Jewish David facing down the Arab Goliath all but evaporated when the roles were reversed). The population was triumphant but not triumphalist. Israel was not, and would never become, a militaristic country. Her minuscule standing army has always depended on the periodic mass call-up of the reserves in times of crisis.

The Six Day War could easily have brought Israel's modern story to a shuddering, blood-drenched halt. For most Jews (and not a few gentiles), the young state's feat of survival against calamitous odds was a near miracle. For the Arab world, however, the outcome was both inexplicable and unforgiveable. They and their allies vowed to reverse it and, with few exceptions, have pursued their aspiration tirelessly ever since.

21

Our group of volunteers was billeted to kibbutz Kfar Blum in the north of the Galilee region where my father's cousin Hattie and her husband Chuck had made their home since the mid-1940s. Hattie had been captured and interned in Cyprus by the British (who at the time held the League of Nations Mandate for Palestine) for the "crime" of attempting to get to the Jewish National Home in 1947. There she met Chuck, who had joined the *Haganah* (the pre-state Jewish army), shortly thereafter. Although Chuck was born in Brooklyn, his family were originally Jerusalemites who had emigrated to America in the late nineteenth century. His *aliyah* was a literal homecoming.

When we first arrived on the kibbutz, our jaws dropped. It was located in a ravishingly picturesque and peaceful spot located close to the Lebanese border and adjacent to the Golan heights from where a Syrian invasion force had been so recently repulsed. The verdant tranquillity of the scene was deceptive; kibbutz life, especially in those days, was harsh and demanding, physically and mentally. Our role as volunteers was straightforward. We were unpaid agricultural labourers, housed in basic wooden huts and fed and watered in the communal dining room along with the kibbutzniks who, for the most part, found our presence there a baffling, unnecessary and often irksome distraction.

We picked fruit (mainly Jonathan apples) for six solid weeks that summer under the tetchy supervision of the orchard manager. This was a challenging experience for us city kids who had rarely undertaken manual labour, let alone wielded a scythe or climbed a high ladder. *Reveille* was at 4.30 am and, after gulping down a mouthful of lukewarm, black, over-sweet tea and a bowl of watery porridge, we were driven in near darkness on tractors out to the orchards. There we laboured for eight long, sweat-drenched hours with a snatched 45-minute break for breakfast. That was the best meal of the day, comprising fruit juices, cheeses, yoghurts, hummus, boiled eggs, freshly baked *pitta* and plentiful fruit and vegetables, but the relentless pressure of the clock denied us the pleasure of properly savouring these gastronomic glories.

In the early afternoons, we fraternised with other volunteers at the poolside and tried to seduce the strikingly attractive local girls who casually (and intentionally) drifted into our sightlines, all the while maintaining a kind of amused and typically *Sabra* (native Israeli) *sang froid*. The more these dusky beauties ignored us, the more we desired them. Sexual mores were known to be joyously lax throughout the kibbutz movement and we were confident that we would soon enjoy a taste of heaven. We were wrong.

Romantic disappointment didn't dent my enthusiasm. I was completely hooked on the kibbutz lifestyle and ethos. This looked to me like authentic socialism – or even communism – in action. All those student demonstrations in Edinburgh amounted to puerile play acting. Here I was living and breathing the real thing. This was the practical realisation of the egalitarian utopia to which we aspired. (That pronoun was the royal variety – for my cousin Richard, sadly, the experience verged on purgatory and we parted company later that summer to embark on divergent life trajectories).

Every mid-afternoon, Richard and I made our way to Hattie's tiny hut where she served English tea and delicious home-baked cake (most of which we disposed of within ten minutes flat) while Chuck, puffing on a clay pipe, recounted colourful stories about his childhood in Brooklyn and his adventures in Israel with Hattie, the love of his life. (Those same stories entertained our children when we visited the kibbutz several times during our sojourn in Israel in the 1980s). I admired Chuck and Hattie hugely. Their commitment to the cause was absolute, sincere and humane. In my eyes, they were much more than amiable relatives but heroic Zionist pioneers.

Later, much later, I was to discover that the kibbutz-centred Labour Zionism of which I was such an ardent follower was heartily detested by millions of so-called *Mizrachi* (Eastern) Jews. These Israelis came from a very different tradition from that of the European *Ashkenazi* culture. They had lived for centuries – in some cases millennia – in the Middle East and North Africa and were deeply antipathetic to an Arab world that had spewed them out in the spasm of antisemitic fury that convulsed the region following Israel's creation. This growing (and largely *Sephardic*) Jewish community viewed, justifiably or not, the state's founding fathers and everything they stood for as elitist, exclusivist and even racist. Ben Gurion's militantly secular socialism held minimal appeal for these traditionally minded Arabic or Ladino speaking Israelis who felt marginalised politically, disadvantaged socio-economically, and alienated culturally.

Menachem Begin, despite his own European *Ashkenazi* origins, brilliantly exploited this undercurrent of ethnic resentment in the 1977 general election when he mobilised the *Mizrachi* masses to turf out of power the establishment left-wingers who, in their youth, had struggled so hard and sacrificed so much to create, defend and develop the state. Begin's revolution exposed the cracks in Israeli society that had been papered over for far too long. Its political and social consequences were immediate and profound, and they continue to reverberate, for better or worse, in the country and around the region to this day.

22

After our stint on the kibbutz, we spent some days in tourist mode, and that gave us the opportunity to explore the ancient alleyways of Akko (Acre) and Jerusalem, gape at the near-naked frolickers on Tel Aviv beach, and contemplate man's inhumanity to man in the unbearably poignant Holocaust memorial known as Yad Vashem.

*

There is widespread misunderstanding about the important role of the Holocaust (*Shoah*) in Israeli national life. It is always there as a reminder, a kind of permanent black cloud on the horizon, a symbol of the disaster that befell the Jewish people in living memory. Contrary to the claim of antiZionist propagandists, however, that mass tragedy didn't cause the State of Israel; the tragedy was caused by the absence of the State of Israel, or at least a guaranteed safe haven for the victims of lethal antisemitism.

Had the British government actually fulfilled its central legal obligations under the Palestine Mandate – obligations that included the promotion of Jewish immigration to the territory and Jewish settlement of the land – millions of lives might have been saved. The British, by appeasing Arab opinion, effectively colluded with Hitler in his Final Solution. No subsequent British government has acknowledged let alone apologised for that betrayal.

The *Shoah* finally ended the long-running debated within world Jewry about the desirability if a Jewish state – and should have done across the non-Jewish world as well. The fact that it did so only patchily represents a failure of the collective imagination of the international community. That is the reason foreign leaders are routinely taken to Yad Vashem, not to *play the Holocaust card* (a despicable phrase that rolls off the tongues of antisemites and their fellow-travellers), but to demonstrate the necessity of translating the otherwise vacuous mantra *Never Again* into a practical means of fulfilling that aspiration by ensuring the continued, secure existence of Israel.

*

Israel is a small but varied country; in that long hot summer of 1967, I wanted to discover every inch of the place, from Dan to Beer Sheva. Hearing spoken Hebrew and seeing road signs in the revitalised ancient language that most Diaspora Jews associated with synagogue and *cheder* (Sunday school) was thrilling beyond words. And everywhere were soldiers – on buses, roadsides, supermarkets, cinemas – those exhausted heroes and heroines who had literally saved the country from oblivion just a few weeks earlier. These were not the sort of Jews I had encountered in Glasgow and I dreamt of joining their ranks one day.

Just after the war, Israelis poured into the Old City of Jerusalem from where they had been violently expelled in 1948 and subsequently barred by Jordan, despite an armistice agreement that had guaranteed them access to Jewish holy places and Mount Scopus (where the Hebrew University and Hadassah hospital were originally located). Yonah Rosen, a social work friend of my father's, and a fluent Arabic speaker, drove us into Ramallah on the West Bank (as the Jordanians had renamed Judea and Samaria after they had annexed the territory in 1948) where we ate a sumptuous dinner in a charming open-air restaurant. I don't recall any hostility towards us on the part of the staff or the local residents though they must have been reeling from the shock of recent events.

Shortly before returning to the UK, we were hosted by kindly relatives – the Sher family – in Kfar Mordecai, a *moshav* (collective farm) in the centre of the country. A notch or two lower, in terms of ideological purity, on the socialist ladder than a kibbutz, the *moshav* functioned as an agricultural community with a strong collectivist ethos. Zvi Sher spent many hours educating us on the byzantine administrative structure of agriculture in Israel and the fierce political debates that raged around him as he struggled, with limited success, to eke out a living from his modest patch of arable land.

Our interest in the technical minutiae of citrus production rapidly became distracted by a far more intriguing matter – my two teenage cousins, Sara and Einat. They were both dark-eyed, olive skinned, long limbed, and beguilingly beautiful creatures. (I was always more fascinated by Sara, which was just as well; her sister later got into serious hot water with the authorities for her extremist political activities – she was rumoured to have joined the Palestine

Liberation Organisation in the days when it was a proscribed terrorist organisation in Israel). The four of us became inseparable, sharing confidences, anecdotes, jokes, songs and the latest Beatles album, *Sergeant Pepper's Lonely Hearts Club Band*. The girls were playful, flirtatious, and sexually alluring while remaining firmly unattainable under the watchful supervision of their parents.

One evening, Richard summoned up the courage to make a pass at Sara, to my chagrin, though I'm (almost) certain he wasn't rewarded for his efforts. I plotted my revenge, conceiving ever more elaborate plans to express my feelings to one or (preferably) both of the girls. These schemes never materialised. Still, despite its chaste nature, this dual infatuation was almost my first intimate non-familial relationship, albeit a deeply unfulfilled one.

23

The importance of that attachment transcended a passing phase of adolescent tomfoolery. My Israeli cousins were my first close female friends of my adult life and so fulfilled the function of essential emotional stepping stones to future relationships. But their role was also quasi-political. They had been reared in a culture that had, it seemed clear to me, moulded their personalities into something wondrous, an attitude to everyone that was refreshingly open, direct and uninhibited. The contrast between their no-holds-barred Israeli *chutzpah* – an untranslatable noun that approximates to "unabashed daring" – and our repressed British diffidence was stark and I, for one, rejoiced in it.

I confess that I probably idealised (and idolised) the country and her inhabitants in my youth, and I still remain a tremendous admirer of their many accomplishments in my maturity. Having been plucked out of my beloved near-native Jerusalem at a tender age, I reflected, with a rueful and slightly envious melancholy, that I had much more in common with my Israeli contemporaries than with my Scottish family and friends.

I had narrowly missed out on their extraordinary if incontestably dangerous journey. Had I been master of my own destiny, I should have accompanied them every step of the way. Instead, I had inhabited a parallel universe that seemed dull, colourless and meaningless in comparison. They had thrown off the shackles of centuries long Jewish passivity and were charging ahead into a bright and pro-actively created future while I was stumbling along ineffectually in my dreary Scottish backwater. Well, what was I going to do about it? I responded with a nebulous and unsatisfactory answer: I would somehow have to lengthen my stride and catch them up.

That first return visit to Israel in the summer of 1967 set me on a course that was to dominate my adult life. I would have to make *Aliyah* (for a second time, technically) as soon as I possibly could. Zionism became all-consuming, the centre of my existence. My first priority was to educate myself. I read everything on the topic that I could lay my hands on. The sheer romance of the achievement – the re-establishment, after two millennia, of Jewish sovereignty in our historical homeland – was irresistible. It was obvious to me that statehood, with all its ramifications, was the only solution to the otherwise insoluble Jewish predicament.

The logic of all this was, in my youthful view, beyond persuasive; it was incontrovertible. Throughout the long agony of the Diaspora, no-one had done the benighted Jewish people any favours despite unfulfilled promises of emancipation and occasional, short-lived, and ultimately unsuccessful attempts to throw off the shackles of discrimination and ghettoisation. Millennia of praying hadn't hastened any form of salvation let alone the promised coming of the Messiah. A single scarlet thread of homicidal hatred – antisemitism – connected the Jewish experience from Roman Emperor Hadrian's brutal mass murder and expulsion of the Jews from their homeland in 135CE to the Czarist pogroms of the 1880s. So they – we – concluded that the time for waiting had long passed. The world was just too dangerous for defenceless Jews. We would henceforth cease to rely on the goodwill of others. Modern political Zionism offered us a tool for forging our own destiny. We would use it to carve a new and exciting future out of a devastating past.

For the record, to avoid a misunderstanding: my embryonic political philosophy wasn't in any sense a narrow, inward looking, tribal preoccupation but one that had a universal resonance. If the Jews could achieve their own freedom, so could persecuted minorities everywhere. In Zionism, the biblical injunction to be *a light unto the nations* had the potential to achieve fruition. I had at last found a just cause, an inspiring vision, a personal passion, and a lifelong obsession. In the process, I discarded my former prejudices and passive world view, along with the naive philosophical premises on which they were so flimsily based. All of these now struck me as ignorant, puerile, complacent and indefensible.

By the age of eighteen, my rapid political transformation (that would today doubtless be labelled radicalisation) was almost complete. I barely recognised the callow, ignorant (and arrogant) youth who had matriculated as a freshman student a year earlier. The more I read, debated and reflected, the more convinced I grew of the rectitude of my chosen path. I was impatient to embark upon it but events conspired to frustrate that plan for another decade and a half.

24

Meanwhile, the rest of the world hadn't stood still. Back in grey Edinburgh, examinations had to be passed, girls dated, parents placated. Second year medicine in those days was synonymous with daily exposure to the clinging formaldehyde aroma of the human anatomy dissection room supplemented by lectures from the world-famous Professor Romanes. He had a reputation as a brilliant if somewhat autistic anatomist who could reproduce at will on a blackboard a cross section of any part of the human brain and spinal cord with coloured chalk. No, I do him an injustice: the drawings would depict the anatomical structures at any stage of embryonic, fetal or postnatal development. An amusing party trick of his was to invite the class to shout out requests – six weeks post-conception, eight weeks, eleven – he was never defeated. His was a unique talent and these virtuosic performances left us awe-struck. Whether they enhanced our medical education or our competence as doctors is another matter.

My clinical (ward-based) teachers didn't impress me half as much. By nature they were irritatingly elusive, always slipping away inconsiderately to see their favourite patients. Exceptions were Sir John Crofton, pioneer of antituberculous therapy, and Professor Gillingham, Scotland's superstar of neurosurgery who was ahead of his time in supporting car seatbelt legislation; and I must mention Dr John McLeod, a delightfully down-to-earth yet erudite general physician who taught us the paramount importance of methodical history taking.

A young psychiatrist, Ian Oswald, succeeded in hypnotising our entire class (though he later got into hot water for paying medical students to undergo pharmacologically dangerous sleep experiments). One of his colleagues, a charming South African friend of my father's called Henry Walton, mesmerised us with his slides about personality development, Freud, sex and madness. One day, he ushered into the lecture theatre a beautiful longhaired woman whom he interrogated to expound the symptoms and signs of hysterical personality (a condition that is nowadays called, mainly for reasons of political correctness, narcissistic or borderline personality disorder). I found his presentations both riveting and unaccountably discomfiting – I suppose it was all a bit too close to home given my father's profession and psychodynamic orientation.

But medical education had become a sideshow for me, paling into insignificance next to the mind-blowing events unfolding in the Middle East. The Six Day War and its aftermath had changed me profoundly and permanently. I joined the university Jewish society, hardly as the contrite prodigal son but proudly and defiantly proclaiming to my fellow members – in case of doubt – that I was now a secular, atheistic, Zionist New Jew. I conceded that religious ritual and observance could provide a useful temporary vehicle for creating and sustaining Jewish national identity but I rejected absolutely any allegiance to Judaism as a faith. Some of my colleagues agreed though many (most?) did not. Nevertheless, all were remarkably tolerant of my solipsistic posturing and welcomed me into the fold with open arms.

I became a committed student activist and very soon found myself serving on the executive committee of the Edinburgh University Jewish society in some official capacity (the details of which elude me). That was no great accolade – the JSoc was a tiny organisation desperate for office bearers – but within a year or two I was elected, this time by a much larger constituency, to the chairmanship of the entire northern region, a confederation of Jewish and Israel societies in Scotland and Northern England. To the surprise of many (including myself), I revelled in the rough-and-tumble of student politics and especially enjoyed publicly threatening the UK national conference of Jewish and Israel societies that I would lead our region into full scale separation from the rest of the country if we didn't get our way immediately. These were absurdly melodramatic, quasi-nationalistic rants but they were generally ecstatically received by my young audiences.

Most of my evenings and weekends became filled with Jewish and Israel-oriented politics. The timing could not have been more fortuitous. Anti-Israel activists, who were numerically small in those days but well organised and funded by wealthy Arab regimes, were gearing up for a sustained campaign assault on Israel's reputation. Israel was branded the aggressor in the recent war, allegedly because she had technically fired the first shot. The "illegal occupation" of Arab (later tagged "Palestinian") lands was maliciously depicted as merely the execution of a longstanding and sinister (though non-existent) Zionist master plan to expand into and eventually control all Arab territory while ethnically cleansing it of all its indigenous inhabitants. These smears were demonstrably untrue but they began to gain traction in some gullible circles, a seemingly unstoppable process that would continue unchecked in academe for years to come.

It was during this period that I began to undertake tentative attempts to defend Israel against the rewriting of history that was well under way by a weird alliance of Soviet-aligned communists, gruesome Arab dictators and a few *Charedi* (ultra-Orthodox) Jewish sects – all cheered on by the traditional antisemites of the far right. (Today, those same malign forces remain in the mix but with the addition of a new red-green alliance of left-wingers and Islamists. Extraordinarily, the message of these bigots is being heard by a growing number of apparently receptive ears. Their lies and half-truths have been repeated so often that many otherwise sane people, especially on the left, now believe them; in the early twenty-first century, the default position of all self-styled progressives is deep and endlessly reiterated hostility to Israel).

From her establishment in 1948, Israel's counter-propaganda efforts were notoriously feeble. They were constrained by a chronic lack of resources, combined with an inadequate appreciation of the importance and scale of the task. We Jews and Israelis would reap the bitter harvest of that failure over many subsequent decades.

25

As the preposterously branded Swinging Sixties drew to a close, I was rescued from the cesspool of Middle Eastern political debate by a few timely distractions. The principal one was music. My student flatmates – all amateur musicians – exposed me to a vast repertoire of magnificent classical music that I had either never heard or never properly listened to before. They propelled me into a lifelong love affair with Mahler, Bruckner, Wagner, Puccini, Brahms and Schubert. The highly competent Scottish National Orchestra was conducted by Motherwell-born Alexander Gibson, whose great contribution to the British musical scene was to launch Scottish Opera. He was probably underrated as a musician – his Mahler's Eighth at Glasgow's Kelvin Hall was a revelation – but he was a brittle character, unpopular with the players, and a drinker to boot. These flaws must have eroded his reputation. But the orchestra invited an impressive line-up of guest conductors – Sir Adrian Boult, Walter Susskind, Jascha Horenstein among them – every season.

I dragged a few girlfriends along to these concerts. Most were underwhelmed but one, a pretty Glaswegian Jewish medical student called Sandra, stayed the course and was even brave enough to accompany me on the supreme musical challenge of sitting through all sixteen hours of Wagner's *Der Ring des Nibelungen*. I had learned all the important *leitmotifs* and tried to teach them to my somewhat bemused girlfriend. I must have bored her to tears. Yet the dalliance flourished (for reasons unrelated to Wagner) and an engagement followed quickly. We held a memorable party, with beautifully catered food and an infinite supply of alcoholic drinks, in the splendid setting of Capelrig House in Newton Mearns.

A quick rewind: I had met my glamorous fiancée at a Scottish Jewish student function in Glasgow. Our Edinburgh contingent was being served food and drink, in a manner unthinkable today, by a posse of female students from the host JSoc. Sandra was, I judged, the standout stunner and somehow, despite my innate shyness, I contrived to engineer an introduction via a table companion. I was instantly smitten and invited her on a date, with little expectation of a positive response. When it came, I was ecstatic. We hit it off and that was that: I had found my soulmate and I knew that my bachelor days would soon be over. Getting hitched, as we called it, seemed to us the most natural thing in the world and so it proved: we didn't look back (at least not for around another three decades). Our relationship didn't merely flourish; it evolved rapidly into a wondrously harmonious, fun-filled and fruitful partnership that was the envy of our friends and the toast of our initially bemused and sceptical parents.

*

In the summer of 1969, I faced a dilemma about my future career. Reaching the mid-point of my medical course, after appreciable intellectual toil, the thought struck me that I didn't actually want to be a doctor. Or rather it re-struck me; I had never intended to be one. Again, I had the sensation of being a fish out of water. Was I the only medical student in history with no desire to wield a stethoscope? I wasn't, but at the time I felt uniquely freakish.

At the end of my third year of studies, I was forced to confront harsh reality. My original aspiration to become a medically qualified scientist had been thwarted by my scoring mediocre grades in the all-important science examinations. I found myself stranded in mid-stream, unable either to move backwards and start again, or to look forward with enthusiasm to the prospect of a lifetime trapped in clinical medicine. In my ignorance, I saw the options as binary: I would have to choose between science and medicine. As I have frequently pontificated to successive generations of sceptical medical students since, these are far from mutually exclusive domains. All good doctors are scientist-practitioners. In any case, a medical course is merely a launching pad for a wide variety of careers, from neurosurgery to medical journalism. Across the range, there is literally something for everyone.

As I prepared, with mounting apprehension, to embark on the clinical studies that comprised the second half of the course, that insight was hidden from my view. All I could discern, as I stood on that fateful crossroads, were two giant arrows and I would have to choose one of them. I predicted that, sooner or later, this quandary would evolve into a full-blown crisis unless I took evasive action – which is precisely what I did in the summer of 1969 in Boston, or more precisely Brookline, Massachusetts.

26

A passing fancy for pathology had prompted me to undertake a short elective period at a prestigious laboratory at Boston City Hospital run by the doyen of American pathology, Professor Stanley Robbins, who happened to be an old friend of my father's. He was an impressive character whose encyclopaedic knowledge of his subject must have been second to none. His vast tome, *Textbook of Pathology*, was known to medical students and doctors the world over as a standard reference work. Moreover, he occupied a niche position close to the very top of the American medical elite and was treated, as I observed at first-hand, like academic royalty in the portals of that temple of Bostonian medicine, the Massachusetts General Hospital.

For a while, I visualised myself as a Stanley Robbins clone, a high-flying pathologist effortlessly straddling the worlds of teaching, practice and research. Could this strange discipline offer the elusive answer I was seeking? A few hours of dispiriting exposure to the malodorous misery of the post-mortem room quickly disabused me of that notion. I'll spare you the details (that are not for the faint-hearted). That was the snag – pathology and dead bodies are locked in an inseparable embrace; you can't have one without the other. Robbins treated me tolerantly enough but sensed that my heart was not fully in it and communicated that subliminal message to me effectively.

So there I was back to the drawing board with the clock of undergraduate training ticking too loudly for comfort. Within three years I would be a junior doctor, a looming fate from which I needed either a means of escape or a cast-iron intellectual justification. If I couldn't pursue a career as a medical scientist, what would become of me? The answer, it transpired, was that I would become a medical scientist. It was just that the particular branch of science that I selected would be at odds with my preconceived notion of a white-coated laboratory boffin patiently unravelling – and solving – the hitherto impenetrable secrets of cancer.

The newly built Harvard medical school campus was located in Brookline directly across the road from my temporary digs in a student residence called Vanderbilt Hall. The central quadrangle of the residence was entirely filled by a clay tennis court on which were performed long, serious matches of a phenomenally high standard. My fellow students were intelligent and unashamedly ambitious young Americans. Without exception, they were disarmingly friendly – one bespectacled young woman invited me to her room where she lectured me earnestly on a feminist tract called *The Myth of the Vaginal Orgasm*. Was she hinting that we might test the hypothesis implicit in the title? (Spoiler alert: no).

As a visiting elective student, I had access to the medical school's extensive library. It was immaculately designed and logically organised with shelves of textbooks stacked neatly in clearly labelled sections. I decided to skip the dubious attractions of the hospital's post-mortem room for a couple of days and explore the written word in this altogether more salubrious setting. Wondering how to pass the time, I alighted on a novel idea: I would perform a cross-disciplinary survey of literally the whole of medicine, starting at *A for anatomy*.

After several hours of pleasant but fruitless meandering through the vast collection, occasionally extracting a heavy volume and flicking through its pages, I paused briefly at psychiatry, the only subject that exerted even the most minimal appeal. I gingerly extracted one of the textbooks and tucked it under my arm. I was torn. My father was a distinguished child psychiatrist and I dreaded the (quasi-Freudian?) ignominy of confessing to him (or anyone else) that I was intent on following in his professional footsteps. But what was the alternative?

By sunset, I became gripped by near panic. Conscious of the rapidly approaching end of the alphabet, I knew that my options were shrinking. Returning the psychiatric tome to the shelf, I moved on to the next section, burdened by the despondency of anticipated failure. That was the precise moment when, as so often in life, a breakthrough occurred when I was least expecting it.

There, in the encroaching dusk, in a quiet, inconspicuous corner of a Boston library, I discovered my future.

27

Public health had a poor image both within the medical profession and across wider society in those days. By general consensus, it largely comprised dull-witted bureaucrats – many of them third-rate doctors – taking an obsessive interest in the gloomy infrastructure of human excretion, specifically involving drains, sewage and the less savoury aspects of personal hygiene. While there was a grain of truth in this stereotype, the subject was, of course, far more sophisticated and wide-ranging. In the field of infectious disease control alone, the discovery and deployment of childhood vaccinations had saved countless lives. For some reason, most of the credit for these major breakthroughs was unfairly accorded to microbiologists rather than the public health practitioners who planned and rolled out the programmes.

Fortunately, my inexperience protected me from prejudice; I had not yet internalised the prevailing negative tropes. What really grabbed my attention, in that steamy Boston mid-summer, was the potential for population-wide measures such as health education, physical planning, vaccination and screening to benefit literally millions of people. Even the most accomplished of super-clinicians couldn't begin to compete with that level of impact. With mounting excitement verging on jubilation, I read everything on that shelf with the growing conviction that I had finally found my true calling.

That conclusion was reinforced by my subsequent exposure to the subject in my later undergraduate years. The Usher Institute for Social Medicine sent students off on short-term community-based projects during their compulsory module there. Most of my classmates regarded this course as tedious at best and a dangerous distraction from *real medicine* at worst. But I loved every minute of it. My group, under the flamboyant supervision of Dr Una McLean (wife of John Mackintosh MP, a rising star of the Labour Party who died too young) was tasked with a review of the care provided at Gogarburn hospital, a ghastly residential institution on the outskirts of Edinburgh that housed hundreds of "mentally handicapped" children in conditions of appalling neglect and squalor. When we turned up with a camera and a tape recorder, we caused near-panic among the staff. To his credit, the medical superintendent permitted us to complete our work, the results of which presumably languish to this day on some high, dusty shelf in the Edinburgh University archives.

Following graduation, I had to jump through the usual hoops of hospital house-doctor jobs and start my postgraduate clinical training. These were mere preliminaries for me, a means to an end – to become a public health doctor. It wasn't an easy choice. Family and friends were openly flabbergasted. However patiently I tried to explain my enthusiasm for this unglamorous discipline and its almost limitless possibilities, they just didn't get it. As with much else in life, perception trumped the truth.

Among the sternest critics of public health was my father. Remarkably, his disapproval didn't deter me in the slightest from embarking on my career and may even have had the opposite effect. In any case, being a stubborn contrarian, I was rather attracted to a subject that most of the medical establishment viewed with barely disguised contempt.

Ed held on to his prejudices about the specialty throughout his life. I don't think he ever resolved the cognitive dissonance caused by his realisation that epidemiology, my chosen academic field, was the basic science of the much-reviled discipline of public health. Even towards the close of my career in the field, he went as far as to launch a scathing public attack on public health doctors – "failed clinicians" in his words – in my presence at a meeting held to commemorate the fiftieth anniversary of his creation of the child psychiatry unit at Yorkhill hospital. I was embarrassed, disappointed and rather hurt by that remark but held my tongue. He seemed blithely unaware both of the tastelessness of his observation or of the implicit slight on his son's choice of profession. (I bear him no posthumous ill-feeling about this as I suspect he was displaying symptoms of a mild age-related dementia that blunted his normally sound empathetic instincts).

Within a couple of decades, attitudes to public health had changed radically (and would later be transformed almost beyond recognition as a result of the coronavirus pandemic of 2020). From the outset, I anticipated that my chosen professional path would turn out to be an unconventional, unpredictable and, in all likelihood, uncomfortable one. On all three counts, I was right.

28

What is happiness? We usually recognise it when it's missing but at the time it just feels like normality punctuated by flashes of grateful awareness. Mostly we float on the surface of a fluffy ether of unconscious contentment. At least, that is how I recollect those hectic early years of proper adulthood and parenthood. Marriage, children, work, travel – the script unfolded with what felt like a natural and pre-ordained certainty though, from this distance, it was hubris awaiting a fall.

The seventies are generally depicted as miserable years in most countries, yet many good things were happening in my life. In 1973, I married Sandra, after an engagement of a couple of years, in the old Newton Mearns synagogue under the nervous supervision of its young minister, Dr Geoffrey Conn. (Such was the emotional warmth of the occasion that the building burnt down to the ground shortly after the ceremony). Against a background of severe economic recession triggered by the Yom Kippur War, in which Arab states again attempted to obliterate the only Jewish one (with near success), we were, as a couple, beyond doubt, extremely happy. Even the frequent power cuts caused by the UK coalminers' strikes didn't succeed in dampening our spirits.

We set up our first home in a bright but rather draughty top floor flat in Dudley Drive in Hyndland and quickly befriended the delightful McLeish couple who lived across the road. Peter had been an old school chum of mine and was the most naturally gifted classical pianist I ever met. He died too young in 2013 in his early sixties. His wife Irene was a warm, friendly soul with an unquenchably optimistic outlook. Some years later, I heard that she had, tragically, become confined to a wheelchair due to multiple sclerosis.

As a junior doctor at Stobhill general hospital, on the north side of Glasgow, I learned to ply my medical trade under the expert instruction of some truly brilliant teachers. Passing the membership of the Royal College of Physicians of Glasgow was a mere formality in that academic hothouse of clinical medicine. After two years, I was a fully accredited physician. I was now ready for the next phase of my career – and life. Moving from Glasgow to London, where I had been appointed to an academic post in epidemiology at St

Thomas's medical school, was a major upheaval but an exciting one. We bought a one-bedroom flat just off Hampstead High Street (for the laughably small sum, by today's standards, of £15,000) and looked forward to the future with enthusiasm.

The first few months in London were spent, frustratingly, in Sandra's aunt Myra's home in St John's Wood following a legal glitch that had delayed our entry to the new flat. Myra could talk for England though I must admit she looked after us royally. When we finally collected the keys to our home, our excitement was beyond boundless.

More thrilling still was the birth of our first child, Ilana, in mid-1976. I won't resort to the usual clichés; we were intoxicated with boundless love for this exquisite miniature human. My response to fatherhood was intensely emotional. When colleagues at work enquired after the welfare of my newborn baby, I was so overcome with excitement that I feared a syncopal collapse. We named her Esther Ilana Bat Daniel at the local *Masorti* (conservative) synagogue (the fiefdom of the controversial and brilliant Rabbi Louis Jacobs), the English version being reversed into Ilana Esther.

To fast forward: the three subsequent arrivals were equally joyful events though I must confess somewhat guiltily that the heart-stopping cataclysm of the first was never quite replicated. We ended up with the perfect brood – two of each. But I won't deny that producing Jewish baby boys was challenging. Millennia of unbroken religious custom clash with modern sensibilities in a specifically, exquisitely uncomfortable manner.

I have never fully come to terms with the *brit milah*, the Jewish circumcision ritual, that we inflicted on our two boys. Sandra and I certainly found it trying though the babies undoubtedly enjoyed it considerably less than their parents. I made impassioned speeches about the need to bring our ancient but outmoded religion into the twentieth century. There was, nevertheless, no question of abandoning the tradition, however irrational it seemed. Nor would I join the chorus of assorted xenophobes and "human rights' activists" who denounced the practice as the epitome of barbarism. I tried hard to rationalise the procedure on health grounds though without much conviction (or hard data).

Ironically, current medical opinion is more supportive of the procedure than at any time in the past. Walk-in, free-of-charge adult circumcision clinics are now widespread throughout sub-Saharan Africa as a highly effective means (according to the World Health Organization) of reducing HIV transmission. The American Paediatric Association has waxed hot and cold over the issue in recent decades but now suggests that the balance of evidence is marginally favourable, though they stop short of recommending it as a universal practice.

Unsurprisingly, European medical opinion ranges from the equivocal to the downright hostile with a pronounced leaning towards the latter, reaching a near-hysterical antipathy in those countries with a pitiful historical (and often contemporary) record of antisemitism. Mere coincidence? I doubt it. Attacking circumcision (along with ritual animal slaughter) is a dog-whistle for diehard racists ranging from covert antisemites to flag-waving white supremacists along with every other strand of bigotry along the way.

29

One of my duties at St Thomas's Department of Epidemiology was to organise the weekly seminar programme. The prospect of taking responsibility for this largely administrative chore initially unnerved me yet it turned out to be highly pleasurable. I was able to dip freely into the large pool of talent that was so abundantly available in London, an extraordinary privilege for a young Scottish lecturer who was making his way in the metropolis. Not only could I select the speakers, I was given a modest budget to entertain them to lunch or coffee after each seminar.

Among the many luminaries I hosted were George Brown, a shy but highly intelligent and original sociologist; Heinz Wolff, an eccentric Berlin-born engineer and promoter of the tilting teapot (for frail or arthritic users) among other curiosities; Denis Burkitt, who discovered an unusual lymphoma in Africa and promoted the high-fibre diet as a panacea for Western diseases; and Steven Rose, a high-flying young biologist who later gained notoriety (along with his wife Hilary) for fanatical anti-Zionism and advocacy of an academic boycott of Israel. My role as the humble seminar organiser taught me two lifelong lessons. First, I discovered that I had good organisational skills. Second, London was *the* place to be. Most of the UK's movers and shakers were based there, or at least were in the habit of passing through. By contrast, Glasgow was a sleepy provincial backwater.

As it turned out, I only lasted two years in the post – and even that was the result of a gargantuan effort on my part – mainly because my professorial boss, Walter Holland, and I clashed incessantly over fundamental issues of science and medical politics. He branded me a "clinical heretic" for advocating a clinical dimension to public health. He claimed that it was impossible to be competent in both public health and clinical practice as each had to be a full-time commitment. Naturally, I disagreed, pointing to the contemporary role models of Sir Richard Doll and Professor Geoffrey Rose among many others. Moreover, I countered that he was being hypocritical in the light of his wandering around the corridors of St Thomas's hospital in a white coat with stethoscope prominently garlanded around his neck, presumably to underline his clinical credentials.

Matters came to a head when I wrote a provocatively worded opinion piece for the *British Medical Journal* arguing that community medicine (as public health was then called) had little future if it insisted on excluding any kind of clinical component from its domain. (Nowadays the UK Faculty of Public Health is more accepting of clinicians than it was then but the specialty has remained resolutely non-clinical – so in a sense Walter and I were both right). The argument became heated and excessively personal but I refused to back down and the article duly appeared in the journal with my home address, rather than the department's, on the strap line. I knew I had reached the point of no return and that I would have to jump before I was pushed and so handed in my resignation shortly thereafter.

I was genuinely sorry to leave under such circumstances. I felt I had just got my feet under my desk and had much more to learn. Nevertheless, my stint at St Thomas's was critical to my professional development as it helped me to hone the basic tools of the academic trade – how to plan and conduct high quality research, structure grant applications, prepare reports and publish scientific papers – and all those skills stood me in excellent stead throughout my future career.

I also discovered something important about myself. I had somehow acquired a steely intellectual backbone that enabled me to stand up to blusterers and bullies who were used to getting their own way. I would encounter plenty more of their ilk in the coming decades and I always confronted them (with variable success) on my terms rather than theirs. How or why this happened remains something of a mystery to me.

30

Although we enjoyed the London life, various unwelcome factors began to intrude. Our miniature Hampstead flat, cosy for two but cramped for three, was losing its charm. During the day, baby Ilana slept in the bedroom while at night we relocated her to the living room. It must have been confusing for her to wake up from every sleep in a different place. We were simply outgrowing our surroundings and concluded that we would have to move home sooner rather than later. Sandra was permanently exhausted by the impossibly competing demands of motherhood and part-time work in general practice. Occasionally she was obliged to take Ilana with her to work and patients were subjected, in the course of their disrobing, to a hilarious (if not always appreciated) running commentary from the fascinated toddler: "Take your skirt off, now your bra, now your panties."

The steaming hot summers of 1976 and 1977 didn't help. Air conditioning in London in those days was as rare as hen's teeth and the overheated populace sweated and panted their way around the city trying to preserve a tolerable distance from their malodorous neighbours in offices, buses, trains, shops and other public spaces. The metropolis, like the nation as a whole, seemed to wilt under the weight of multiple sources of stress: a plummeting economy (largely caused by the OPEC's cynical use of oil to try to force the West to apply pressure on Israel), along with increasing levels of poverty, industrial unrest, rising crime, and an extremely nasty IRA bombing campaign. Harold Wilson unexpectedly resigned as prime minister and James Callaghan briefly and unsuccessfully took the helm, paving the way for the new cyclonic force in British politics that was Margaret Thatcher.

Malcolm Gladwell hadn't yet published *The Tipping Point* but most people understood, from their own experience, what it meant. We reached ours when we returned home one evening after a day out to discover our pretty Hampstead flat submerged under water. A faulty cistern in the unoccupied property above had caused a catastrophic flood. For a few weeks we returned, as homeless refugees, to Sandra's benevolent aunt Myra in St John's Wood that stretched her (and our) endurance to its limits and beyond. That was our irreversible tipping point: goodbye London, hello – somewhere, anywhere, else.

The small matter of how to earn a living had to be addressed. Having resigned from my London lectureship, I was essentially unemployed and had to find a means of supporting my family. An advertisement in a medical journal for "radio doctors" in Australia looked enticing. We had little choice, so I gratefully seized the job offer. Within a few weeks the three of us were ensconced in a bright, spacious flat in Bondi, Sydney, right next the famous beach that struck us, disappointingly, as a vast and featureless playground with minimal attractions. But it suited us perfectly for the few months of our residence there.

Australia had no national health service to speak of and much of the healthcare was private, or at least insurance based. By working anti-social hours as a locum GP (with locally recruited drivers whose company through the long shifts was a rather mixed blessing), I earned an obscene amount of money. The work itself was undemanding medically, apart from the occasionally scary confrontations with drug addicts and prostitutes in Kings Cross (the city's crime-ridden red-light district) who sought to manipulate me into prescribing hard drugs such as pethidine and morphine. This was my first contact with opiate addiction, a blight that had yet to reach the UK but was by then widespread in the US and Australia.

At the end of each eight-hour shift, I would guiltily empty my pockets of wads of ten and twenty dollar notes. We were almost literally swimming in money. The challenging hours were a minimal hardship as our gorgeous baby daughter ensured, from the day of her birth, that normal sleeping patterns were but a fond memory.

31

As (almost) everyone knows, Sydney is renowned for its exceptional visual beauty. It's a scenically thrilling city, thanks to its natural seaside setting and superbly engineered human habitat. The exotic flora and fauna are a constant delight and the sun always seems to shine. Despite its short history and relative paucity of high culture, many millions of European immigrants regard it as the nearest thing to paradise on earth.

Fleetingly, the idea of settling in Australia was an appealing one to us. Within a matter of months, we had formed a few solid friendships and had made contact with a sprinkling of family and acquaintances who had migrated from Scotland. A former academic colleague from London offered me an exceptionally well-paid post as a senior administrator in one of the New South Wales' teaching hospitals. Our new friends urged us to take the leap into the not-so unknown; for them it was a no-brainer. I was flattered and tempted. Sandra was more circumspect. The seductive Australian dream beckoned – a detached villa, complete with large garden and pool, a comfortable lifestyle in a verdant Sydney suburb, and a salary sufficient to fund both an affluent lifestyle and regular return trips to the old country. Furthermore, the Jewish community was large and lively – kosher meat has never looked nor tasted so good – and heart-warmingly Zionist.

But there were at least two serious downsides to settling in the southern hemisphere. We knew that both sets of parents would have been horrified at the prospect, and that my ambition to migrate to Israel would have to be postponed indefinitely. After some token agonising, I graciously declined the offer. Through a stroke of good fortune, I discovered that the NHS in Glasgow was advertising public health traineeships that looked tailor-made for my purposes. With more than a pang of regret, the three of us were soon homeward bound again to the gloomy vistas of Clydeside.

*

I completed my public health training under the beneficent guidance of Dr George Folwell, Glasgow's brilliant but somewhat eccentric public health director. A warm-hearted man with a permanent twinkle in his eye, he had a sharp, analytical mind that could forensically dissect the essence of any complex issue. So formidable was the combination of his professional ability, managerial acumen and emotional intelligence that he had no difficulty in bending irascible senior doctors and administrators to his will without them even being aware of it.

He also had an impressive gift for turning his insights into memorable and amusing aphorisms. Among the Folwellisms that impressed me most were those relating to the tribulations of medical politics: "Let's not discuss this delicate subject in front of the children"; "You two go behind the bicycle shed later and sort it out between you"; "People think that what I do is supremely clever but it's all Brownian motion"; "Don't get carried away with self-importance – you were the fifth choice." His career advice was sound too, his most perceptive maxim being: "Remember, doctor, it's later than you think." I didn't believe him at the time, but it turned out to be accurate; I've recounted it often to successive generations of medical students, trainees and colleagues.

I suspect he approved of my contrarianism as he frequently asked me to write him a memo ("Daniel, give me a piece of paper") about some controversial matter or other. He was as scathing as I was about the direction public health was taking ("It's a form of self-indulgence for doctors") and wasn't afraid to adopt unpopular positions. From the start, I was open with him about my plans to emigrate to Israel and he never tried to deflect me from that ambition. Perhaps he admired my idealism. He predicted, with extraordinary prescience, that I'd return to Scotland. "By all means swan off to the Negev and have your great adventure if you must, but you'll be back, mark my words."

32

I did swan off to the sunny Negev (more of which shortly), but not before writing two epidemiological theses (both on neural tube defects) and publishing a respectable number of scientific papers. My research output was well enough admired throughout my long career to propel me up the greasy academic pole though in retrospect I am quite harsh on myself as I struggle to identify anything especially noteworthy, let alone strikingly ground-breaking, among my publications.

More significantly, I also produced, with a little help from Sandra, another two offspring, providing brothers as company for Princess Ilana; Peter arrived in 1978 followed by Ethan in 1980. (Pamela didn't appear until 1983, by which time we had moved to Israel). Living in the midst of this expanding family was deeply satisfying and a huge delight, if an endlessly demanding one. This is no exaggeration. I can't recall a single day of real strife either between the siblings or between parents and children. Perhaps I have just forgotten. Sandra and I should take credit for getting something right as parents (although how can one tell?). We always set clear boundaries for the children and these were rarely crossed. Discipline was never an issue and we both steadfastly eschewed physical methods such as smacking (running against the grain of most of our peers in those unenlightened days).

Our flexible working arrangements enabled us to organise our timetables in a way that ensured an equitable sharing of parental tasks. I was an expert nappy-changer and probably ahead of my time as a fervent believer in a strong paternal presence in family life. Grandparents were often on hand, and regularly called upon to assist with school runs, baby sitting or crisis management. They provided terrific role models for us when our turn came. Both sets of grandparents established a routine of vast weekend family meals – Rena and Henry's on *Shabbat*, Helga and Ed's on Sunday – and the children thrived on the lavish treats and undistracted attention.

From mid-1978, we had rented a largish, undistinguished looking detached villa in Newton Mearns, a sprawling suburb on the southern edge of Glasgow. The house was surrounded by a vast acreage that was ideal for allowing toddlers to expend their energies but proved a lawn too far for my limited gardening skills. We settled down into a typical middle-class suburban lifestyle for the next three years that was sometimes dull but never unpleasant. Our social life flourished and we contributed our share to the endless (and to my taste tiresome) cycle of Saturday night dinner parties with friends. Weekends were spent maintaining family ties with occasional jaunts into the Scottish countryside. Money was tight (and often borrowed) but the next pay cheque was always around the corner to save the day. That satisfying if unexciting pattern might have continued for several decades. It was not to be; a discontented subterranean rumble was disturbing the foundations of our suburban idyll.

Throughout this period, I was growing increasingly restless to get to Israel. Sandra realised that she would have to accommodate that all-consuming obsession if there was to be a future for us together. The Camp David accords between Israel and Egypt were signed in 1978 and there was a widespread feeling that an era of peace and goodwill was about to dawn. Yasser Arafat's Palestine Liberation Organisation had other ideas and stepped up their cross-border terrorist attacks from Lebanon. As so often, the prospect of peace didn't dampen the violent impulses of Israel's politicidal foes (as wrongly and consistently predicted by too many foreign commentators) but fuelled them. Peace was the last thing that Palestinian extremist groups, whose existence depended on ceaseless mayhem, would welcome. Yet the Arabists of the Foreign Office, the BBC and *The Guardian* stubbornly stuck to the morally bankrupt line that only further Israeli concessions would blunt Arafat's murderous incursions into Israel. Appeasement wasn't a word any of its advocates used in relation to that policy but that's exactly what it was. Unsurprisingly, Israeli politicians were disinclined to adopt that advice.

The mounting violence was worrying but insufficient to deflect us from our (or more accurately my) intention to make *Aliyah* at the earliest possible opportunity. I set the wheels in motion and arranged an appointment with the local Jewish Agency *shaliach* (emissary) who handed me a thick sheaf of forms. These didn't deter me in the slightest – I think he was genuinely flabbergasted when I returned them meticulously completed and signed within twenty-four hours. We had taken the first step on our way to the Promised Land.

It's often said that there are both push and pull factors motivating Diaspora Jews to start new lives in Israel. In our case, the overriding impulse was a positive one – to make a tangible contribution to the strengthening of the reborn national homeland. That was certainly how I felt, and I believe Sandra did too. Antisemitism played no direct part in this decision. But there was a subtler form of bigotry at work, a sense that the very existence of the state of Israel was somehow illegitimate, even among some of our own middle class, Scottish, gentile peer group.

A single episode illustrates this soft racism. We had been invited to a birthday party by a couple with whom we'd been moderately friendly for several years. Within days of the event, we were suddenly uninvited via a phone call to Sandra. The reason? Among the guests would be an Arab student and the hosts were concerned "about Daniel's views on Israel." Unsurprisingly, that particular friendship came to an abrupt end there and then. Mildly offensive behaviour of this sort was fairly rare, but it was a portent of things to come, and would eventually burgeon into the full-blown antisemitic antiZionism that manifests itself as the BDS (boycott, divestment and sanctions) movement, and all the associated accoutrements of hate. But in those early days, the symptoms were mere irritants and we didn't take them too seriously. Oh, the foolish innocence of youth....

33

When the Israelis definitively ascertained that I was genuinely seeking permanent employment in Israel, at least three universities offered me a position. That was wonderfully gratifying – and flattering – but posed a major conundrum. I was naturally drawn to Jerusalem, so redolent of my childhood memories. Haifa and Tel Aviv both had their appealing aspects, not least the Med. But I quickly plumped for the newly established Beer Sheva medical school for the sheer romance of the desert and everything that it symbolised for the Zionist project. David Ben Gurion's rallying call resonated with me: *Unless we conquer the Negev, the Negev will conquer us.* I wasn't deterred by that challenge – how tough could living conditions be in a medium-sized town a mere hour and a half's drive from Tel Aviv? (It was a rhetorical question, of course, but it shouldn't have been; we had no clue what we were getting ourselves into).

Following an influx of highly educated Russians, Israel at that time was a grossly over-doctored country that didn't need more medical graduates, though most of them tended to gravitate to the large urban centres leaving rural communities underserved. But Beer Sheva was no ordinary medical school. The founding Dean was a charismatic if egocentric administrator called Moshe Prywes who had grown tired of the Jerusalem Hadassah hospital's conservative ways and wanted to create a new kind of doctor, one that was firmly community-oriented and dedicated to serving disadvantaged groups.

I soon made the happy discovery that almost everything about the increasingly world-renowned Beer Sheva Experiment was radical – its philosophy, curriculum, teaching, assessment methods, recruitment, and community relations. For me, it epitomised the pioneering spirit of Israel. I loved its idealistic and highly cost-effective motto: *Those who serve, teach, and those who teach, serve.* Above all, Prywes believed that public health and prevention were central to medical education and that the medical school would embody that belief assertively and uncompromisingly. The epidemiology department had the kind of elevated status normally accorded to cardiac surgery in conventional medical faculties. For me, all of this was pure nectar. I couldn't wait to get started.

Our journey to Israel in late February 1981 was unexpectedly riotous. The five of us (including eight-month-old baby Ethan) flew on the only direct flight from Scotland to Israel – a packed, specially chartered football supporters' plane from Glasgow to Tel Aviv as Scotland happened to be playing Israel in a World Cup qualifying match. The flight also coincided with our elder son's third birthday. Sandra had ordered a birthday cake to be served mid-flight. As soon as the fans spotted its appearance, word rapidly spread down the aisle and within seconds the entire company burst into an uproarious and amusingly dissonant rendering of Happy Birthday to the accompaniment of a torrential shower of five-pound notes that floated, like cascading leaves from an autumnal forest, onto the head of the delighted birthday boy.

The fans were good-natured, boisterous and extremely drunk. The border officials at Ben Gurion airport were so bemused by the arrival of this large band of singing and dancing Scotsmen, complete with kilted bagpipers, that they decided to dispense with the usual entry formalities. The gates were thrown open and we were all waved through to the luggage reclaim area. There we parted company with the Tartan Army, by now our best friends, and were bundled, with our possessions, into a large taxi by an affable little Anglo-Israeli (called Wally something), representing the British Olim (Immigrant) Society.

Two hours later we were delivered to a bleak, concrete estate – a large immigrant absorption centre on the edge of Beer Sheva – that was to be our home for the next nine months. We were handed a welcome pack of sheets, blankets, towels, plastic crockery and cutlery, carbolic soap, and a polystyrene baby bath. After being ushered into our three-roomed flatlet, we collapsed exhausted onto unyielding iron bunks where we all fell asleep instantly. The day had been long and eventful, our most memorable family birthday ever.

34

For Sandra and me, living in the absorption centre was a trying experience. Everything in our tiny flat was absolutely basic. We had no creature comforts beyond running water, a primitive gas stove, a few items of crude furniture and some bare light bulbs. It was like finding ourselves suddenly abandoned in a high-end refugee camp. Still, it cost almost nothing (which was just as well as we had arrived in Israel with a considerable bank overdraft) and we were treated humanely enough. The children regarded the whole thing as a grand adventure and were looked after most of the day in a well-staffed kindergarten where the two older ones rapidly acquired a smattering of Russian and Yiddish from their Russian classmates. Sandra and I tried to learn some basic Hebrew in the *ulpan* (language school) in the mornings after which we set off, with baby Ethan in tow, to practise the language with an army of bureaucrats in the afternoons.

Much of the day's business was frustrating beyond endurance. The list of tasks was long and seem to lengthen faster than we could tick off our list. We had to register at various government ministries for everything from an identity card to a national insurance number and were obliged to join the *Histadrut* (trade union federation) – I proudly kept my red membership card for years – to access the health service. I was faced with the additional worrisome complication of securing temporary exemption from army service.

Every government office was overcrowded and understaffed. Worse, the officials (who almost invariably chain-smoked) were bad-tempered and aggressive, though they usually softened at the site of our infant son who was a permanent appendage on these outings. Many of the clerks were themselves recent arrivals from Eastern Europe and had brought with them a Soviet-style contempt for the general public, particularly *olim chadashim* (new immigrants) like us who hailed from the affluent West. Few of these clerks spoke English and our Hebrew was too poor to make much of an impression on them. We wasted aeons of time being harried from pillar to post around Israeli officialdom. Those were not happy days but somehow we preserved our British stoicism and got through them relatively unscathed. I had to start work quite early on to earn an income and that offered me an additional, crucial emotional lifeline.

As soon as I was introduced to my new senior colleagues in the epidemiology department, I felt at completely at home. These were outstanding academics and decent human beings to boot. My boss, a recently retired senior army medical officer called Lechaim Dagan, was a soft-spoken, serious man and the most meticulously disciplined scientist I had ever met. He quickly roped me into the undergraduate teaching programme and gave me responsibility for several major research projects, the most challenging of which was the evaluation of a programme designed to improve primary healthcare for the semi-nomadic Bedouin population of the Negev. I didn't quite catch on at the time, but Dagan was sending me, unprepared, into a political minefield.

Providing basic clinical services, let alone a range of more sophisticated preventive interventions, was virtually impossible when a large proportion of Bedouin families had no fixed abode. The only rational solution was to settle them in permanent towns and villages, but that involved destroying their centuries-old tradition of nomadism. The result was that the government was caught in a no-win position, simultaneously criticised for neglecting the needs of the Bedouin and for trying to meet them. I vividly recall a field trip to the newly established town of Rahat where several families had prematurely taken possession of their half-built homes. These were destined to become substantial dwellings, much larger than the average Jewish home in the nearby development towns of Yerucham and Ofakim, or Beer Sheva itself. What especially intrigued me was the sight of goats, camels and donkeys wandering freely around the interiors of the skeleton structures while the humans camped in goatskin tents outside. Whether the unconventional hierarchy that privileged animals over people remained after the houses had been completed I never discovered.

Classical music of all kinds was a very big deal in the epidemiology department. Everyone seemed to play an instrument – Dagan himself was an accomplished violist and violinist – and I was immediately co-opted as a second violinist into the regular Saturday morning chamber music group in the neighbouring village of Omer. That was probably the highlight of my week. The standard of music making was extraordinarily high and I struggled to keep up with this gifted group of amateur musicians. Otherwise, leisure and cultural opportunities in the Negev were severely limited.

The visual charms of the city were also somewhat elusive. Beer Sheva itself – self-styled capital of the southern region – had sprouted, as the local joke went, from a one-camel to a two-camel town over a couple of decades. The quaint but dusty old city had originally been built by the Turks to administer the Negev region and had never been properly resourced subsequent to the Ottoman departure by either the British or Israeli authorities.

By the mid-eighties, much of Beer Sheva had degenerated into what could accurately be characterised as a vast slum. Radiating outwards from its unprepossessing core were clusters of soulless housing estates that had been designed by architects whose briefs were uninhibited by trivia such as aesthetics. Large numbers of mainly Moroccan Jewish refugee families had been shunted into substandard housing close to the town centre with little regard to their long-term needs and those of their communities. The squat, ugly concrete buildings were only partly ameliorated by the local council's commendable efforts to enhance their city with copious palm trees, desert flowers and green public spaces.

I mustn't exaggerate; the municipality had created some worthy institutions. There was a tiny archaeological museum, a respected Hebrew-language theatre and a decent, though small, music conservatory with a concert hall where a fine chamber orchestra, the Israel Sinfonietta, gave weekly performances. But our overriding impression was that we would struggle to bond with this tough desert town. We fully accepted that Beer Sheva had a great future; our more immediate problem was how on earth to deal with its present.

35

Life in Beer Sheva offered no shortage of daunting challenges. As we had been forewarned (though it didn't really help), the Negev weather was extreme, soaring mercilessly into the mid-forties in summer and dropping below zero at night in winter. Air conditioners were noisy and inefficient though a solar panel heated our domestic water for free, long before the technology had been heard of in Europe. The frequent dust storms, blown in from the North African deserts, darkened the skies and stung the eyes. The aroma from the toxic fumes of a nearby chemical factory had a nasty habit of permeating clothing, skin and saliva. Many drivers wrapped their cars each night in canvas "pyjamas" to minimise sun, sand and pollution damage.

This whole undertaking was quite unlike anything else either of us had ever experienced – or imagined – and I confess that the initial novelty wore off within about a fortnight. *Settling down* into this unforgiving landscape wasn't at the top of our agenda; our paramount objective in those first few months was survival, physical and emotional.

Our three usually ebullient young children were overawed at first but rapidly embraced the child-friendly Israeli ethos and lifestyle. Despite the constant security alerts, including regular bomb scares in our neighbourhood, they enjoyed a freedom to roam and play that had been unknown to most British children for the previous half-century. Watching them set off for kindergarten and school triggered warm memories of my Jerusalem childhood. In that unlikely desert landscape, they blossomed in a manner that would have been inconceivable in Scotland. Within weeks, they were speaking a rudimentary form of Hebrew and were, to all intents and purposes, Israeli children. They looked much healthier too, with their tanned limbs, healthy skin and shining eyes. It was an astonishing transformation.

Truthfully, they were adapting to their adoptive country much better than their parents. The absorption centre was getting us down. Negotiations with the Jewish Agency (the organisation charged, from the days of the British Mandate, with the task of settling Jews in the country) turned into a battle of wills. When we finally secured, at a greatly subsidised price, a newly built flat in an adjoining neighbourhood called Shechunah Tet, we were overjoyed. It really didn't matter one jot to us that the place had an alarmingly unfinished look, that live electrical wires protruded from the ceilings, that the whitewashed walls and tiled floors were bare, or that our much-missed personal possessions that we had shipped from the UK had not yet arrived having got stuck in bureaucratic logjam in a Haifa dock – these were all soluble problems. We were making progress at last. With financial help from parents, who flew over on an emergency mission or two, we were somehow able to furnish our new home to a reasonably comfortable standard – though if I could show it to you now, *luxurious* would not be the first word to issue from your lips.

The flat was bright and fairly spacious by the standards of those days but we quickly discovered that it required vigorous, twice-daily cleaning due to the continuous accretion on every surface of that pesky desert dust. It also suffered periodic infestations – even the tiniest crumb of food left inadvertently on the marble kitchen top attracted a swarm of ants and other unidentifiable beasts within the hour. (Try getting that message across to small children who universally regard a procession of ants marching across the floor as one of the wonders of the world). As for the mysterious plumbing arrangements, well let's not go there…

The great outdoors offered unexpected hazards too. We had to warn our offspring off their playful habit of overturning stones in case a scorpion jumped out to offer a nasty handshake. Mosquitoes weren't a great nuisance, but various other biting flies were. As for the heat, it was a near-permanent, oppressive presence apart from the respite of short winter. Dehydration was a constant threat. Normal levels of water intake were inadequate: the kids were soon chanting a cute little rhyme *Yellow pee is bad, white pee is good* (a ditty that sounds, I assure you, much better in Hebrew). We had no domestic phone line – this was long before the mobile phone era – and no car for the first year. Communication and travel were both, of necessity, severely restricted.

Home is wherever you want it to be, as the saying goes. We were creating a home in the desert and were determined that it should feel like a real one. I like to think we succeeded, more or less. But the effort came at a cost, and not just a financial one.

36

Within weeks of our arrival in Israel, we had been befriended by several English speaking (mainly American) *olim* (immigrants) who, despite being deeply religious Jews in a modern Orthodox way, seemed unperturbed by our relative secularism. That is one of the most surprising features of Israeli society: the contentious religious-secular divide doesn't result in social segregation or serious inter-communal tension with the (arguable) exception of the *Charedi* (ultra-orthodox) Jewish military draft issue.

Over time, we steadily developed an affection for Beer Sheva and its extraordinary desert setting. Adapting to a new environment is always hard but we felt we were coping reasonably well. Above all, the children were happy, and they were our top priority. But a sandfly or two had sneaked into this otherwise balming oriental ointment. One was money, or rather the lack of it. Insane as this must surely sound, we arrived in Israel with little cash and substantial liabilities. Our migration process had been funded via a large bank loan. We soon made the disagreeable discovery that the daily cost of living, while lower than in the UK, was far from trivial. Luxuries such as cars and television sets were subject to enormous taxes that doubled or tripled their prices. Decorating and furnishing our flat proved extremely expensive.

The result was predictable: with each passing year, we became mired ever deeper in uncontrollable debt. Generous handouts from our parents kept us afloat for a while but the crunch came when my UK bank threatened to take possession of our London flat that had been languishing on the market, empty and unsold, for a year. Just maintaining the property in habitable condition was a continuous drain on our shrinking resources.

Poverty corrodes the soul and our eventual return to Scotland was prompted less by any diminution of our commitment to Zion than by looming bankruptcy, among the first indications of which was the imminent collapse of our credit rating. We couldn't contemplate sacrificing our children's future on the altar of an impractical ideology, however worthy.

These mounting financial woes coincided with worrying news from home about my mother-in-law's health, both physical and mental. The cancer that would eventually kill Rena had not yet been diagnosed but was making its unwelcome presence felt. In its early stages, a mild dementia emerged. At first her behaviour appeared just marginally eccentric but her perturbing emotional lability became an increasingly prominent feature. Once the diagnosis was made, Sandra experienced mixed emotions. On the one hand, her mother's illness could be properly treated. On the other, her partial relief was offset by growing anxiety about the future. Her mother's prognosis was uncertain at best. What should we do?

I was conflicted but Sandra was not. Two return visits to Glasgow (one of which was for giving birth to Pamela) hammered home to me the unmistakeable message that my wife had left her heart in Scotland. If I valued our marriage, I knew that a point of no return would soon be upon us when we would have little choice but to pack our bags and go. We never openly argued about this but debated the pros and cons into the wee small hours night after night. Sandra reminded me of an uncomfortable truth – that she had agreed, from the outset, to try living in Israel for a year without commitment to the longer term. I, by contrast, had glossed over the fact that I had viewed *Aliyah* as the ultimate objective.

Had we grasped the unpalatable truth that these contrasting visions were fundamentally irreconcilable and risked tearing us apart? If we did, we failed to express them clearly. That reticence was doubtless born of fear, conscious or otherwise. Separation was, after all, an outcome neither of us wished to contemplate. And so the inevitable happened and an undeclared war of attrition ensued. Frankly, I was never optimistic about winning and perhaps I didn't want to. I was being mercilessly pulled in two opposite directions. I knew I somehow had to face the reality of our family's dilemma, but I was reluctant to follow its logic to any sort of practical conclusion. After all, my commitment to Israel was unconditional, wasn't it?

Gradually, over a period of months, Sandra wore down my resistance. The decisive final straw took the unexpected form of a military sign in large Hebrew lettering in Tel Hashomer on the outskirts of Tel Aviv.

But I am getting ahead of myself….

37

Almost all young adult Israelis, except for *Charedi* Jews and Arabs – are conscripted. That observation needs qualification – the non-*Charedi* Jewish and Druze citizens are conscripted while the Bedouin can (and often do) volunteer. The non-Druze, non-Bedouin Arab population may undertake a parallel form of non-military national service though relatively few do so due to the social and political taboos against it in their community. (There is nothing racist about this policy; it was formulated early in the state's history to avoid the risk of an Arab soldier being sent to war against his family members across the border).

I had always known that, as a medically qualified Israeli citizen, I would be liable for army service. That alone would have deterred most of my British contemporaries from visiting let alone choosing to reside in that war-ravaged country. On hearing of my dilemma, numerous friends said: "So you obviously won't be going then," and reacted with dumbstruck incredulity when I replied that, on the contrary, I was more than ever determined to do it.

For me, serving in the IDF wasn't a drawback but a privilege. I would wear it as a badge of honour, a purposeful gesture that would elevate my Zionism from theory to practice, from the armchair to the battlefield. My advancing years (I was approaching my mid-thirties) were no protection, given my profession. All armies need doctors and the IDF needed more than most at that time due to an ongoing national shortage of medical graduates. To the immigration authorities, I was a *returning minor* as I had originally immigrated as a baby in the 1950s. When I re-entered Israel in 1981 openly and proudly bearing the country's passport, the army were immediately alerted to my presence and, sure enough, the relevant documents were stamped, and I was handed a sheaf of (incomprehensible) explanatory papers by the border officials.

The dreaded brown envelope dropped through our letter box some months later. Knowing its likely contents, I carried it around in my breast pocket for the rest of the day before succumbing to curiosity. My Hebrew was just about adequate to discover that I was being "invited" to report to the local draft office. I presented myself there on the appointed day.

It was a truly surreal experience. First, the other recruits were mostly teenagers who viewed my appearance there as mystifying. Second, nobody actually talked to me directly or even made transient eye contact for two hours. I was duly registered, processed, interviewed, measured, medically examined, and finally injected with unidentified vaccines before being dismissed. The roughly scrawled note I was handed was barely decipherable but I gathered that the army had assessed me as having no military value until I had become more settled in the country and, most crucially, become proficient in the Hebrew language. That outcome was a tremendous (if temporary) relief.

*

Two years later, in November 1983, another brown envelope dropped through the letter box. Inside was a slip of paper demanding my attendance a week later at the main army induction centre in Tel Hashomer, the large army base on the outskirts of Tel Aviv. When I arrived, I found there a sprawling collection of wooden huts scattered across a nettle-strewn wooded and only partially shaded parkland.

I am not ashamed to admit today that I was shaking like a leaf as I entered the compound though I tried hard to conceal my fear from the outside world. Bearing arms was not something that I had ever expected to do, nor had it figured prominently in my self-identity as a Zionist. But I understood that the Jewish state would not have come into existence, nor survived for long, without an army. That, however, was an abstraction; what was happening to me now was all too concrete.

My mind raced in tandem with my accelerating heartrate. What would military service actually be like? Would I cope with its unknowable physical and mental demands? What would become of me at the end of this first day? Would they send me to a training camp? Would I find myself in the midst of the current shooting war in Lebanon? How would I cope with army discipline? How often would I see my family? Would I be injured, or even killed, on the battlefield? These multiplying, frightening, unanswerable questions were inundating my tired brain as I waited long hours in raggle-taggle queues of chattering Israeli youngsters squinting anxiously at each other in the low winter sun. At each office window, when I eventually reached it, a sullen and uncommunicative uniformed clerk inspected my assorted papers, stamped them contemptuously, and gestured me, wordlessly, to move on to the next hut.

The penultimate stop was the quartermaster's store. Young soldiers, barely acknowledging my presence, insolently tossed in my direction various items of clothing and equipment, including a bulky drum-shaped rucksack that I gathered I was expected to lumber around with me for evermore. Finally, an older and gentler female officer stamped the date of discharge on my induction papers, murmuring a few words of encouragement that turned out to be wildly over-optimistic: "Don't worry, Daniel, it will all pass very quickly."

I examined the piece of paper with apprehension verging on panic. My sentence was eighteen months. Of course I knew that was the prescribed length of service for a doctor of my age, but I had clung to a sliver of hope that it might be cut in half at least. I had heard stories of such things happening. Well, it was not to be, and an ancient Scottish exhortation formed on my lips: *you'll just have to thole it, man*. There was one upside to my predicament – the clock had started, and every passing second brought me nearer to my discharge. I brooded over that notion with minimal conviction. Everyone who has (compulsorily) donned a uniform, whether for military or judicial reasons, knows this truth: time seems to stand still, every minute feels like an hour, and every hour like a day.

38

I wasn't instantly dispatched, as I'd long feared, to basic training. The army needed generalist military doctors for immediate clinical duties and I would acquire, they assured me, the full array of soldiering skills at the officers' course at some point during my service. Despite its impersonality, the process of induction was not quite as random as it seemed.

Because of my academic status, I was briefly whisked off to be interviewed by a senior air force scientist (an aeronautical physiologist as I recall). I was hardly wined-and-dined though I was treated to a remarkably tasty lunch by army standards. He offered me the option of a stint at a prestigious and somewhat shadowy research facility in the north of the country but my lack of enthusiasm (due in large part to the thought of having to complete at least one parachute jump in my first week) quickly stymied that prospect. To be honest, I didn't really have enough information on which to make a sound judgement. The air force base looked modern and well-maintained, and I learned later from colleagues that I would undoubtedly have enjoyed a far higher level of creature comforts throughout my service had I accepted that invitation. "The air force is the *crème de la crème*, nothing like this dump – you should definitely have gone there," was the firm but unhelpful verdict of my fellow IDF doctors.

The army's southern command desperately needed doctors at a Negev medical base that was less than ten minutes' drive from my home. When they imparted that information to me, it was music to my ears. Perhaps I should have asked for a day or two to give myself time to think. Fearing that the offer might be time limited, I jumped at the chance to serve in the Negev. The die was cast. I was told to report to my base the following morning at eight.

A bored sentry waved me through the gate of *Charap* (the Hebrew acronym for the army's medical corps), Base No.543. This was a ramshackle collection of low buildings set in the midst of a barren dustbowl just outside Beer Sheva. As I stood perspiring in my new olive-green uniform under the blisteringly hot sun surveying an uninspiring cluster of wooden huts, I found ample cause to regret my hasty rejection of the air force. Following a sign pointing to *General Clinic*, I surveyed the ramshackle centrepiece of the camp

– a square courtyard surrounded by an elevated walkway beyond which were about half a dozen consulting rooms. A paramedic spotted me and, on confirming my identity, ushered me into one of the empty rooms where I was instructed to await the appearance of the commanding officer.

The doctors' offices were primitive affairs. I gingerly eased myself onto a wobbly upright chair behind a rickety table and gazed at the dingy surroundings. They were hardly a sight to lift the spirits: a worn-out leather examination couch, a small fan humming ineffectually in the corner, a small plastic bin, and a clapped-out fluorescent strip light spluttering overhead. Large winged insects buzzed and slapped against the wire meshing of the window frantically seeking respite from the unforgiving sun.

I mopped my brow and tried, unsuccessfully, to repulse an incoming tide of negative emotions. This desolate place would presumably be my home for the next year and a half. I had feared physical danger as a soldier in a war zone. Here the hazards were hardly life-threatening but no less real and would likely pose a major threat to my mental health. How would I survive this heart-sinking challenge? The answer was banal in its simplicity and logic. I would deal with it as best I could because I would have no choice.

An inner voice sternly admonished me for flirting with self-pity: *You had a choice, Steyne, you and no-one else took this decision, and here is the consequence so accept responsibility and get over it.*

39

For the first few months, life at the base was mind-numbingly dull at best, dyspeptically aggravating at worst. My ostensible function was to act as a primary care provider to the thousands of youngsters who had been plucked from the bosoms of their families and thrown into a stressful military cauldron. I tried to adopt the role of a benign family doctor who would tend to their clinical and psychological needs, but I soon discovered a different reality. I was, in effect, the gatekeeper to *gimelim* – the highly sought-after military sick lines that exempted the soldiers from all routine duties. In my naivety, I initially dispensed these slips of paper with thoughtless abandon. The result was predictable.

By day two, I was the most popular medical officer in the entire Israeli army. A queue of hopeful supplicants, eager to exploit the largesse of the new Scottish doctor, awaited me – and only me – as I arrived at the clinic every morning. By the third day, the queue was snaking around the block. This scenario was unsustainable, naturally, and within a week it was brought to a juddering halt. My immediate superior, under irresistible pressure from increasingly incensed field commanders, banned me outright from issuing any further *gimelim*. I argued, with as much conviction as I could muster, that my first responsibility was to alleviate human suffering rather than to provide cannon fodder for the army.

I knew I was being obstinate, melodramatic and contrarian. The commanders had a perfectly valid point – they needed soldiers or the whole army would have disintegrated. And I was well aware that some of my patients were expert manipulators. At the very least, I protested, we army doctors were being subjected to a major conflict of interest. The response from my superiors (and most of my colleagues) was cynical laughter.

"Listen, Steyne," barked my commander, "you have no conflict of interest here. None whatsoever. Your duty is to the army. Here you are not primarily a doctor; you are a soldier. That is your priority. You are first a soldier, second a soldier, and third a soldier. Got it?" He neither expected, nor received, an answer.

*

By far the most depressing part of my army service were the regular callouts from the Beer Sheva *Katzin Ha'ir* (City Officer). This involved accompanying a social worker and a driver to the homes of unsuspecting families to convey the grim tidings that they had lost a loved one in the line of duty. The knock on the door from the army is the event that all Israelis dread above all others. Many of the victims were youngsters in their teens or twenties, male and female. The fatalities mostly occurred either in battle or during training although a significant number had been caught up in terror attacks, usually suicide bombings. There were also suicides, road traffic injuries, and a sprinkling of sudden deaths due to a variety of undiagnosed medical conditions.

We army doctors reluctantly took turns to assist in the discharge of this appalling obligation. We visited these homes at all hours of the day and night. Our role was purely supportive – to provide medication (usually a sedative) or first aid to relatives who were confronted with this nightmarish scenario. How can such unimaginable grief be medicalised? In truth, we contributed little other than to stop well-meaning onlookers from exacerbating an already intolerable situation. Approaching a deserted street in a slumbering suburb or village at 2am, in the full knowledge that we were, within a matter of minutes, about to shatter for ever the lives within, was almost unbearable.

I witnessed many harrowing scenes. It has lately become fashionable in some circles to sneer at Israeli families sunbathing on the Tel Aviv beaches while apparently ignoring the daily suffering their army allegedly inflicts on Palestinians. This wicked caricature is supposed to convey an insight into the "asymmetry" of the conflict. It is a grotesque distortion of the facts. If anyone dares to suggest, in my presence, that Palestinians are the only victims of this endless bloodletting, they will receive a searing counterblast from someone who knows differently. (I have held many such high-voltage conversations over the years and, without exception, the sneering critics have been quickly silenced).

That life-changing trauma apart, I couldn't complain unduly. At least I could get home at a civilised hour on most days and that was a great privilege for any soldier, but the chronic tedium began to take its toll. During those eighteen months, I would much rather have been somewhere – anywhere – else but I gritted my teeth and got on with the job. With each passing hour, I was moving closer to D-day, my date of discharge. All the conscripts kept a personal "calendar of despair" on which we scored off the dates as each day came and went.

I had to keep reminding myself what I was doing there. I was serving, albeit as a medical officer, in *Tsahal*, the legendary Israel Defence Force. In the eyes of many military experts, this was the most efficient and effective army in the Middle East, perhaps in the world. If that were true, I ruminated, what in heaven's name were the others like? Anyone who has faced cognitive dissonance will understand my perplexity about this.

Eventually, the penny dropped. The army was actually a huge machine with innumerable cogs and wheels that had to be oiled, repaired and replaced as rapidly and efficiently as possible. I was dealing, in the main, with the rejected components, the damaged misfits that risked clogging up the whole system. The *Charap* bases were peripheral to, though necessarily supportive of, the real army. I came to regard the *Charap* clinics, uncharitably, as repositories of a hidden, unsavoury underbelly where a motley crew of inadequates and incompetents congregated in largely vain attempts to extricate themselves from the rigours of military life. And all of these lost souls sought solace from the only place available to them in the full knowledge that any magnanimity the military doctors might dispense would offer them, at best, a temporary respite from their troubles.

The harsh fact is that all military conscripts suffer hardship of one kind or another. It's an occupational hazard. By the end of my first year of service, I thought I had experienced my fair share. Yet again, I would be proved wrong. Mine had scarcely begun.

40

I had been forewarned that I would, at some unspecified point, be sent to an officers' training course but had put that prospect out of my mind in the hope that I would be left to my own devices until my last day of service. That was wishful thinking.

One day in early 1985 I was handed an order paper to report to the senior course commander the following week. There was no advance notice and no discussion. The medical officers' course was held in a large base in the town of Rishon LeTsiyon near Tel Aviv. From the moment I drove through the gate, I sensed that I had entered a different world from that of the Negev *Charap*. This looked and felt, for the first time in my service, like a real army.

The instructors knew what they were about and projected an impressive aura of confidence and competence. The trainees were doctors from a variety of specialties and nationalities. Discipline was strict and the days long, especially so due to the early start from home. One of my medical colleagues from the Beer Sheva base, a bubbly American-Israeli girl called Janice, had also been enrolled on the course and accompanied me on the long drives. She was pretty and I enjoyed our daily conversations. This arrangement incurred, naturally (though entirely needlessly), Sandra's jealousy when she learned about my glamorous travelling companion.

*

Throughout most of these journeys, we listened to Israeli popular music. I'd never been a great fan of the genre but in the eighties I became addicted to what became known as a golden age of Israeli song. Among my favourites were Ofra Chaza, Chava Alberstein, Yardena Arazi, the Parparim, Arik Einstein, Yehoram Gaon and Shlomo Artzi. These performers had the knack of conveying the constantly fluctuating national mood through an intensely powerful combination of musical technique and emotional artistry. They all deserved a global platform but only Ofra Chaza successfully breached that inexplicably impenetrable barrier. Unfortunately, her success was all too short-lived; she succumbed to AIDS-related pneumonia at the age of forty-two.

*

The trainees' work programme was intense, demanding and mostly interesting. I enjoyed all the field exercises, except for the route marches though the verdant Israeli countryside; these took their toll on our backs, arms, legs and, above all, feet. One evening I returned home exhausted after such an ordeal and could barely remove my boots, so severe was the pain from numerous friction blisters. The three older children gathered around their complaining father as Sandra gently removed my footwear to reveal the reddened, swollen and bleeding tissues underneath. Ilana, Peter and Ethan audibly gasped in unison, fascinated and horrified in equal measure, as their mother patched me up as best she could in readiness for the next day's exertions.

There were more physical challenges to come though not all of them were as demanding as the marches. For several weeks we were stretched, physically and mentally, to the very outer limits of our endurance and we had to stay constantly alert. I was handed an M16 rifle and taught how to shoot at a target (a task I found surprisingly easy to master), take the weapon apart, clean the components and reassemble them quickly under stress. I took the gun home every evening and stored it under my bed, warning the children of dire consequences if they so much as breathed on it. This was a matter of simple domestic safety, but I had an added incentive: the penalties for the misuse or neglect of an IDF-issued weapon were draconian.

The days flew past. We learned map reading, military strategy, communication codes, and the names of weird-looking bits of metal attached to armoured cars. Above all, we were drilled repeatedly in battlefield medicine, resuscitation techniques and casualty triage. There were numerous exercises, and these were, more often than not, highly entertaining.

At the end of each module, we were thoroughly tested. The practical assessments were straightforward, but the verbal and written ones exercised my Hebrew language skills beyond breaking point. The examiners knew this, of course, and took full account of it – they candidly admitted that they couldn't afford to fail me. Somehow, I clambered over the modest bar they had set and I graduated as a lieutenant, in front of my instructors, classmates and family, at a brief passing out ceremony. The grand climax of the evening was the presentation of the award for the class's outstanding soldier. That wasn't me, in the unlikely case you're wondering, but I was pleased as punch with my hard-won pips.

For some reason, I had been slow to make the connection in my mind between my newly promoted status and the likely future direction of my army career. As a doctor, I had been conscripted as an officer. That gave me a few basic benefits, but it was really quite meaningless in terms of my status in the organisation. To become a "real soldier" I had to jump through the many hoops of the officer training course. Until I'd passed that milestone, I was a lowly jobbing generalist; after it, I was considered battle ready. I had been warned by colleagues about this critical transition but was in no rush, once back on home turf, to draw my superiors' attention to it.

By contrast, the army knew exactly what it was doing and acted fast. Within a matter of days of returning to my regular desert posting, I was summoned to the base commander's office. He shook me warmly and disarmingly by the hand (always an ominous sign), ushered me (even more worryingly) to a seat and imparted his news. Now that I was fully trained, he gleefully informed me, I was ready for much greater things. I had now earned my passport out of the Negev. Surely I didn't want to stay in this boring backwater for the remaining months of my service?

As I tried to muster a coherent response, he stopped me in my tracks. No, he answered for me, what I really needed was to move up to the next level; in short, to fulfil my potential as trained army medical officer in a different and altogether more exciting setting. They had, I would be pleased to learn, decided to send me to war. What war, you may ask? I didn't as I knew the answer only too well.

It's time for a drop of history.

41

For the first thirty years of her existence, Israel had not enjoyed a single day of peace. After three (or arguably four) wars, some of the neighbouring Arab states realised that the hated Zionists could not, at least in the foreseeable future, be destroyed militarily. Egypt's leaders, having been subjected to a succession of humiliating defeats on the battlefield, reluctantly concluded that diplomacy might prove more effective.

Following the peace moves between Israel and Egypt in 1977-78, in response to President Sadat's offer to address the Israeli *Knesset* (parliament), a furious Palestine Liberation Organisation stepped up the tempo of terrorist attacks on Israeli civilians from their bases in Lebanon. (Contrary to *Guardianesque* fantasies, Palestinian terrorism has generally been fuelled rather than dampened by signs of impending peace that they view as heralding the death knell of their central cause, namely the destruction of Israel). Some of these "resistance actions" – notably the northern coastal road massacre of 1978 – were monstrous in their random cruelty and violence.

The mastermind of these atrocities, PLO chairman Yasser Arafat, had established a personal fiefdom in southern Lebanon, a heavily armed state within a state. To the eternal shame of the United Nations and many countries around the world, the Kalashnikov-wielding, grinning Arafat was neither condemned by nor ostracised from the international community for his disgraceful behaviour; on the contrary, he was feted as a hero and given a platform for his violent extremism more than once on the floor of the General Assembly. With the backing of oil-rich Arab states, and neighbouring Syria, though not of the Lebanese people or government, he proclaimed himself leader of the "rejection front" that would stand by the Arab League's nihilistic 1967 Khartoum declaration – no peace, no recognition, no negotiation.

Because Lebanon had been weakened by years of civil war, that formerly serene little country was viewed by Arafat and his cronies as the ideal launching pad for escalating attacks across the border. Small-scale Israeli incursions against PLO bases achieved only temporary lulls in terrorism. Throughout this period, the PLO was gaining strength. When Shlomo Argov, the Israeli Ambassador to the UK, was seriously injured in an assassination attempt by a PLO splinter group in 1982, Prime Minister Begin and Defence Minister Sharon ordered the army to cross the northern border and push out the PLO from southern Lebanon. That early phase of *Operation Peace for Galilee* worked well enough and was supported by most Israelis. The defeated Arafat and what remained of his paramilitary infrastructure soon decamped to Tunis. Unfortunately, the rest of the campaign was badly mishandled by the army, under erratic and incompetent political direction, and rapidly became mired in disaster. Casualties on both sides rose steeply and morale on the Israeli home front quickly crumbled.

The turning point came when Sharon and Begin were blamed (however unfairly) both at home and abroad for the Lebanese Christian Phalangist massacre of Palestinians in Sabra and Shatila. This gruesome event was a propaganda coup for the PLO and critics of Israel have exploited it to the hilt ever since. Some people have suggested (though I don't fully agree) that it marked the point at which the international community turned sharply hostile to Israel and her supporters. The sanctimonious leader writer of *The Guardian* demanded (and I paraphrase) that *all Jews should hang their heads in shame*, apparently oblivious to the racist nature of that collective condemnation – a fate that the Lebanese people, the Phalangist militias and the world's Christians were pointedly spared. The war had always been deeply unpopular in Israel and by late 1984 the army was desperate to withdraw since it was losing soldiers regularly to suicide attacks launched by the newly formed and ultra-fanatical Islamist militia, Hezbollah.

This was the nasty, low-intensity, asymmetrical and dangerous conflict into which I was thrust in the summer of 1985.

42

The night before my journey north, I spent several hours discussing the morality of the war with colleagues and friends (though not my family – I had been ordered to keep the details of my deployment secret from them). Many of them were furious with the government and were ready to take to the streets to voice their outrage. When an anti-war demonstration was organised by the nascent Peace Now movement (of which I was a signed-up founder member), hundreds of thousands flocked to central Tel Aviv. Some estimates put the total turnout at half a million. It was the largest protest in Israel's history.

Ariel Sharon, former war hero and already a cult-figure in Israeli politics, had been found "indirectly responsible" for the Sabra and Shatila massacre by the Kahan commission (though Jeremy Bowen of the BBC and other journalists of his persuasion have ever since been unable to resist the temptation to drop the all-important *indirectly* prefix). After much prevarication he resigned as defence minister and was effectively banished from national politics for twenty years. His (ostensible) boss, the prime minister, escaped the wrath of public opinion. I was never a Begin supporter but had credited him with the extraordinary peace deal with Sadat of Egypt. I suspect many others felt the same. Nevertheless, the Lebanon imbroglio was stretching my forbearance to breaking point. If I, like so many Israelis, was unsympathetic to the turn the conflict had taken, should I refuse to obey my orders and risk a prison sentence?

Frankly, I never seriously considered being a conscientious objector. For all that the government's war aims had become mangled by the reckless Sharon and Rafael Eitan, his compliant chief of staff, Israel was not and never had been the aggressor. An implacable enemy, whose declared aim was Israel's destruction, had become entrenched uncomfortably close to her northern border and was perpetrating horrific terrorist attacks on a regular basis on her citizens, with barely a murmur of protest from the international community. I concluded, after much soul-searching, that the war may have been seriously mismanaged, but it was – by a whisker – legally and morally justifiable. (Whether it was politically smart or militarily advantageous was another matter). And if I refused to go, another poor sod would surely be sent in my place so where was the morality in that? No, for all my qualms, I would do it. I took a deep breath and set all my reservations temporarily aside.

My orders were to travel by bus, with a rifle and steel helmet, to the northern town of Metula (right on the border with Lebanon) and report to the military post there. Sandra was grim-faced when I told her I had to leave home for a few days and our parting was strained, almost bad-tempered; she wasn't fooled for a moment by my evasiveness. I promised to call her as soon as I could. The journey took several hours during which I wrote my "dear family" letter, as all soldiers entering a combat zone were ordered to do, in case we didn't return home. (I used the back of a postcard that is still in my possession somewhere). When I arrived at the border post, I was told to wait until the next morning when I would be transported to an IDF base in Southern Lebanon.

The scene I beheld there was one of organised chaos. Soldiers of all ranks were milling around an array of vehicles, small and large, in apparent random motion. I had no idea what was going on. Someone with a plan was presumably in charge but I couldn't work out who that was or what was expected of me. Eventually, I located a makeshift office where a surly clerk stamped my orders and sent me to a tin hut where I would spend the night with other stray soldiers awaiting further instructions.

Having grabbed a vacant bunk, I struck up a conversation with a crusty reservist from Tel Aviv who shared with me his news that his wife had just delivered him a son. I congratulated him with the traditional *Mazal tov* to which he retorted grumpily, "Why?" That reaction genuinely flummoxed me.

"Aren't you happy about your new baby?" I asked.

"Yes, of course, but at the same time I'm sad, very sad."

"Why," I asked again. With a shake of the head came a devastating answer.

"We've created another soldier."

We both fell silent. I thought I should try to lighten the mood. "I'm sure that by the time he grows up there will be peace." The soldier smiled ruefully at me. "You haven't been long in this country, have you doctor?"

43

I've always attracted mosquitoes. Apparently they are drawn to the aroma of certain people. (My mother suffered the same affliction so it may be a genetic quirk). They also, I can confirm, congregate in army facilities in vast numbers. On one occasion, I was relocated temporarily from the Negev to a base in the centre of the country. There I was dive-bombed by swarms of the creatures throughout each night. Only the liberal application of jungle strength insect repellent saved me from being devoured entirely though I still managed to sustain numerous, excruciatingly painful bites on my face, neck, shoulders and arms.

My Metula experience was only marginally less excruciating. After a poor night's sleep incurred primarily by my resolve to hold the buzzing devils at bay, I stepped out of the hut to catch some warming sunshine when I thought I heard my name called by a distant, disembodied voice.

"Dr Steyne, where are you? We need you, now."

A harassed sergeant took a quick squint at my papers and led me to an open jeep on which was mounted a sizeable machine gun.

"You see that beauty? You'll be in charge of it. Climb in."

I threw my kit bag into the back seat and took up my place next to the weapon. A well-built, bespectacled man in his forties dressed in ill-fitting combat fatigues sauntered up to the vehicle and, saying nothing, clambered into the driving seat. I gathered that there would be just two of us on the journey.

My companion turned out to be a very senior officer, a lieutenant general, I think, who eventually introduced himself with a brief handshake (saluting being almost unheard of in the Israeli army). He pointed at the weapon. "You know how to use this?"

"Well," I stammered, "I vaguely remember the theory, but I've never actually fired one."

My answer clearly unsettled him. After a prolonged, weary sigh, he delivered a thirty-second tutorial on its use and instructed me to stay fully awake and keep my finger on the trigger.

"Open fire on anything that moves. If you hesitate, we'll both be goners."

"Understood." I nodded vigorously, trying to persuade both of us that I was in full control of the situation.

This was a far from ideal induction to my combat duties. Disconcertingly, the starter took several minutes to ignite the engine, but we finally set off, swaying and bumping on the primitive suspension, and crossed the border into Lebanon in total silence. In the hazy early morning light, the rolling countryside beyond the impressive presence of Mount Hermon looked remarkably similar to the Galilee region of Israel but after a few miles we were driving through much more barren terrain, a striking contrast to the manicured orchards and forests we were leaving behind us. I saw no local inhabitants whatsoever. They had either fled as a result of the fighting or were keeping a low profile.

Every half hour or so, my officer-driver picked up his walkie-talkie and conducted a clipped, bad-tempered, and largely incomprehensible conversation with what I presumed was a central communications centre. I was tired after my restless night and struggled to avoid dozing off. I wondered whether I should engage the general in conversation but decided against, focusing instead on my delegated task of scanning the horizons for signs of activity.

The blue waters of Lake Karoun injected a splash of colour into the otherwise bleak landscape, and within a couple of hours we had reached our destination. It was a flat-roofed concrete building on two floors – perhaps a school or community centre – located bang in the middle of a tiny deserted village. I was greeted cheerfully by the chief paramedic with a mixture of curiosity and sympathy and assigned a lower bunk on the ground floor. This was to be my home for the next ten days or so. A young paramedic gave me a tour of the base, ending with a peek into the shower cubicle – an unexpected luxury in the circumstances, notwithstanding the cluster of oversized rats scurrying around the skirting boards.

This wasn't so bad, I reflected, as I gingerly tested the springs of my bed with my aching backside. No sooner had I removed my boots and was preparing for a few minutes rest to recover from the wearisome journey, when we were all (no exceptions) summoned to an urgent meeting with the base commander.

44

He was a short, bald man, probably not much older than me, but his furrowed brow had prematurely aged his face. The thought struck me that he looked the complete antithesis of the New Jew of Zionist mythology; here was not so much the fearless, battle-hardened fighter ready to take on the world, but the demoralised family man weary of having to fight yet another war.

He gestured to us, about thirty soldiers in all, to sit as he pulled up a rickety chair and sat on it back to front, gazing wordlessly into the middle distance as if gathering his thoughts. Or perhaps the silence was deliberately designed to raise the tension. If so, it worked. When he spoke, his words carried an authority that belied his modest appearance.

"Guys, listen carefully, I have something very important to tell you. Not far from here, just yesterday, one of our young soldiers was abducted, tortured, and killed. I won't trouble you with the gruesome details. By all accounts, he was a gifted young man – a classical musician, I believe. He had a glittering career in front of him. More importantly, he was someone's son, brother and sweetheart. His death has devastated his family and his community. And here's the relevant point – it was completely avoidable. He had wandered, against standing orders, into the local village to try to pick up a bargain in the *souk*. Instead, he picked up something else. Something he wasn't looking for. A slow, agonising death. He no longer suffers, thank God, but his family will suffer for the rest of their lives." He paused and mopped his perspiring brow with a grubby handkerchief.

"Why am I telling you this? Because that young man could have been any one of us. It has been brought to my attention that some of you have been purchasing goods – radios, cassette recorders, cameras – on the black market in the village next door. I won't name names. You know who you are. But this must stop, now. Not only is that behaviour in violation of your orders, it puts everyone involved at risk. If you get a knife in your back, what should I say to your parents? How will I explain to them that I permitted you to risk your lives unnecessarily? How will I live with myself as your commander? You have no mother and father here. I am your mother and father. And I have to do everything in power to protect you, not just from the enemy (and God knows he is dangerous enough) but from yourselves. Better to return home safely without that camera or cassette player than not to return home at all. As from today, the black market does not exist. It's finished. Is that clear? Questions?"

I looked around the room, but all eyes were fixed on the floor. I felt dissociated from the scene, as if I were acting a bit-part in a long-running soap opera whose principal characters I had never met. The emotional atmosphere was heavy enough for a relieving thunderstorm that never came. There were no questions or comments and the commander took the silence to signify assent.

He stood up. "Good, this meeting is over." The group dispersed rapidly, though exactly to where was a mystery to me. A few of the company loitered in doorways and lit cigarettes. I stored my rifle under my bunk and wandered into the yard. It was really just a patch of overgrown grass about a hundred metres square surrounded on all sides by the squat buildings of our temporary base. I quickly took my bearings and, feeling an irresistible call of nature, headed for the latrines that I knew were at its far end.

I'd reached about halfway across when someone shouted, "Doctor, where are you going?" The gruff voice belonged to a guard on the roof who was pretty agitated.

"Just popping across to the toilet," I replied. "Is that a problem?" It obviously was.

"Without a weapon? Are you mad? You'll be a sitting duck."

"Fine, calm down, I'll go back and get it."

The guard shook his head in exasperation. "I won't be calm if you get blown to pieces. You're not in England now. You need to learn quickly here, doctor."

I did. My first lesson was that nothing, not even normal bodily functions, could be taken for granted in this surreal, parallel universe.

45

My unit was a standard mobile medical support team comprising mostly paramedics, a handful of doctors and a few multipurpose non-medics who were there to provide support and protection to the group. We were on constant standby for "action" (though no-one ever explained precisely what that meant). I discovered, after persistent enquiry, that our main role was to rush to an incident out in the field in which injuries might have been incurred. The prospect filled me with apprehension. Though I had just been trained in battlefield medicine and was confident enough in my basic clinical skills, confronting the real thing was a daunting prospect. It's one thing to demonstrate your competence in a simulated exercise, it's another altogether to do the same under fire.

Military gurus explain that one of the great strengths of the Israeli army is the verisimilitude of its exercises. One of these sticks in my mind. Shortly after arriving at the *Charap*, I was dispatched for the weekend to a group of reservists in the Negev who were accompanying, as was their usual role, a tank regiment. As dusk fell, the radio crackled, and we were sent "to war." Flares were hoisted and the tanks started firing in rotation towards unseen targets. It was all rather exciting and a touch scary. When I asked one of my colleagues whether this could be a real shooting war rather than an exercise, his curt reply was far from reassuring: "Who knows?"

I reflected on that episode as I braced myself for the real thing in an actual theatre of conflict. As it happened, there was no serious fighting in our zone during my time there and I wasn't summoned to treat traumatic injuries. Others in the unit weren't so lucky. Without much prompting, they gave vivid accounts of harrowing scenes of death and injury on the battlefield. This gloomy ritual of military storytelling fulfilled two purposes. It acted as a kind of group therapy for the soldiers, many of whom were struggling with post-traumatic stress as a result of their experiences. And it helped pass the time.

*

One of the paramedics described to me how he had been driving a mini-ambulance containing three or four soldiers and an injured fighter when they came under mortar fire. He stopped the vehicle and screamed at everyone to get out and throw themselves under the chassis. There wasn't much space under there and one of the reservists was a little slow in taking cover – he suffered a direct hit and was incinerated on the spot. His remains were returned to his family in a plastic bag.

On another occasion, my staff sergeant recounted a ghastly incident during a training exercise in which his commanding officer was seriously injured by "friendly fire." Late one night, the lieutenant had decided to check the perimeter of their makeshift base in the woods when he encountered what he thought was an animal, perhaps a boar or a fox, prowling in the bushes. He drew his pistol and moved stealthily towards his target. There was no animal in the undergrowth – just a young guard completing his final circuit of the night. The private panicked when he caught sight of a figure in the shadows, the handgun glistening briefly in the moonlight. He opened fire with his Uzi and shot the commander's right arm clean off.

I heard many such accounts, some of which were sleep-disrupting in their horror. Every Israeli family has heard them while almost no-one outside the country has the faintest inkling either of their existence or of their searing impact on the national psyche. That's a shame because it diminishes the international community's ability to exhibit minimal empathy – so capacious with regard to the Palestinians – towards Israelis and their unending, soul-destroying security nightmare.

*

The long Lebanese days passed with mind-numbing tedium. Our longed-for sleep was interrupted by a compulsory two-hour stint of guard duty every night. Conversation was intermittent and cursory as everyone was permanently tired and nervous. The combination of boredom and fear is not a good one. Such was the all-pervasive sense of lethargy that I and my colleagues began to yearn for some action, just for the sake of killing time rather than the enemy.

I tried hard to relax (if that isn't an oxymoron) and undertake some constructive personal reflection. One of the more experienced reservists encouraged me to focus on this as a form of therapeutic meditation or "clearing the head" as he called it. I was sceptical. My head was becoming more cluttered with incoherent worries with every passing minute.

Thankfully, at least an hour or two each day was occupied performing some basic clinical duties. We ran a makeshift medical clinic in the backyard that accepted all comers – after a thorough security check – and that offered me welcome if brief diversions. Now and again, a soldier or civilian would turn up with a symptom that needed attention and I was asked to function as a kind of all-purpose GP on these occasions. The presenting problems were usually fairly trivial – eye infections, coughs, sore throats, sprained ankles – and easily dealt with. My patients were mostly young men, some uniformed, though on occasions they would have an elderly parent or sibling in tow who had been dragged along for a consultation. In keeping with the ethical code of the IDF, we treated everyone – Jews or Arabs, Lebanese or Palestinians, Christians or Muslims, soldiers or civilians, friends or foes. Most of the time I didn't know which of these categories I was treating, nor did I care.

46

Everyone on the makeshift base, from the most senior commander to the lowliest private, was permanently irritable and pessimistic. We complained continuously to anyone who would listen (or just to ourselves) about the bedbugs, the stinking toilets, the rat-infested showers, the inedible food and the military idiocy of our continued presence in this remote backwater. All we wanted was what all soldiers in history have ever wanted – to go home and sleep.

None of the mundane tasks I had to perform was my idea of fun but I especially loathed guard duty. It seemed to come around every day and most nights, disrupting sleeping patterns and, most damagingly, morale. Our job was to patrol the roof in pairs, identify potential attackers and sound the alarm should we spot anything untoward. As far as I could tell, everything in this environment was untoward. If you stand stock still on a rooftop in an unfamiliar landscape in the middle of the night, I guarantee that you'll hear and see (or hallucinate) all kinds strange happenings. Our challenge was to separate illusion from reality.

I felt the burden of responsibility intensely. The sky was a magnificent sight, replete with streaking comets and multitudes of stars of all shapes and sizes that looked near enough to touch. But astronomy was a potentially lethal distraction. Our senses were strained to detect sights or sounds much nearer to hand. Were these noises caused by animals, birds, a rustling breeze, or an impending attack? There were no rules to help us, other than the order to maintain complete silence at all times, and we felt powerless to exert real control over our surroundings in any meaningful sense. Time stood still and heartbeats raced, and the night eventually passed. The first faint glimmerings of dawn were a blessed relief marking our rescue by the rising sun. In truth, daylight was no less dangerous than the black night but at least we would be able to see our assailants.

Even when we were mercifully freed from the rota of the dreaded roof patrol, life was seldom peaceful for long. One night, I was rudely awakened from a (rare) deep sleep at about 3am by the thunderous rattle of automatic gunfire. At first I assumed I was dreaming. The explosions sounded extremely close and could surely only signify bad news. With much cursing and flailing, we all jumped out of our bunks, hastily donned whatever footwear we could locate and rushed, rifles in hand, outside into the cool air.

For a minute or two, there was utter confusion; men were shouting, gesticulating and running in all directions to no obvious purpose. I stood still while I tried to assess the developing drama. There was little to see – the enfolding blackness of that night looked much the same as all the others – so we had to rely largely on our ears, and they didn't prove much of a help. Our working hypothesis was that we were being drawn into a firefight with unseen terrorists lurking in the bushes, but it soon became obvious that we weren't. The gunfire had ceased and there were, thankfully, no signs of injuries or of an enemy. After the initial chaos, word spread rapidly that we could relax. It transpired that the whole thing had been a carefully planned contrivance, an unannounced exercise conducted with startling realism by the platoon commander to test our readiness to repel an assault. He achieved his objective. We had failed the challenge miserably and he wasn't shy in telling us.

"What an absolute disgrace!" he barked. "You were far too slow. For at least thirty seconds, not a single one of you showed his face. Is this an army base or a holiday camp? If that had been a real attack, we'd all be dead. Not good enough. Go back to bed. We'll review this sorry mess in the morning."

Shaken and chastened, we trundled back to bed. The episode, for all its seemingly capricious cruelty, had the desired effect. Our collective alertness soared. The roof-top guards were doubled up. And from that night on, we slept in our boots.

47

That was, more or less, the extent of my war. I never participated in direct contact with the enemy nor was I called upon to treat battlefield injuries. I suppose I was mildly disappointed though simultaneously relieved at my good fortune. The war may have been petering out but the casualty rate was, if anything, higher than ever. But I didn't obsess over such matters. My real focus, in common with every other soldier in that forlorn place, was on the agonisingly slow countdown to the blessed day we would leave. Enervating boredom gradually gave way to eager anticipation.

When the great moment finally came, we were loaded into two open army lorries and warned to remain alert, stay silent and be ready to return fire at all times. Suicide bombings against Israeli forces by Hezbollah had become epidemic and the risk was a very real one. We drove off in an unfamiliar state of mind, precariously perched between euphoria and dread, rifles with their safety catches off lightly resting on our laps. I had never known a bunch of Israelis to remain speechless for so long.

The three-hour southward journey (that felt to us more like a week) passed without mishap. The joyous feeling of crossing the border back into Israel's manicured landscape was indescribable. With a collective whoop, we cheered and sang, drunk with survivors' relief. We hungrily consumed the sight of the friendly countryside around us. Each and every one of the familiar, squat makeshift huts that comprised the ramshackle Metula army base were as ravishing to our eyes as the Taj Mahal.

I will say this for the Israeli army: they treat all new recruits, regardless of background, status or role, with equal and almost callous indifference, but if you put your life on the line for them, they will respond with unequivocal, generous and near-palpable respect. As we climbed off the truck, my commander shook my hand, patted me on the back and bade farewell. "Go home and rest, doctor, you deserve it."

I didn't need to be told twice. With a minimum of fuss, the members of our platoon bid each other the usual ritual farewells and dispersed in multiple directions. I slept fitfully on the bus to the Negev, the journey that I had at times doubted that I would ever make. Despite my bone-crushing fatigue, I was exhilarated. Standing at the end of our dusty street in north Beer Sheva, I gazed at the passing traffic, glanced at the indigo sky and offered a silent thanks – to whom? (Not to a deity, certainly). I was home. I'd only been gone a fortnight but that meant nothing. I was a new man, metaphorically reborn and literally impatient to restart my life. Moreover, the world around me, though superficially unchanged, would never be quite the same again.

I stood there at the doorway of my flat, haggard, exhausted and dishevelled in my grimy uniform, clutching the paraphernalia of war. I couldn't help grinning like a mischievous child. The concrete block of flats that housed our flat had never glowed in the early evening sun with such wondrous beauty. The welcome I received from my family was rapturous.

"My God, Daniel, how you stink. I just knew you were in Lebanon," Sandra sobbed. The children were puzzled, perhaps even awe-struck at the dramatic if temporary unrecognisability of their soldier-father. But, as always, they (unlike their parents) took it all in their stride.

I showered, changed, ate quickly and collapsed into bed. The next morning, refreshed and dressed in civvies, I was still smiling, intent on savouring every last drop of pleasure at the miracle of my re-entry into the arms of my loved ones. I had never felt happier and my euphoria seemed to envelope the whole family in a blanket of grateful contentment.

I had no way of knowing then that we would all have to cope with the unanticipated, subversive implications of this episode for the rest of our lives.

48

Shortly after my return from Lebanon I was discharged from the army. On my final day, I travelled by car with a Russian fellow medic, tipsy on vodka, to the same Tel Aviv base where our military careers had begun a distant eighteen months earlier. The event was almost anticlimactic, so often had I strained to conjure up every detail in my imagination. Having returned our uniforms and completed the bureaucratic necessities, our papers were stamped, and we exited the camp under an archway emblazoned with the words in large Hebrew lettering *Welcome to Reserve Duty*. It was over. Clutching my documents, I glowered defiantly at the sign and made an inward promise.

Readjusting to civilian status was a challenge. Inflation had by then rocketed to nearly a thousand percent per annum. The cost of living index was announced in the middle of each month and that was followed by an avalanche of price increases; the trick was to do the monthly supermarket shopping on the day before the index was announced to exploit the lower old prices. But we were running to stand still. We could scarcely afford the mounting domestic bills let alone attempt to furnish our modest flat adequately or to contemplate family holidays. Every day we sank deeper into debt.

My parents continued to offer a degree of financial assistance that was never matched, to my distress, by an equivalent level of emotional support. On one visit, they had been cool to the point of iciness. Sandra was becoming understandably agitated about her mother's deteriorating health back in Scotland, and she bore the brunt of looking after four young children (as the youngest, Pamela, was now on the scene) while juggling with part-time medical work. I was struggling to reintegrate successfully into my academic job. The two major projects that I had led before being drafted had been handed over to colleagues and I found myself scratching around for the remaining morsels of research and teaching to which nobody else laid claim. Project grants were hard to come by and staff morale was low.

The wider environment was scarcely more inspiring. Israel was ill at ease with itself. The daily grind to make ends meet was taking its toll on the country's populace. Life in Israel is never easy but there are definable points in time when it becomes well-nigh intolerable and this was such a moment. The bitterly polarised and destructive political divide caused by the war had become an unbridgeable chasm. Public demonstrations, led most by the leftish *Peace Now* movement of which I was a proud member, were commonplace. Terrorist incidents were on the rise. A humiliated Arafat, sitting in exile in Tunis, was steadily raising the temperature of his anti-Israeli rhetoric in anticipation of the mass violence of the first *Intifada*. The optimism of the 1978 peace deal with Egypt had all but evaporated. The treaty itself had survived but it was a "cold peace"; Egyptians, despite having regained all the territory (and some) that had lost to Israel in a war that President Sadat had launched, were not yet prepared for the genuine rapprochement with their northern neighbours for which Israelis had fervently hoped.

The national spirit was lifted briefly by the unexpected release of a group Russian Jewish dissidents, the so-called *refuseniks*, the most internationally renowned of whom was the diminutive and brilliant Anatoly (now Natan) Sharansky. The Soviets had grown tired of their restless Jews and started to drip feed exit visas to the more troublesome activists. A massive international campaign on behalf of Soviet Jewry, under the banner of the slogan *Let My People Go*, had been running since the 1970s (in which Susan had been an active participant). The bad publicity was becoming a thorn in the side of the Soviet regime. We noticed a growing number of Russian speakers in our neighbourhood of Beer Sheva. Within a few years, the floodgates would open and more than a million Russian immigrants (many of whom were non-Jewish) would settle in Israel, increasing her population by about a million and a half.

49

The children were (mostly) oblivious to our growing family crisis. Or if they were troubled, they hid it well. Because we had two of each, the girls and boys often paired off with each other along gendered lines as a matter of course, and doubtless offered strong mutual support. Ilana and Peter had a tendency to mentor their younger same-sex siblings and that may have helped them all get through the crisis. Who knows? I certainly don't.

What I do know is that we were exceptionally fortunate in having given to life to four remarkable human beings. Here's what I wrote about them in my autobiographical prose-poem of 2019:

They entered and changed the world for evermore.
Never for an instant would I pick one out for praise,
For all were favourites, each with special gifts.
How to summarise a lifelong loved one
In a sentence or two? It patently can't be done
Yet I must try, or this moment will pass me by
To my eternal regret. If they should chance
Upon these words, I trust they'll understand.

Ilana, with her beauteous, caring warmth, was spoiled
No doubt by doting parents, though it never showed.
Peter, our quirky free spirit, wreathed us all
In wistful smiles concealing a deep-flowing wisdom.
Ethan, whose awe-inspiring grasp of facts
Enthralled us with his endless child-like wonder.
Pamela, sharp as a pin, suffering no fools gladly,
Wrapped her protective heart around us all.
We, their parents, tend to view them as a whole,
This supremely talented, divine quartet
That plays the heavenly music of the spheres,
Spun by both our double helices enjoined
To craft pure gems, each one a miracle of humanity.

Meanwhile Sandra and I were becoming gloomier by the day. The stable, happy future that we craved was drifting away, like a will-o-the-wisp, into the far horizon. Something would have to give. With every passing day, returning to Scotland became less of an option and more of an inevitability.

After prolonged prevarication, and not a few fraught marital conversations, we embarked on the tricky task of informing friends, colleagues, employers, and – most distressingly – our children of our impending departure. The news was greeted with surprise, dismay and sometimes anger. In some circles, the act of emigration (*Yerida* or *going down*) was regarded as treacherous. The otherwise benign dean of the medical school, as I broke the news to him, deliberately turned his back on me in an act of contemptuous disapproval. At some level, I probably agreed with him. My rationalisation for leaving was quite straightforward: I felt I had no choice. I had dragged my heels over this decision for long enough. I knew that any further delay would both bankrupt us and put my marriage in serious peril. In truth, I had probably made up my mind to leave on the day of my army discharge.

I harboured no animosity towards the army. On the contrary, I was grateful for that period of my life. I felt privileged to have served in the IDF and to have had the opportunity to express my support for the homeland in a practical way. In the course of my service, I met Israelis from all walks of life and heard their very different and often remarkable stories. Even the hardships had their positive aspects as they had taught me that I was capable of withstanding more severe stress than I had ever imagined possible.

*

I had absolutely no idea that I would shortly be thrust, unwillingly, into another hate-filled environment – a Scottish university – and would be obliged, out of necessity, to adopt and hone a new "career" as advocate for Israel. I was about to find myself on another front-line – this time an intellectual and ideological one – facing a different but equally fanatical enemy of the Jewish state. I would be ill-prepared and would have to embark on a steep learning curve. Fortunately, my years in Israel turned out to be the best preparation anyone could undergo for this new type of low intensity but nevertheless potentially lethal conflict, for that was when I would discover another great gift my military experience had handed me: I had acquired credibility with both Israelis and her adversaries, an asset that became decisive in the face of growing anti-Israeli activism in university campuses, trade unions, churches, the media and NGOs throughout the world.

A central plank of the Israel-haters' strategy was the alleged criminality of Israel's army. What the accusers didn't know (though they would soon discover) was that I was an unusual adversary for a simple reason. When confronted with the modern blood libel of Israel's "disproportionate" response to threats to her security, I had a huge advantage over my opponents – I'd had direct personal experience of serving in the IDF. No-one who hasn't served can defend an army's behaviour more effectively than a former member of its ranks. I knew of the centrality of the army's *purity of arms* dictum and its practical translation into the avoidance or at least minimisation of civilian casualties.

*

Our departure from the country was shambolic. We scrambled to give away or sell, for pin money, most of our flat contents and prepare for the journey back to the UK. Our close friends and neighbours, the Goldsteins, took it upon themselves to help us tie up the multiple bureaucratic and financial loose ends. We gave no thought to the future except that we had to get on that plane to London.

I had accepted an academic position at Glasgow University starting in the summer of 1985 and so faced an immutable deadline. For the two younger children, this was all just another adventure. The two elder ones were not so easily fooled. Peter kept his counsel and withdrew into himself. Our eldest, Ilana, aged nine, was distraught; I observed her tearful farewell to her friends with a heavy heart. It was obvious that she loved her Israeli life, was progressing well at school and had just been granted the accolade of the "outstanding pupil" of her class. To her credit, she never blamed her parents for this cruel twist of fate, but she retained an unshakeable affection for Israel and often expressed an aspiration to return some day.

Were we making a terrible mistake? Perhaps, but the decision was by now irreversible. Until the very last moment, I announced to colleagues and friends – and almost deluded myself into believing – that we would return within a year or two, but I couldn't sustain the pretence for long.

On the morning of the journey, a cluster of family suitcases were deposited at the doorway. There were eight, far too many. I arbitrarily pulled out four of the heavier ones and declared, to some consternation, that they would have to stay. The protests were fairly muted. We never saw those suitcases, nor their contents, again.

As metaphors for our hasty departure from the Jewish homeland, resulting in some hazily recalled but important family baggage being unwillingly but necessarily left behind, they could not have been more apt.

PART 3

50

Our newly purchased bungalow was located in a quiet, tree-lined street in the Glasgow suburb of Giffnock – "the most beautiful place on earth" in the words of the wonderful *chazan* (cantor) Ernest Levy, a Holocaust survivor and near neighbour. I had looked at a couple of properties on a short preparatory trip to Glasgow earlier in the year and had made up my mind, almost impulsively, that this was the one for us. Sandra had delegated to me the heavy responsibility of making a unilateral choice, a reflection perhaps of her desperation to get back to Scotland at any price.

By UK standards, the house was cramped and a little shabby; to our Israeli eyes it was palatial. Because the rear of the property was blessed with an unhindered south facing outlook across an enormous open space, we were able to enjoy gazing out at the vast sky and, especially, the innumerable spectacular West of Scotland sunsets. Was this heaven on earth? Not quite, but a reasonable approximation. It suited us just fine. We settled quickly into the rhythm of our new life despite the multiple irritations that always accompany such an upheaval. Both sets of grandparents were ecstatic at the return of their prodigal family. Only now that I have grandchildren of my own can I appreciate the anguish that the two-thousand-mile separation of the generations must have caused them.

We enrolled the children in the local Jewish primary school where they received some basic Jewish and, much more importantly, Hebrew language education from British and Israeli teachers of varying competence. The three older ones renewed old friendships and quickly formed new ones. As usual, the resilience of all four was wondrous to behold. That gave us enormous comfort. The unfolding tragedy back in the homeland did not.

By now, Zionism and Israel had become more of a religion to me than Judaism itself. From the relative tranquillity of that verdant Glasgow backwater, I followed Middle Eastern matters obsessively. Events there seemed to be set on an unstoppable downward spiral. During violent uprising known as the *First Intifada* (1987-1994), the British media turned mercilessly on Israel. Since the start of the Lebanon war in 1982, many journalists had opted for a simplistic geopolitical analysis that attributed most of the evils of the Middle East to Israeli malfeasance. An example: the banal cliché *one man's terrorist is another man's freedom fighter* was regularly deployed in a manner that implicitly endorsed violence by Palestinian extremists; it also revealed much about the prejudice of its proponents. Their take on terrorism was that it was an inevitable consequence of "the Illegal Israeli Occupation" and its associated repression. By contrast, the commentary on Israeli wrongdoing was never so forgiving. That was the laziest way of reporting a complex conflict; it involved signing up to the Palestinian victimhood narrative – lock, stock and barrel.

As American journalist Thomas Friedman explained in his book *From Beirut to Jerusalem*, the truth was the reverse – the Israeli repression was a consequence rather than a cause of the violence. So benign was the pre-*Intifada* occupation that the PLO became concerned that the Palestinian population was sleepwalking into full integration into Israeli society. I knew this to be so, given the ease with which we could drive through the West Bank and even Gaza in the 1980s. Tens of thousands of Israelis indulged in the daily pleasure – to the satisfaction of Palestinian merchants – of shopping in the *souks* of Hebron, Jenin, Ramallah and Gaza city. In those days, neither Israelis nor Palestinians were encumbered by checkpoints or barriers as there was no need for them. Today this basic historical fact is widely acknowledged in both Israel and the Palestinian territories, and just as widely discounted abroad.

Historical veracity has never obstructed the global media war against Israel. It has continued unabated to the present day with perhaps just a couple of brief pauses (the signing of the Oslo Accords in 1993 and the assassination two years later of prime minister Yitzhak Rabin). The result of truth-bending reportage is predictable: well-meaning people, lacking sufficient knowledge to filter the wheat from the chaff of biased media coverage, increasingly hold Israel largely or exclusively responsible for the continuing conflict and for the suffering of the Palestinians – "the victims of the victims" in Edward Said's seductively glib and misleading phrase. Historians of the future will scratch their heads at the way the truth was so easily perverted by so many for so long.

51

While we're on the subject of history (and when aren't we?), let's look briefly back at the nineties. It wasn't long ago, but the world's memory is short.

The plausible-sounding land-for-peace formula, conjured out of the successful precedent of the negotiations with Egypt in 1977, was *the* core idea of the Oslo Accords of 1993-95. Israel handed land to the Palestinians but didn't get peace. That should have been the top news story of the decade. Instead, foreign correspondents competed with each other to magnify alleged Israeli wrongdoing while minimising any Palestinian blame for what they misleadingly labelled the escalating "cycle of violence." After Israeli prime minister Rabin's assassination in 1995, the more rightist Likud party returned to power amidst widespread predictions that Israel would adopt a hard line, uncompromising position and renege on all of her remaining Oslo commitments.

Astonishingly, the opposite happened. In an attempt to restore momentum to the peace process, Israel's new prime minister, Benjamin Netanyahu, implemented the Wye River Memorandum of 1998 that involved further Israeli troop withdrawals, including from Hebron (Judaism's second holiest city) and its environs. He received little credit for this act of political and military courage either at home or abroad. For his part, Yasser Arafat agreed to end incitement against Israel and her citizens and resume negotiations. He did neither. Israel's dovish posture, it transpired, merely encouraged Arafat and other extremists in their belief that the enemy was on the verge of capitulation. With the knowledge of – and sometimes connivance with – the newly created Palestinian Authority, terrorist attacks on Israelis were stepped up, including horrific suicide bombings on Jerusalem buses. One of these occurred while our eighteen-year-old son Peter was visiting Israel (who thankfully called home as soon as the news broke). At last, surely the world's media would be forced to admit that there were also Israeli victims in this endless conflict.

I reflected angrily that dead Israelis (aka Jews) were the only ones likely to attract British sympathy but I was proved wrong by the bizarre media and political reactions to the nightmarish scenario that was unfolding in Israel. This sustained Palestinian campaign of terror became known as the *Second Intifada* (2000-2004) when over a thousand Israeli civilians were blown to smithereens on buses, in supermarkets, cafes, hotels and shopping centres. One of the victims was a close friend of our younger daughter Pamela; he was a 19-year-old Scottish student called Yoni (whose grieving parents agreed, in an act of transcendental compassion, to donate his organs to a Palestinian recipient).

The daily atrocities were committed by well-organised gangs of thugs claiming allegiance to a range of "resistance" organisations, notably Tanzim, Hamas and Islamic Jihad. The whole bloody business was instigated and coordinated by Arafat, a venal dictator who was continuously excused, feted and even idolised by his legion of supporters in the West. These useful idiots were actually dictating the foreign policy of around half the world's governments. Israelis, understandably, expected the Palestinian campaign of mass murder to change the climate of world opinion. It did – against Israel. Not only did the carnage fail to stop the kneejerk blaming of Israel, it reinforced it.

As the IDF tried to contain wave after wave of indiscriminate killings that were unleashed against the Israeli people from their notional partners in peace, the Palestinian casualty count inevitably started to rise. Tragically, some of those were civilians (inasmuch as they could be identified as such) who had got caught in the crossfire. This provoked the moral indignation of leader writers around the world, especially in western Europe, to a degree that the Israeli casualties had not. Israeli protestations that vast majority of Palestinian civilian deaths were accidental rather than deliberate cut no ice whatsoever.

The conventional explanation for the media and political hostility to Israel was that the IDF's allegedly disproportionate response was creating more Palestinian than Israeli victims. The comparative body counts may have been factually correct, but so was the Israeli argument that all the deaths were a consequence of Palestinian violence. That defence was dismissed outright by the sanctimonious liberal commentariat – *"the numbers speak for themselves,"* they shrieked. This kind of crude moral arithmetic is still invoked today and has never, to my knowledge, been applied to any other conflict in history. The automatic assumption, that the good guys are defined by their sustaining fewer casualties than the bad guys, would make no sense at all in relation to, say, the Allies' confrontation with the fascists during the Second World War, or the NATO air assault on the Serbs in Kosovo. The absurdity of this position becomes obvious on just a few seconds' reflection.

Yet absurdity increasingly rules when it comes to journalistic or political attitudes to Israel.

52

My pipe-puffing boss at Glasgow University's newly created Social Paediatric and Obstetric Research Unit was an intelligent and ostensibly jolly Yorkshireman called Andrew Bender. I had met him a couple of times previously and we had got on well. Although we later had our differences, I will always be grateful to him for scooping me out of the inhospitable Negev desert and slotting me instantly into his embryonic research team. I had one competitor for the advertised Senior Lecturer post – his name escapes me but he later became quite famous – so the outcome of the interview was far from a foregone conclusion. I knew I'd have to perform well or at least competently before the distinguished selection panel, an occasion that has all but faded from memory with the exception of one tiny and possibly relevant detail – I wore a smart new suit.

I worked hard from the outset and made rapid progress, all of which was self-motivated. I had to rebuild my career from scratch (as the UK medical authorities totally discounted my time in Israel) and I set myself the target of establishing a solid academic reputation within five years. In the end, I stayed at the SPORU for ten but that was probably five too many. Bender became jealous and fearful of my burgeoning success, that stood in stark contrast to his own indifferent productivity, and he soon turned from friend into nemesis. I had to fight hard to unshackle myself from his chains.

He wasn't an evil person, just vain, controlling and, I believe, deeply insecure. Most of Bender's appointees were bright young men whose absolute loyalty and unquestioning obedience he demanded. That included their sitting at the metaphorical feet of the master at the local hostelry for interminable hours on a Friday evening while he pontificated on the ills of the world and his gold-plated solutions for righting them. I participated in this social ritual a few times but found it tiresome in the extreme, so I found excuses to give my apologies and stopped attending.

Even in the more formal office setting, the behaviour of most of the junior staff towards their mentor struck me as unhealthy. They were excessively deferential to the point of sycophancy. More than once, I thought I detected a frisson of homoeroticism in the exchanges between them. I just didn't fit this mould and had no intention of attempting to do so. Because of my pointed aloofness, I was regarded with growing suspicion and even coldness by most of my colleagues and above all by Bender himself, who increasingly resented my attitude.

More significantly, I couldn't bring myself to respect the man intellectually. I concluded very early on that he was a second-rate researcher and that any time I invested in attempting to work closely with him would be wasted. That did not bode well for a productive long-term professional collaboration. Nevertheless, I gave it my best shot, sacrificing several tedious days at a time, inhaling billowing clouds of pipe smoke, and straining to make sense of his elaborate, speculative and wholly untestable theories of health, disease and the state of the world. I felt that was the least I could do out of gratitude, if nothing else, for his having appointed me to the post.

This approach worked reasonably well at first but over time I became deeply dispirited. Bender's oppressive presence was stifling my creativity and threatening to obstruct my academic progress. I realised I would have to take decisive action to preserve my sanity. I set about gradually distancing myself from him as best I could while maintaining a minimum degree of cordiality on a day-to-day basis. He sensed my unease and didn't take kindly to it. Still, I believe I managed the consequent tension adequately enough. My chosen strategy was certainly a high-risk and somewhat lonely one but it proved effective and professionally liberating. I soon struck a seam of unprecedented scientific productivity.

By now I was well on the road to achieving virtually all of my objectives – publishing, teaching, influencing – bar one: I had no research grants. That was because Bender had warned me when I arrived that I was ineligible to apply due to the directly funded, government-controlled nature of the unit. That was a blatant lie, almost certainly a diversionary tactic to sabotage my prospects of promotion (as all academics are judged on two crucial indicators of success: publications and grants). I was incandescently furious when I discovered his deception. I channelled my rage into an escape plan that ultimately reached a triumphant conclusion.

53

The first major fruit of our relocation to Scotland was my medical consultant salary. It was about double, in real terms, the Israeli one. I learned, not for the first time, just how right Mae West had been when she mused: *I've been poor and I've been rich and rich is better.* Sandra also landed a satisfying and well-paid senior NHS post in family planning and psychosexual medicine. For the first time in our lives, we had a respectable disposable income, and dispose of it we did with gusto and rapidity. It took many years to pay off the substantial backlog of accumulated debt, but we owned enough assets to reassure the banks that we were at least theoretically solvent for the purposes of daily life.

So there we were, living the middle-class dream as a two-car, two-holiday family with a comfortable house in a swish Scottish suburb. We were determined to squeeze every drop of enjoyment out of our new-found good fortune while it lasted. We had finally won the glittering prizes, or so it must have appeared to our family, friends and colleagues. After the extreme austerity of Israel, we wanted to savour every moment. I don't believe we were ever slaves to materialism; as doctors, we were too grounded in the knowledge of the transient and fragile nature of the human predicament. As if to remind us of that reality, the health of both of Sandra's parents spiralled downwards rapidly and they soon both succumbed to mortal illness. The loss of her mother, at the relatively young age of 65, was an especially cruel blow to Sandra, coming as it did just a couple of years after our return to Scotland.

Nevertheless, there was much laughter, joy and contentment in the Steyne household that offset that sadness. We could finally afford some decent clothes, food and furniture. We threw ourselves with energy into the rough-and-tumble of family life. Raising four children was a formidable (and exhausting) if fulfilling challenge. I had the flexibility to work at home and carry my fair share of the burdens of parenthood. Occasional aggravations and challenges intruded but we shrugged them off without much difficulty. The extended family provided a welcome and frequently deployed safety net of childcare and, when needed, financial support.

Shabby old Glasgow, at that time, was a city undergoing a remarkable economic, architectural and cultural renaissance. Music, as always, came to dominate whatever leisure time was available to me. A newly appointed Estonian conductor, Naemi Järvi, was making waves with the Scottish National Orchestra, and Scottish Opera was in its heyday. Playing violin-piano duos with my father was a regular weekend delight. I signed up for a few piano lessons that failed to ignite whatever latent talents for that instrument I might have possessed. But my teacher's daughter happened to play in the Glasgow Chamber Orchestra (*one of Scotland's finest amateur ensembles* according to their publicity blurb) and, to my delight, I was quickly co-opted into the second violin section. I remained a faithful rank-and-file fiddler with the GCO for nearly three decades.

If you really want to bond with the great classical orchestral repertoire, don't just listen to recordings or attend concerts – play it. It's not a privilege open to all, of course, but it was to me and I made full use of it. There is no greater thrill than participating in the production of the wondrous sound generated by a decent orchestra, even an amateur one. (Not far behind is the pleasure in listening to elite musicians interpreting scores that you have actually played).

The children were faithful attenders of our performances throughout the eighties and nineties. They weren't always as fully absorbed in the music as I would have liked – Ilana had a habit of listening through earphones to pop music on her Sony Walkman throughout the concerts – but they never complained, at least not within my earshot. Leaving the orchestra in 2013 was an emotional wrench far greater than I could possibly have imagined. I received a moving, unforgettable send-off from my fellow musicians. At my final rehearsal, I was obliged to make a short speech. It was sentimental and wholly unmemorable but the players responded as though I had delivered the Gettysburg address. I had to struggle exceptionally hard, moist eyed, to maintain some semblance of composure as I contemplated the end of an era.

54

The euphoria that had followed our relocation was short-lived. Because the family finances were beginning to creak, yet again, I worked late evening shifts as a locum family doctor. Even though I was driven to every home visit, these sessions were stressful and at times potentially hazardous. The heroin epidemic was digging its claws into vulnerable young Scots and the out-of-hours doctors were regarded as a soft touch for opiate prescriptions – those who didn't play ball were subjected to threats or worse. I was never assaulted but suffered some near misses. Even uneventful sessions took their toll as I regularly returned home at 3am or later, facing the prospect of four hours sleep, maximum. I was permanently exhausted as a consequence. This lifestyle was clearly unsustainable, and I set about searching out an alternative source of extra income. I found it in an unexpected place.

A young Malaysian trainee in public health had joined our unit and we immediately struck up a warm friendship. His name was Philip Chu. I learned from him that the ethnic Chinese were subject to systematic discrimination in his home country and were widely viewed by the locals as "the Jews of Malaysia." Philip and I were kindred spirits. We both needed cash urgently and, after a series of long discussions over coffee, concluded that there might be room for an entrepreneurial enterprise in 1990, when Glasgow would be the designated European City of Culture for a year. We toyed with several ideas, eventually settling on one unlikely candidate: we would write a restaurant guide (under the penname of Daniel Phillips).

We couldn't identify any competitor publications on the market, other than *The List* magazine, so we drew up a book proposal that we circulated to a few promising-looking local publishers. Without awaiting their response, we launched the project. Philip had no real interest in food and never ate out so I was on my own, with the willing help of family and friends, in field-testing hundreds of restaurants, hotels, bistros and cafes all over greater Glasgow. It was an expensive caper but one that I predicted would, if successful, repay our investment handsomely.

We filtered this indigestible mass of eateries down to a short list of a hundred. These formed the core of what would become our *Guide to Eating Out in Glasgow*, published by an unconventional local publisher called Richard Dear. (He was an eccentric character. When we had signed the contract, his parting words were: "I must be mad – and sincere apologies for the farting dog"). Philip and I were stunned; we were about to be published restaurant critics. The public would decide whether or not our gamble had paid off. To everyone's surprise, not least ours, this slim paperback was a hit and instantly entered the Scottish bestseller lists. We sold around ten thousand copies in the first month alone. The royalties were derisory – Dear had driven a hard bargain given our lack of a literary track record – but at least the expenses were tax-deductible. And therein lies a tale.

The four editions of the guide that were published over the next eight years generated the wrath of the tax authorities, who were obliged to send me annual cheques amounting to several thousands of pounds. Eventually their patience snapped and they launched an investigation. I was summoned to an awkward meeting at my accountant's office in the course of which the inspector waved random receipts in front of my nose demanding that I justify their inclusion in my tax return. Luckily I was on sparkling form that day and the officious little man had to concede that I had argued my case well. But I spent an anxious few weeks awaiting their final ruling that, when it came, exonerated me from any wrongdoing.

Sadly, my co-author Philip didn't live beyond the first edition. He was diagnosed with an aggressive form of colon cancer to which he succumbed at the tragically early age of forty-two. He had contributed little to the process of reviewing the restaurants or writing the books but without his inspiration, support and cajoling, they would never have seen the light of day.

55

By 1990, having recently turned forty, an insidious restlessness began to grip my soul. I had been churning out a large number of high-quality scientific papers and monographs and generating substantial research grants – against my boss's wishes – so my five-year plan had paid off handsomely. Moreover, I was increasingly travelling the world to symposia and conferences on the back of this academic prowess. In short, I was by now a large fish in a small pond and needed an escape route. The strategy I conceived was to establish a research unit of my own and lead it brilliantly, applying the negative lessons that I had learned through closely observing my incompetent boss. How, when and where I would implement this programme were questions to which I had no answers.

The opportunity presented itself in 1993 when Bender was informed by his Scottish government paymasters that women and children were no longer a national research priority. I don't believe that was strictly true – it was almost certainly a ploy to push him out – but it had a dramatic impact on my career trajectory. At a stroke, my research contribution to the unit was officially deemed irrelevant. That was the moment of crisis I needed as it gave me the pretext to announce my imminent departure.

With the encouragement (or possibly incitement) of the University's professor of paediatrics, Findlay Cormack ("Finn"), I submitted a short proposal to the faculty of medicine to establish a new academic entity with a catchy acronym, PEACH – the paediatric epidemiology and community health unit. Its purpose would be to carry the banner for research on public health aspects of obstetrics and paediatrics that had been suddenly marginalised within Bender's fiefdom. Finn offered me an office and a shared secretary in his department at the children's hospital, Yorkhill, a crucially helpful gesture that turned the theoretical concept into a tangible reality.

The acronym won the day, I always believed, though the fact that I was astute enough to avoid demanding start-up funds was probably the real dealmaker. My proposal gained the support of the dean of the medical school who ensured that it was granted a free passage, on his nod, through the various university committees. I was ready to launch my venture.

The nascent PEACH unit, under my founding directorship, was scheduled to open its doors in late 1995. All that remained was for me to organise as smooth a transition as I could manage from one role to another. That was a pipedream. The move turned out to be traumatic in the extreme. By the early summer of that year, my relations with Bender, already chronically strained, were verging on open warfare. My spectacularly successful initiative, and especially its skilful piloting through the shark-infested waters of the university's bureaucracy, had become a *cause celebre* in the medical faculty and that must have incensed him.

A second source of friction around that time was a highly provocative interview I gave, on the record, to a colleague who was making an educational video about the challenges of conducting medical research. I discussed, on camera, how to cope with what I described as "a common scenario, one that I am currently experiencing," in which a senior colleague behaved unhelpfully or even obstructively towards a junior one. I suspect Bender saw the film.

To add insult to (his perceived) injury, I had poached my long-serving secretary, Rina, from under his nose. In those days, secretaries were essential to the smooth running of any office and there was always intense competition to secure the services of the good ones. Rina wasn't good at her job, she was outstanding – and Bender knew it. I think he was stung by the double betrayal: mine, for stealing from him a highly talented staff member, and hers, for colluding in the plot.

One day he called me into his office, pointedly declining to offer me a seat. After subjecting me to his usual protracted ritual of pipe-lighting while I stood in silence, consciously taking as shallow breaths as I could to avoid inhaling the polluted air, he announced solemnly that he needed to requisition my office for some unspecified purpose. Urgently. He demanded that I remove or dispose of its entire contents and leave the premises within one week flat. This was an unnecessary and aggressive final act of contempt from a man who had posed as my friend a decade earlier.

I was unfazed. Bender's petulance had played straight into my hands just when I was searching for a face-saving exit strategy. His ultimatum fitted the bill nicely. I smiled, nodded, and left the room wordlessly. We never spoke again.

56

Some people make enemies as easily others make friends. I don't as a rule. The Bender affair was, and remains, an aberration. I regret that it happened but I can't see how it might have been averted. By nature I prefer cooperation to confrontation, possibly to a fault (though I do admit – with more than a *soupçon* of defiant pride – that I'm increasingly combative nowadays when it comes to causes dear to my heart). I felt I had to stand up to this bully or he would have trampled all over me. At the same time, I recognised in him a useful foil, an obstacle for me to push back against, and so he served as a timely if uncomfortable motivator of my career progression. And progress it did.

With the help of a colleague, an affable Cockney community paediatrician called David Merton (who briefly made a futile bid for a share of the founding directorship), the PEACH unit grew, on the strength of a string of successful grant applications, from a staff of three to twenty-six within five years. In 2002, we were joined – as a result of the lobbying of the newly appointed professor of child health – by a high-flying English paediatrician, Charlotte Bright. She was terribly posh, a Roedean-educated jolly-hockey-sticks kind of gal who revealed, on several occasions, an unfortunate streak of (probably unconscious) racism in her world view. Nevertheless, we worked pretty well as a team and the fledgling unit evolved into one of an elite group of such centres in Europe and the only one of its kind in Scotland.

Over the same period, Andrew Bender's empire disintegrated and was seamlessly absorbed into the university's academic public health infrastructure. In retrospect, my timing had been perfect and I found myself fulfilling all of the professional objectives I had set myself. I was – and still am – proud of that achievement. As I write, the unit is being dismantled (in my absence) by former colleagues (including, regrettably and perhaps revealingly, Merton and Bright) in cahoots with penny-pinching administrators endowed with what I can only describe as stunted minds. But I take great satisfaction from the fact that it produced some fine and important work in the first two decades of its existence.

Glasgow was a founding member of an international network of birth defect registries that called itself EUROCAT, led (I joke not) by one Professor Lechat. He was a genial Belgian who took a liking to me and we got on famously. I greatly enjoyed my frequent trips to Brussels, a much-maligned city that is blessed with a rich cultural heritage as well as the most alluring chocolate shops in Europe. EUROCAT's scientific quality was exceptionally high and the work invariably enjoyable. The intellectual setting was a natural one for me as I'd written two theses and more than a dozen papers on the subject of congenital anomalies, mainly neural tube defects and Down Syndrome.

Before long I was playing a leading role in the organisation and was elected (though I wasn't entirely sure why) by the twenty or so European registry leaders to the prestigious position of Secretary General. Apart from the collaborative research, some of which turned out to be highly productive and at times even ground-breaking, there were notable perks – international travel, memorable haute-cuisine dinners and a delightfully sociable atmosphere. I learned a great deal from my colleagues, including the art of extracting substantial research funds from the vast bureaucracy that was the European Commission; it was a crucial skill that I would put to effective use in the future.

Some years later, I used the EUROCAT model to create a comparable network closer to home that I named BINOCAR (the British Isles Network of Congenital Anomaly Registers), again demonstrating that a good acronym is worth a thousand words. This was hosted by the UK government's Office for National Statistics and was widely hailed as a major epidemiological resource for researchers and healthcare planners. And it was another large feather in my professional cap.

57

My second major research passion was injury prevention. It was a neglected field in those days, partly due to the all-pervasive and, in my view, dangerous fatalism that "accidents will happen." My interest in the field was ignited by an incident that impinged directly on my family.

One day, my daughter Ilana's close friend Joyce, aged twelve, was almost killed by a speeding van as she crossed a road adjacent to their school; she escaped with a fractured skull (and possibly some mild brain damage) but it was touch and go for twenty-four hours. I contacted the local police to urge them to take action at the hazardous junction but they declined. Their defence was that they were unable to institute traffic calming measures there as there had been no fatalities at that particular spot for several years and so it didn't meet their criteria for intervention. This reasoning struck me as ludicrous and unacceptable. That was when I decided to try to launch an injury research programme.

After a few false starts, I managed to extract a large grant from the European Commission to support several multi-centre projects with resonant acronyms, the most memorable being EURORISC (European Review of Injury Surveillance and Control), EUROSAVE (European Review of Suicide and Violence Epidemiology) and EUROMOTIVE (European Monitoring of Transnational Injury and Violence Epidemiology). These ambitious, and generally successful, projects established my reputation as a major player on the international injury prevention stage. I was soon being invited to lecture around the world, with expenses-paid trips to far-flung locations offered as incentives, and found myself, for the first time in my career, in constant demand as an expert advisor to research councils, health authorities, local councils, NGOs, governments and even the World Health Organization (yes, it is – or should be – spelt with a Z even in English English).

We can never predict precisely how we will be judged by future generations. I like to think I have made a significant impact on epidemiological scholarship. My research contributions to knowledge were fairly modest though posterity will be the ultimate judge of that. I never really regarded myself as primarily a researcher but rather as an academic public health practitioner in the broadest sense. If I had to hazard a guess, my most important legacy will be my innovations in the unglamorous fields of teaching and service development. I was (and I hope still am) a relentless innovator in these fields, perpetually seeking out new perspectives on old problems and offering novel ideas about teaching public health to medical and other healthcare students, as well as urging local and national government to adopt imaginative solutions to strategic challenges. Most of my ideas were impractical and never saw the light of day. Nevertheless, a few were implemented and may have made a lasting, positive impact.

Creativity lay at the heart of all my academic and service activities, a fact that was recognised only by one person in the universe – me. (That may appear to you to be an excessively solipsistic and even arrogant statement and you would be right, but it's a view that was born of necessity; I wouldn't have been able to progress on my chosen path had I doubted my own worth for a second). The prestigious Glasgow medical school seemed institutionally incapable of absorbing new ideas and the NHS was equally impervious. Their unresponsiveness didn't deter me as I'd always understood the brutal reality that I was on my own, professionally speaking.

If I could address an audience of the bright-eyed and bushy-tailed young academics of the future, I'd say this: all my personal professional achievements were hard won and were the fruits of my labour and mine alone. In academe, we all pretend to play lip-service to the collaborative ethos. But we also all know that the truth is much bleaker. I had to struggle to progress every inch of the way, in the face of the unremitting hostility or (at best) indifference of my seniors and colleagues. There's a famous saying in the Ethics of the Fathers: *if I am not for myself, who is for me?*

My version is somewhat blunter: *if I am not for myself, I am well and truly sunk.*

58

It is peculiarly difficult for me to recapture the true essence of those intermediate years. Family life was all-consuming and there was little time for reflection. The endless procession of school runs, shopping, socialising, working, sleeping – punctuated by spasms of pleasure or pain depending on largely uncontrollable external events – demanded action not philosophising. The children all performed successfully (and frequently outstandingly) at school, had busy and (as far as we could tell) contented social lives, and never posed insoluble dilemmas or challenges.

Those two and a half decades from 1976 to the millennium – the span of a generation – flew by. Birthdays, anniversaries, festivals, bar/bat mitzvahs, came and went with many smiles and a few sighs. Summer holidays were spent, often with grandparents, in France or Spain or Israel, apart from occasional forays further afield – to New York, and then a round-the world trip, the excuses for which were those special birthdays that cannot be ignored. Throughout this period, marital relations were, superficially at least, placid; the unnoticed or unacknowledged undercurrents of unease never seemed real enough to cause either of us concern. The stream of existence flowed on, clear and sparkling, its progress hindered only lightly by the occasional rough pebble of untoward incident or unavoidable impediment. Such was our life and I was inexpressibly grateful for it.

In his epic novel *The Magic Mountain*, Thomas Mann describes the paradoxical sensory illusion of time, whereby a busy calendar, racing past the participant in a flash, appears elongated in retrospect, so packed is it with memorable events, while an empty one, stretching indolently and seemingly endlessly towards an unseen horizon as it is experienced day-to-day, becomes drastically compressed when later recalled. Our experience was the epitome of the former. We were perpetually busy, often frantically so; children had to be ferried around the city to and from school, to sporting fixtures, swimming and music lessons, and a ceaseless round of sleepovers at friends' homes. All of these had somehow to be integrated into the normal humdrum business of shopping, medical and dental appointments, socialising, and a thousand-and-one other pressing demands on our time that often necessitated an ultra-rapid response. This relentlessly frenetic activity inevitably obstructed our view of the changing tempo and texture of life. There was no possibility of looking to the future with any degree of clarity. We understood only that our most precious resource – time – was disappearing so fast that we could barely catch our breaths.

And then, quite suddenly, around the turn of the millennium, the treadmill slowed, and with a few short years had all but ground to a halt. The children were entering adulthood, acquiring skills, finding partners, leaving Glasgow and setting up home in London. Everything connected to the long-established routine of our lives seemed to be changing beyond recognition. It was disconcerting at first but no more than that. In 1998, we moved house, buying a ludicrously spacious art deco villa in upmarket Whitecraigs just when we should have been downsizing (although that purchase turned out to be an unintentionally shrewd financial investment).

The first tremors of an even greater domestic upheaval were imperceptible to us but the tectonic plates that underpinned the Steyne family were slowly shifting. I can't pinpoint the precise moment when we realised that trouble was afoot: a sharp word here, an exasperated frown there, a succession of tiny and apparently trivial clues gradually edged their way onto our radar. Eventually, and belatedly, the penny dropped, and we became aware that something troubling was happening. Initially, in outright denial mode, we just carried on. This is quite normal, we mused, all families find change challenging and we'll deal with it in our own way.

Exactly how we would set about dealing with it came as a deeply unpleasant surprise to everyone, not least ourselves.

59

When prime minister Yitzhak Rabin was assassinated in 1995 by an extremist Jew, the morale of the Israeli and Jewish people slumped to an historic low. It was a moment of indescribable shock and despair for Israelis and all who cared about the country. (I comforted myself in the knowledge that there had been many previous nadirs in the annals of Zionism and we had survived all of them).

I don't accept the contention, promoted enthusiastically by "expert" commentators who hold Israel solely or largely responsible for the Arab-Israeli conflict, that this disaster ended the peace process just as it was getting off the ground. That view, for which there is scant evidence, is so widespread as to be almost axiomatic in western media and academia. It holds that peace can only be achieved through Israeli concessions and that these have been repeatedly obstructed by events in Israel – such as the assassination of Rabin, or the precipitous resignation of Olmert, or the illness of Sharon – aided and abetted by the irredeemably, indulgently pro-Israel United States.

Rabin had undoubtedly been a reluctant peace partner of Yasser Arafat's, with good reason, and was steadfastly opposed to the creation of a potentially irredentist Palestinian state on Israel's doorstep. During the *first intifada*, Rabin had been a ruthless and at times brutal defence minister as he sought to suppress the relentless escalation of Palestinian violence. As a young officer during the War of Independence, he (along with Yigal Allon) had controversially implemented the expulsion of the Arabs of Lydda and Ramle to create a safe passage for the army from Tel Aviv to Jerusalem. (This event has been used maliciously to demonstrate that Israel expelled all the Arab refugees during that war; in fact, that episode was an exceptional one that was expected to be a temporary measure. It was certainly never part of an overall strategy of ethnic cleansing as Israel's enemies claim).

Like all leaders, Rabin made mistakes and regretted many of them later. Nevertheless, he was a visionary who sought peace and commanded the trust, respect and affection of friend and foe alike. As defence minister in the 1980s, he had been my ultimate boss during my army service (when I heard him speak live at least once) and I regarded him as a kind of father figure, as did many Israelis. His loss was described as irreplaceable. It was certainly a huge blow to Israel. But it didn't undermine my commitment to the country; on the contrary, my resolve to defend her in the only theatre of the conflict to which I now had unfettered access – the war of ideas – was stiffened.

In 1985, as a newly appointed academic in Glasgow, most of my colleagues viewed my Israeli past as a kind of exotic cultural appendage. They were intrigued that I had just arrived from a place that was as alien to them as the far side of the moon. What I didn't realise, though soon discovered, was that their curiosity was partial, conditional, and destructive. They viewed Israel as the embodiment of a highly suspect and probably fascistic ideology, Zionism, and could never properly relate to Israel as a living, breathing, normal country filled with people like themselves who just wanted to be left to live their lives in peace. Almost all were left-of-centre, devoted *Guardian* or *Independent* readers who had unconsciously internalised many of the reflexive anti-Israel posturings and prejudices of these papers' journalists, and of the liberal-leaning media in general.

One of the thousands of things I don't understand (*pace* Bill Bryson) is how intelligent, educated people can suspend their critical thinking and permit themselves to be led, *en masse*, up the garden path by the fashionable rantings of media celebrities. Yet many do this willingly and fervently. As Robin Shepherd astutely observed in his underrated book *A State Beyond the Pale*, for such people their political opinions are moulded entirely by their chosen peer group in a manner reminiscent of mediaeval religious fanaticism.

From the start of my long academic residence in Glasgow, I had enough sense to steer clear of Middle Eastern politics in general, and my service in the Israeli army in particular, during polite conversation with academic colleagues. I would gently guide discussions towards what I naively assumed was the much safer territories of research, teaching and public health. Israel remained a permanent preoccupation of mine, but I accepted that I was now an observer rather than a participant in that drama. My contribution to humanity would have to focus henceforth on international research, teaching and career building. Israel would have to take a back seat. Nevertheless, I couldn't fully absolve myself of responsibility for seeking to banish the widespread ignorance about the country that I encountered at almost every turn.

Around 1987, I delivered a departmental seminar on medical education in Israel entitled *The Beer Sheva Experiment* that was well enough received. The smallish audience comprised overseas postgraduate doctors plus a couple of curious local academics; the latter later expressed a collegial interest in the technical and pedagogic aspects of my talk and seemed content to ignore its contentious geopolitical context. That offered me the welcome prospect of a reprieve from endless political argument but, even then, I sensed that it would be temporary. How right I was. The hounds of hatred were champing at the bit, growling and straining at the leash, sinews primed for the signal to attack at the earliest opportunity.

They – and I – didn't have long to wait.

60

I had kept in a touch with a handful of my old colleagues at the Ben Gurion University of the Negev. One of these was an American-born sociologist called Aaron Aronofsky. His wife, Helen, was an academic psychologist who had worked with my father in Jerusalem in the 1950s (and with whom I had co-authored, in the 1980s, a paper on alcoholism in a Negev development town).

Aronofsky was a distinguished figure in the Beer Sheva medical school who had shot to international prominence as a result of his ground-breaking *Sense of Coherence* theory of health. His seminal theoretical paper on the subject had, for some reason, become flavour of the month among medical sociologists and the wider public health community. Its focus was on the factors that protect and promote health rather than prevent disease so perhaps this resonated with the desire of the social medicine community to distance itself from the medical model.

Aronofsky's coinage of the term *salutogenesis*, the health promoting process, caught on like wildfire. I've tossed it into many a discussion with medical students. When lecturing, he would always set out to explain his theories with reference to his earliest memories of his New York childhood when his mother (or perhaps father or grandfather) would ask, on hearing some major piece of news on the radio, "Is this good for the Jews or bad for the Jews?" That gave his parents and extended family their sense of coherence. We all pose a version of that question to ourselves. It scarcely matters what the question is, merely that it is important to us. I had lobbied hard for Aronofsky to be invited to Glasgow to give a talk and the local seminar organisers had agreed. I was looking forward the occasion.

Others were not so enthused – and weren't shy in saying so. A few days before the scheduled event, word reached me via a colleague that there was *a bit of a problem*. What was it? "We hear that Aronofsky is extremely right wing" was the conspiratorial response. I was staggered. Within that academic peer group, to be labelled *right wing* is to receive the Mark of Cain and nothing the hapless bearer of this label can say or do carries any credibility thereafter.

"He's not remotely right wing," I protested. But my rejection of this false "fact" that everyone around me regarded as gospel truth was dismissed. As so often in discussions about Israel, my narrative collided with theirs and reality lost out. Aronofsky had been a founding member of a leftish protest movement called *Peace Now*. I knew of this group as I had been among the first to join them and had participated in several demonstrations against the 1982 Lebanon war when I had lived in the Negev. The allegation was risible; it was worse than a smear, it was pure fiction. What was the motivation? I speculated, reluctantly, that this could be mindless anti-Israelism, a modern, mutated form of antisemitism.

I refused to let the matter rest and challenged colleagues to offer verifiable evidence of their charge. They couldn't. But one did warn me that a boycott was in the air. Unfortunately, he was proved right; the turnout for the event was embarrassingly small. Our guest took it philosophically, politely rejecting my proffered hypothesis of political prejudice. My diagnosis was, however, correct. This knee-jerk contempt for all things Israeli became increasingly prevalent throughout the ensuing decades in all UK universities and spread later to trade unions, the media, the arts, churches and political parties. I know this because I've been battling it ever since.

Around this time, another odd episode occurred. The faculty of medicine contacted me to ask whether I would be willing, given my background, to host a Middle Eastern guest, a visiting doctor. There were no further details but I agreed. Such requests were fairly frequent, and I always went out of my way to accommodate them.

The guest turned out to be Syrian, a country with whom Israel had long been at war. That didn't bother me but his name did – a Dr Arafat. A coincidence? No, he was indeed a relative (a cousin I think) of the despicable Yasser. It transpired that Dr Arafat worked for UNRWA (the United Nations Relief and Works Agency) in the Palestinian "refugee camps" of Syria. He was charm personified. I decided to inform him immediately of my association with Israel to avoid any embarrassment. He took the news calmly. Sandra was rather anxious when I invited him home to dinner but all went well. We had a brief political discussion in which we agreed that two states would be the only answer to the conflicting territorial claims of Jews and Arabs. (That consensus surprised me; perhaps Dr Arafat had decided to acquiesce in my defence of Jewish sovereignty out of respect for his host rather than any genuine political conviction).

I can't help reflecting on how or why this incident came about. Was it ignorance on the part of the faculty, or stupidity, or malice? I'll never know. One of my colleagues, Graham Walsh, the professor of general practice, was a longstanding pro-Palestinian activist. I suspect he may have been behind the move, perhaps in an attempt to flush out what he presumed to be my implacable anti-Arabism. If so, he would have been disappointed.

That's one of the most depressing features of the conflict: pro-Palestinians usually loathe Israelis and (too often) Jews (aka "Zionists"), while pro-Israelis rarely hold comparable prejudices (as opposed to harbouring plenty of grievances) towards Arabs, Palestinian or otherwise. For the former, the conflict is and always was a zero-sum game – a hopeless foundation on which to try to build peace.

61

When I reached my half century in the spring of 1999, I point blank refused to accept it. This is one of those family jokes with a dark centre. When I claim that my birth certificate must be wrong, I am jesting, of course, but I am also deadly serious. The humour enables me to objectify, metaphorically, my fear of death, or, more precisely, my love of life. Like most of my fellow human beings, I can't contemplate the end of the great adventure with equanimity. I try to think of each birthday as a day to celebrate the achievement of having survived another year, though I've never found that view especially comforting. The passage of time is one of those existential questions that won't take no for an answer. The problem is this: I genuinely can't understand what happened to all those decades. My nostalgia for the past is a futile attempt to capture the transitoriness of lived experience, and I become disquieted when I discover that I just can't, however hard I try.

That year, I decided to take my family – or most of them – on an extravagant birthday trip to New York for a long weekend. It was an exhilarating, wonderful adventure that bathed me (and I hope them) in pure pleasure. Highlights included the Museum of Modern Art, absurd breakfasts at the packed local deli, a couple of terrific restaurants, and an equally tasty musical (Irving Berlin's *Annie Get Your Gun*), albeit in the air-conditioned iciness of a Times Square theatre for which we were sartorially ill-prepared.

Yet my backward glance at that American holiday is a slightly ambivalent one. We all adored New York and were so reluctant to leave that we almost missed our return flight to London. But it was also just about the last time we would enjoy each other's company as a fully integrated, well-functioning family unit. Although we were thankfully unaware of their existence, dark clouds were already gathering across the clear blue Manhattan sky, and they had nothing to do with the impending (and largely fictitious) Y2K computer threat that was dominating the media. Standing on London Bridge watching the extravagant Millennium firework display, I pondered the future of my marriage and was filled with despondency.

A destructive pathology had somehow, over time, insinuated itself into our relationship by stealth and had already wreaked appalling, irreversible damage. We had both missed (or perhaps stubbornly ignored) the early symptoms let alone diagnosed the ailment – until a point of no return had been reached. We talked and talked and listened and listened. This was intended to be a mutually therapeutic unburdening of a load whose existence we had barely suspected. The therapy failed. Over time, we reached the reluctant conclusion that we'd somehow taken a wrong turning and that we would have to act decisively to get our lives back on track.

In the subsequent months, we explored the dwindling options. Saving the marriage was the obvious priority yet the idea was discarded quite early on in the proceedings. At some point in this process, almost without really meaning to, we agreed we had arrived at the logical, unavoidable endpoint: separation. We decided to keep talking, and then to tell the children when the time was right. We knew it would be a wretched business but that it would be preferable to get the whole rotten business over with sooner rather than later.

62

If I give the impression that I managed to take the unravelling of the marriage in my stride, it would be the wrong one. I like to believe that I possess an inner strength, a steely resilience of character that has proved capable of withstanding assaults on its integrity on numerous occasions. I had been dragged unwillingly across continents, beaten by sadistic Scottish teachers, sent into a deadly war zone with a gun and a tin helmet, and treated with racist contempt by jealous work colleagues. Yet I was completely unprepared for this test. An emotional maelstrom was brewing around me, and it was unlike anything I had ever experienced or anticipated. It was at once terrifying and exciting but mostly the former. I just couldn't visualise existence without the crutch of what had been the closest relationship of my life, one that had lasted three decades. Still, I was a survivor and knew I would ultimately survive it. My priority now was damage limitation.

It was a genuinely painful and confusing time but somehow we found ourselves navigating our way through it. Just before the storm broke, we received some cheerful news. Ilana and her boyfriend, Jonny, announced their engagement. The wedding was, according to tradition, an irrepressibly happy one. Everything proceeded, with only a few minor glitches, as planned. The setting (the now demolished Glasgow Albany hotel) was impressive, the meal suitably festive and the klezmer-style music (the excellent Gregory Schechter band) loudly and Jewishly celebratory, with much spontaneous laughing, clapping and dancing.

My father, Ed, chaired the proceedings, slightly uneasily I thought, and my mother Helga sat at the top table somewhat frozen-faced as was her custom on these set-piece occasions. Our guests were generous in their compliments. Jonny's parents were fulsome in their praise of the event. ("I have no words," confided his dad to me as we stood side-by-side at the urinal, a comment that, I realised later, might have been double-edged).

The after-dinner speeches were clever, amusing and touching. I wasn't at my best but I don't think I disgraced myself either. Ilana, as expected, insisted on speaking and thanked her mum and dad for, among other things, being "normal parents." Her mum and dad, at that precise moment, felt far from normal and wholly unworthy of the sobriquet. We stole a brief guilt-laden glance at each other but otherwise disguised our discomfort well.

The young couple headed off to the East Coast of America on their honeymoon while we retreated to our Scottish lair to nurse our emotional (and financial) wounds. As all who have experienced it will know, living with a partner from whom you are separating is a unnerving scenario. In the early stages, when reconciliation is not entirely implausible, cohabitation can continue after a fashion. But after a certain point has been reached, there's only one possible direction of onward travel. The centrifugal force is irresistible. I didn't try to resist.

Sandra's method of coping was to focus on the practicalities: we needed to reach an agreement about the splitting of the spoils of a decades-long partnership. We achieved that result with stunning rapidity. More difficult, by far, was breaking the news and managing the distress of others – the children, my parents, relatives, friends, colleagues. I think we handled this process as well as anyone could – in other words, miserably. Our patient, gentle explanations didn't cut much ice, but we couldn't legislate for that.

When the terrorist attacks on the Twin Towers changed history on the morning of 11th of September of that pivotal year of 2001 (cruelly coinciding with my father's 80th birthday), the sense of mounting global foreboding that followed on the heels of that colossal, unfathomable atrocity shook us out of our self-absorption, providing an unwelcome and haunting distraction from our fast-developing domestic woes.

63

My most pressing objective was (for me) a novel one: to find myself a bachelor home, and urgently. My budget was modest, but I didn't need much space and the prospect of downsizing from a large villa to a modest dwelling held no terrors. After a few wild goose chases, I found an ideal two-bedroomed, newly built flat in the Yorkhill district of the West End of Glasgow, just a few minutes' walk from my office. My new home was located on the top floor of a modern block and was equipped with what estate agents call a Juliet balcony overlooking a reasonably pleasant, tree-lined square.

*

Separation and divorce are wretched traumas. The impact on all of the family, including my parents, was shattering. It had a deeply disrupting effect on the children and on their well-being. How serious was the damage? Who can tell? The initial pain subsided but it was followed by a prolonged and inescapable sadness. I've often asked myself whether any of this could have been avoided and have reached the conclusion that it probably couldn't. That realisation offered cold comfort and I expect that both Sandra and I will carry a sense of guilt about it to our graves.

    I comforted myself with the thought that every cloud had a silver lining. Mine was boringly predictable. I had married young and so, having been unexpectedly gifted a second chance at youthful galavanting, I seized it with both hands. I had become dimly aware of the growing fad for online dating and resolved to investigate its potential. This turned out be a distinctly mixed blessing. I confess that I experienced both pleasurable and humiliating encounters in just about equal measure. Many were frankly silly to the point of hilarity. No, I won't recount them. I must draw a discreet veil over my "social" activities in the ensuing few years.... Sorry, reader.

*

As a form of displacement activity, I invested all of my time and energy into my new home. I stubbornly declined any help with interior decorating or furnishing. I arranged everything according to my taste – *subdued modernist* I pretentiously described it – and settled down to enjoy, and (if possible) savour, my newfound freedom.

And so my flat gradually moulded itself to my needs until the fit was as comfortable as I was entitled to expect. Of those few visitors to whom I granted the privilege of crossing my threshold, almost all made a similar pronouncement: *This place needs a woman's touch.* I dare say they were right, but I was more than content with my limited interior designing skills and created my domestic *mise-en-scène* in a manner that reflected my tastes and preferences rather than those of well-meaning but irritating would-be advisors.

The bedroom was functional and bright with a tiny *en suite* bathroom fitted with a high storage cupboard and a long mirror of the necessary height (oh rapture!) to frame all six foot plus of its principal occupant. These little luxuries had been repeatedly denied to me in all of my previous homes. Soon, I also had a spare bedroom-cum-study properly bedecked with a convertible sofa, musical instruments and a desk. My cosy living room doubled as a home cinema with a large screen TV. Once the CD and radio stereo system was up and running I was (almost) happiness personified.

The kitchen came much lower down my list of priorities, but I never lacked for a kettle, tin opener or colander (once I discovered what that object was). Washing and ironing were major challenges, so I delegated those to our longstanding cleaning lady, Cheryl, who journeyed loyally across town once a fortnight. Finally, a carefully selected sample of my favourite paintings, many of which were completely ill-suited Scottish rural landscapes that I had acquired as hand-me-downs from my parents, adorned the walls.

I was now well on my way to forging for myself a new and, I promised myself, reinvigorating future.

64

Having firmly bonded with my new abode, I rapidly adjusted to the rhythm of my reinvented daily life and discovered a capacity for self-sufficiency that had lain dormant for decades, probably since my student days. The short walk from home to work meant that I could rise at 8.30 and be at my desk by nine. I essentially treated my flat as an extension of my office. My secretary and I hatched a conspiratorial code for disguising my intention to work at home – "Rina, I'll be in the annexe today if anyone needs me."

Two lively West End arteries (Byres Road and Dumbarton Road) were located just a few minutes' walk from my front door and they were packed with a tempting and constantly changing variety of fast food outlets, cafes, pubs and restaurants. *I will never have to cook again*, I reflected, as soon as I stumbled upon this culinary fairground. Nevertheless, I did manage to acquire some basic cooking skills. I developed the knack of turning out a decent cheese and mushroom omelette, a rudimentary pasta, an impressive range of microwaved potatoes and even, on occasion, a succulent, lemon-drizzled portion of baked salmon. (My all-time favourite – a self-indulgent regression to early childhood – was a dish I could reproduce at will: runny fried eggs, mashed potatoes and baked beans).

My neighbours were mostly reasonably civilised, despite the predominance of university students in the block, and I was rarely troubled by noisy revelries or late-night slamming of doors. Being on the top floor, adjoining an external gable end, I soon discovered that I could play CDs and practise my violin as loudly and as late into the night as I wished as no-one else seemed to hear or care. A nearby commuter railway line was a potential source of disturbance, especially at night, but my ears quickly re-attuned themselves and magically filtered out virtually all of the rattling of iron wheels on tracks every five minutes or so.

We have reached the early noughties. My parents had grown elderly and frail. They both remained intellectually sharp to the end and I greatly enjoyed their company, especially the regular violin-piano duos with Ed, but the ageing process was inexorably taking its toll. As the years progressed, they required more of my care and attention, and I dutifully obliged. My two siblings offered moral support from a distance of several hundred miles but couldn't really participate in the (metaphorical or literal) heavy lifting.

In late 2004 Helga was diagnosed with oesophageal cancer, an aggressive and incurable disease that you would hesitate to inflict on your worst enemy. The symptoms (difficulty swallowing and weight loss) would have set alarm bells ringing had she mentioned them to us (or her GP), but she chose to remain silent. I'll never understand why – that diffidence probably cost her life. She must have realised how poor the prognosis was, but she was a fighter – "I'm not ready to hang up my boots yet" – and opted for major surgery rather than radiotherapy. And how she fought, ultimately to no avail. After a disastrous series of operations, complicated by a dose of MRSA (an untreatable hospital-acquired infection), she was discharged home with a long plastic tube connected to her stomach into which was pumped a milky mixture of nutrients every few hours. She had a love-hate relationship with the device ("That little machine keeps me alive") but her quality of life lay in ruins.

You can guess the rest. Her rapid decline was excruciating to observe. Within a matter of weeks she was cachectic and depressed. As she often ruminated, that was no way to live. Who could disagree? Further heroic surgery was ruled out and would probably have been futile in any case. Her firm and oft-expressed desire, that we all respected, was to die at home. She stopped breathing quite suddenly in late 2006 in her eighty-third year. We were all distressed at this news yet also relieved that her unconscionable suffering had ended.

Unhappily, my father's was just beginning.

65

Ed was stricken by the loss of Helga, naturally, and I feared that he would struggle to make sense of his continued existence after this bereavement. So profound had been the bond between them that its rupture was more than he could bear. Overnight, life had become literally meaningless for him. I can recall only one brief period when he seemed to regain his old *joie-de-vivre*.

About a year after Helga's death, I organised a ten-day trip for the two of us to Israel. We travelled the length and breadth of the country, meeting relatives and friends, sharing anecdotes from the past, and speculating about the unknowable future. Ed loved every minute of it and was determined to see as many people and as much of the fast-changing country as he could. He (and I) guessed, correctly, that it would be his farewell visit though I don't think he ever explicitly articulated that thought.

In 2008, he was diagnosed with cancer of the larynx, an uncannily similar disease to his late wife's. Whether there was any causal connection, I suppose we'll never know. I concocted several hypotheses, the most (arguably) plausible of which was to attribute their illnesses to the daily pre-prandial dry sherry that had been part of their domestic ritual for around five decades.

Never a particularly religious man, in the conventional sense, Ed faced his bleak prognosis with a resigned dignity coloured, I sensed, with a tinge of relief that he wouldn't have to endure the lonely desert that his life had become without his beloved Helga. On my frequent visits to his Giffnock flat, I did what I could to offer him comfort as he grappled with the debilitating side-effects of repeated rounds of chemotherapy and radiotherapy. His medical advisors were refusing to throw in the towel and I urged him to give their treatment programme a fighting chance. He was unconvinced but indulged us all.

Even on his gloomiest days, we were never short of topics of conversation. These ranged freely across family matters, British or Israeli politics, literature and music, and he was never shy about expressing trenchant views on all of them. His mind was as laser sharp as ever and he had a real talent for diagnosing the irreducible essence of any contentious issue. Over time, however, he seemed to lose some of his former energy and the silences between us grew longer and longer. I soon learned to recognise a characteristic facial expression, a kind of fatigued exasperation with the world around him, that was my signal, after a ritual glance at my watch, to leave him to his private thoughts.

On one such occasion, a Sunday morning I think, we had chatted, animatedly, about various subjects, focusing on the amusing exploits of his growing tribe of great grandchildren, when something unusual happened. Outside, a typical West of Scotland rainstorm was brewing and I took that as my cue to hit the road. I had just started to gather up the detritus from our coffee and biscuits when Ed raised the palm of his hand as if signalling to oncoming traffic: "Wait, Daniel," he implored. "Don't go just yet. Please sit down." Naturally, I complied with this uncharacteristic instruction. By now the rain was pounding on the windowpanes, whipped up by intermittent squalls of whistling wind.

"Just listen to that dreadful weather. You shouldn't go out into that storm. And I'd really love another cup of coffee," he said. "Will you join me? If you have time?"

66

"Let's talk about Israel," he began. My eyes widened.

"Gladly. It's a big subject."

"Of course. Look, Daniel, I know you feel passionately about it and Zionist history and all that, but I want you to put emotion aside for the moment. Can you do that?"

"I don't know." I was baffled. Ed spotted my discomfort.

"I don't mean that you should stop believing in the cause. It's a fine cause. But ideals are one thing, reality another."

I nodded slowly. I had an inkling of what was coming.

"Your mother and I, in our youth, were great fans of Herzl and of left-wing Zionism in general. That's why we joined Habonim. It was an exciting, utopian, revolutionary ideology. We were intoxicated by it. Anything and everything was possible. Or so we believed. For us, making *Aliyah* felt like a necessity. Does that make sense to you?" I was about to answer but Ed was in full, unstoppable flow.

"When we got there, to Jerusalem I mean, we made two very important discoveries. One was that the whole business of *Aliyah* and putting down roots in the homeland was much, much harder than we anticipated. The sheer grind of daily living, of dealing with the bureaucracy, of coping with the threats of violence, of rearing a family in a harsh environment...." His voice trailed off and he gazed into the middle distance as if recalling a troubling memory.

"I can confirm all of that," I said. "We went through the same trials and tribulations thirty years later."

Ed straightened his back and stared at me as if I were imparting highly improbable news. Almost as quickly his features relaxed again. "Ah yes, of course. You know all about it. You and Sandra didn't have an easy time either. But bear in mind, we were there almost at the start, when the state was finding its feet. Nobody knew if the experiment would work. There was a constant fear in the air that the whole thing would come crashing down."

"It must have been a desperately scary time for you and Mum. Especially with two young children to look after."

Ed ignored my interjection. "What was even worse – and this was our second important discovery – was the sheer sense of failure, betrayal even, when we left. *Yeridah* really was a dirty word in those days. Even close friends and family treated us with contempt for considering leaving let alone actually going through with it. But it had to be done, we had no choice. And we paid a price."

"And I suppose you felt guilty about it?" I prompted gingerly. Ed glowered at me, as if he held me personally responsible for his discomfort at the memory. "Guilty? Oh, yes, I did, certainly. More than guilty, much more. It felt like treason. The hardest decision of my life. But your mother? Not a bit of it. She was thrilled to leave. She couldn't get away fast enough."

For a few moments, we sat in total silence. It was a welcome respite. By now, I was sure a major revelation was coming.

"When we got back to Scotland, we had to readjust our thinking. Our Israel project had been a failure, there was no getting away from that. Helga was determined to put the whole experience behind us and look to the future. Only to the future. Don't live in the past, Ed, she scolded me. And I agreed with her, up to a point. That was why we didn't make a big deal of our Zionism when you were growing up. I suppose we feared you might become stricken with the bug and we'd have to watch you and your family go through the whole damn, miserable thing again."

I laughed. "Well, that plan worked well, didn't it?"

Ed's expression didn't alter a millimetre.

"Yet I couldn't turn my back on the country. So I didn't. I helped out, as best I could, here and there. Passing messages between Israelis in Scotland, acting as a courier. Mundane stuff, nothing dangerous. You know about that, of course."

I did and nodded.

"But it was never enough."

"How do you mean?"

"Well, I assumed that establishment of a Jewish state was the main challenge, and once that vision had been realised, the whole business was done and dusted. Unfortunately, it wasn't. I was too optimistic. Look at what's happening today. Israel is still at war with fanatics who will never accept her. And the country is so vulnerable, so fragile. It could all end tomorrow."

He paused and looked directly at me. "You picked up the torch and I'm pleased about that. I should never have dropped it. I'm sure you won't make my mistake."

67

Ed endured a further couple of rounds of radiotherapy with characteristic patience following which he was admitted to the wonderful Prince and Princess of Wales hospice in Carlton Place, Gorbals, ironically just around the corner from the street where his rabbinical grandfather, the family's founding patriarch in Scotland, had set up home just over a century earlier. He was comfortable in his final home and regarded the staff of the hospice as his friends. Those were difficult months for all of us. He died peacefully, under heavy sedation, in September 2009 just short of his eighty-eighth birthday. I was now, at the age of sixty, officially an orphan.

Although he was not a religious man, Ed – in stark contrast to Helga – had been a great enthusiast for many of the traditional rituals of Judaism, including the *Kaddish*, the Jewish prayer for the dead (that doesn't, incidentally, mention death or the deceased). I accompanied him to *shul* (synagogue) regularly for a year following my mother's death precisely for that reason, to recite the prayer.

And so I performed the same duty for him when he passed on. In the process, I rediscovered my proficiency at reading, or rather singing, the *Haftarot,* the prophetic Hebrew passages accompanying each *Torah* reading. Because few of the sparse and ageing congregation were competent enough to do this, I was frequently called up to the *bimah* (podium) where the scrolls were read and, overcoming my secularist convictions, quite enjoyed these experiences, nerve-racking as they invariably were.

Glasgow's celebrated Garnethill *shul* was Scotland's oldest and its neo-Byzantine design created a special atmosphere of comforting, nostalgic grandeur. It is appropriately described as Scotland's "cathedral synagogue." The dwindling band of members were mostly as irreligious as me but all of us felt that the place was a special one and deserved to continue, not so much for the purposes of worship but to affirm the ineradicable place of Jews in Scottish history. I don't believe there's an equivalent survivalist impulse in most other religions.

Garnethill celebrated its 140th anniversary in 2019 and is somehow managing to renew itself by acquiring a handful of new and relatively young members. Unusually, it has no rabbi or clergy of any kind these days – all of its services are conducted by a small band of enthusiastic volunteers – and therein may lie the key to its continued success. I always enjoy my rare return visits to the old place; it's like entering a time machine. I can just about visualise the anxious little boy sitting in his pew, surrounded by hundreds of swaying, praying congregants (some top-hatted during the High Holy Days) draped in their blue-and-white prayer shawls. The child is wide-eyed with wonder at the exotic sights and sounds around him that are somehow both intimidating and heart-warming at the same time. Later, the fast-growing teenager, now superficially a little more confident and assertive, would seek to make discreet eye contact with one or more of the impossibly elegant young women gazing down at him with mild curiosity, and sometimes more, from the ladies' gallery.

*

A relevant aside: I bristle when I hear Jews described as belonging to a *faith* community. Judaism is not primarily concerned with faith. Rather it focuses almost exclusively on behaviour by requiring the fulfilment of divine commandments (*mitzvot*) to the greatest extent possible. There is no word for religion in Hebrew – the word *da'at* means knowledge (though Israelis tend to use it as a synonym for religious belief). The word for Jew (*Yehudi*) depicts a territorial rather than religious attachment as it originated from the state of Judea (*Yehuda*), the southern part of the original Jewish homeland. There's also no specific word for Judaism in the Hebrew language, or rather it's ambiguous as the word that is usually employed, *Yahadut*, has two meanings – Judaism and Jewry.

All this may sound somewhat esoteric, but it has major emotional, practical and even political consequences for the way Jews "practise" their Judaism. Throughout the history of the Diaspora, that began when the Romans kicked most of us out of Judea in the second century CE, Jews have tended to regard their Judaism as a portable identity card or passport through life rather than as a system of beliefs. Certainly many, perhaps most, of the early political Zionists perceived it that way. Judaism had kept the flame of Jewish identity and peoplehood alive when the geographical territory of Israel had become a distant collective memory. Now that Jewish sovereignty has been restored, we are free to discard the religion (if that's what it ever was) and reclaim our national identity in the homeland. Many Jews, especially those who live in Israel, have done just that and live unashamedly secular though fully Jewish lives.

The phenomenon of national or socio-cultural Judaism is vitally important to most Jews, including those living in Israel, yet is almost unknown to (or misunderstood by) outsiders. You can't be an atheist Christian or Muslim but you can certainly be an atheist Jew while fully integrated into the community and wholeheartedly accepted as a participant in all its activities including synagogue worship. Many Jews are content to take full advantage of that hyper-inclusiveness. A survey of regular synagogue attenders in the UK some years ago revealed the surprising finding (to some) that a substantial majority of such people admitted to holding agnostic or atheistic beliefs.

Today, I regard myself, like the Zionist pioneers and many modern Israelis, as a New Jew, a post-Judaic national-cultural Jew, entirely comfortable in my non-religious Jewish identity, though I am still drawn to some of Judaism's domestic rituals (such as lighting the *Shabbat* candles or the Passover *Seder* meal) in a kind of folkloristic, nostalgic and utterly areligious way.

Many Jews, especially those of an observant bent, heartily disagree with me but I, and the many others of my persuasion, have never been ostracised from my community for these views. In any other major religion, we would be regarded as irredeemable heretics. Our disagreement is expressed vehemently but respectfully. That's not a problem for either side: we're a disputatious people and are always up for a robust, well-argued debate. It's what we do and what we've always done. After around four millennia of practice, we're getting pretty good at it.

68

By 2011 and newly parentless, there was little to keep me in Glasgow, apart from my work and that too was spiralling headlong downwards. Maintaining morale had become intensely challenging; I knew I was reaching the end of my full-time working career and it seemed pointless to embark on major new projects in the circumstances. Furthermore, I was being virtually ignored by my dual employers; neither the university nor the health service seemed remotely interested in any of the numerous innovative proposals I was putting to them. As my enthusiasm and energy hadn't waned, this was indescribably frustrating. A continuous stream of new ideas flowed from my pen (of the computer keyboard variety).

My proudest invention was a revolutionary teaching method – the clinico-epidemiological conference – that integrated the teaching of clinical medicine with public health (a concept that was later taken up enthusiastically by several medical teachers around the world including those at the newly established Bar Ilan medical school in Israel's Galilee region). Another smart notion (or so I convinced myself) involved my drafting of a comprehensive injury prevention plan for Scotland. The Scottish government (to which I had been seconded part-time in the mid-noughties for three years) were, to my great disappointment, mind-numbingly unresponsive.

Following an enjoyable and productive sabbatical in London in 2010, out of which emerged two substantial academic books on public health, my eyes were firmly set on a move south to join my children as soon as I could organise it. That became possible in 2013 when my financial advisor discovered that I had massively over-contributed to my pension scheme and was headed for a gargantuan tax bill unless I submitted a letter giving the requisite three months' notice to retire.

When I hinted at my intentions to my colleagues, the general reaction was underwhelming. They all but held the front door open for me and handed me my coat. In truth, I was deeply irritated by their coolness towards my announcement, given the long decades of highly productive service I had devoted to both the NHS and the university. They could have at least feigned mild disappointment at my announcement but they plainly couldn't be bothered. That indifference, more than anything else, fully vindicated, in my own mind, my decision to quit.

My disillusionment with campus life was compounded by the growing cacophony of antisemitism. Naked Jew-hatred was always rare in Scotland but Israel-hatred was another matter; targeting the Jewish state with obloquy was a safer bet, a fig-leaf for an unfashionable racism that dared not speak its name. It has been aptly described as *alibi antisemitism*. Whatever the motivation, its impact was poisonous. Whenever the subject of the Middle East arose, I had to brace myself for an onslaught of falsehoods and libels. The experience was nothing new for me but its mounting ferocity was becoming intolerable.

This was no mere criticism of the kind one might level against the perceived misdemeanours of any other country, but a bucket-load of extreme, vicious and, at times, frankly unhinged propaganda designed to demonise and delegitimise the only democracy in the Middle East. Over the years, the denunciations morphed seamlessly from the political to the ideological and finally to the tribal. The targets were initially Israeli public figures, then Zionists and finally – you guessed it – Jews.

I'd prefer not to dwell on this unsavoury subject so let me give you a just a miniscule taste of what I endured. On one occasion, a fellow professor informed me that Gaza was "the largest concentration camp in the world." On another, a senior colleague informed me that he had sussed us out: "You Jews," he announced smugly, "underreacted to the Germans during the war and now, as compensation, you're overreacting to the Arabs." On a third, my abuser expressed surprise that antisemitism should be considered taboo at all as, "after all, the Jews killed Christ." That was the first time I could recall being subjected to that classic racist trope since my primary school days.

According to these self-appointed moral philosophers, there was a common factor to Jewish misfortune and to the suffering that we (or the Israelis) inflicted on others – we were always assuredly to blame. I was haunted by this recurring yet unanswerable question: if their anti-Jewish language was intemperate in my presence, what was it like when I was out of earshot? I struggled to maintain my composure in the face of these grotesque assaults, and I think I largely succeeded, but they grew in frequency, intensity and venom with every passing week. In retrospect, my efforts were doomed to failure.

I had always tried hard to ensure that my responses to these provocations were calm, measured, civilised and, above all, evidence based. It was to no avail whatsoever. My opponents were unmoved by my protests, including my corrections of their countless factual errors, choosing instead to channel their considerable intellectual energies into the much more exhilarating pastime of piling insults on Israel in an almost maniacal fashion. They tended to operate in packs of three, thereby ensuring that I was outnumbered and easily shouted down if my counterattacks threatened (as they often did) to hit the tender spots of their ignorance, bigotry or malice.

Eventually, I concluded that I had only one recourse if I were to preserve a scintilla of self-respect. Early retirement offered the only prospect of a reasonably dignified exit from academe. The pension mishap provided an appealing pretext and I couldn't wait to avail myself of it.

PART 4

69

Finding a new home was (again) a key step towards my personal reinvention. In 2012, I bought an attractive but tiny flat in North London that served as a *pied-à-terre* in the capital for my increasingly frequent visits. Its main attraction was a south facing stone balcony overlooking a verdant if rather cluttered landscape. In early 2014, I relocated from Glasgow to the metropolis fully and finally.

*

Leaving Scotland was a wrench – it had after all been my home for most of my life – but a relatively painless one. I had been a huge Glasgowphile since my great uncle Moss ("Moush" as we knew him) converted me in the 1960s to the cause through his fascinating mini-lectures about the city's history, culture and architecture. Where he sourced his treasure trove of information was always a mystery. He attributed his encyclopaedic knowledge of the city to his extensive research in Glasgow municipal council's superb Mitchell Library and there was undoubtedly some truth in that. But his erudition transcended mere academic knowledge; his colourful anecdotes reflected a deeper and more intimate understanding of places, events and characters than could ever have been captured on the pages of dusty reference books.

For years, I had raged against Glasgow's inexplicably poor media image in the rest of the UK. Eventually, I reached the sombre conclusion that many of the negative stereotypes were well deserved. For all its virtues, Glasgow was undeniably a provincial city that had never fully appreciated let alone achieved its potential, nor was it ever likely to recapture its once-lofty *Second City of the Empire* status. I'd done enough tilting at municipal windmills; I would bid farewell to the *Dear Green Place* without rancour or regret.

Yet I couldn't avoid experiencing a faint pang of sorrow at the realisation that my departure marked the end of something important – an epoch rather than an era. It had begun in the 1890s when my great-grandparents had immigrated to Scotland from *Der Heim* (the large Czarist-designated Russian Jewish ghetto known as the Pale of Settlement), set up home in the Gorbals, and put down strong familial and commercial roots in a rain-battered, windswept outpost of north western Europe. Their foresight transformed the outlook for their progeny from one of grinding, dangerous poverty in an Eastern Europe *shtetl*, that would ultimately become a literal death-trap for those who stayed behind, to a dull but infinitely more secure middle-class respectability in the urban Scottish Lowlands.

I've always fought hard against the seductive lure of excessive nostalgia, with only partial success. The past isn't just a foreign country, in LP Hartley's words, but is too often a depressing, emotionally stunting and hazardous domain. Here I was in my mid-sixties, resolved to resist the temptation to gaze longingly backwards but to focus with confidence into the unknowable void that was the future. No-one summed up my mindset better than former Israeli president Shimon Peres who exhorted his traumatised people to "remember less, dream more."

*

My snug "bijou residence" in Belsize Park was superbly located in a converted terrace house in Steele's Road, a street populated by acting celebrities and within easy walking distance of excellent parks as well as the bohemian villages of Hampstead, Primrose Hill and Camden Town. That was the good news. There were, however, quite a few negatives.

The cost of living in London was about a third higher than Glasgow's. I was alarmed to discover that proximity to my fellow Londoners exacted a price: an anally retentive upstairs neighbour vehemently objected to my music practice and was far from shy about expressing his disapproval. Welcome to London, I reflected. It may be a huge, exciting city, often acclaimed as the pre-eminent global capital, but it's also an overpriced, heavily polluted and grossly overcrowded one. Its population increases by around a hundred thousand every year. Like the proverbial rats in a cage, there are just too many of us and we tend to turn on each other for catharsis.

70

I had no intention of vegetating in retirement. Nowadays sixty-five (the standard British retirement age) is not considered old, after all. Yet the spectre of mortality is, actuarially, an ever-present fact of life. Too often, friends who had trodden this path soon had earth trodden on them – they met an unexpectedly early demise. Not for me the allure of the golf course or country walks or evenings down at the local pub. To keep my mind and body active, I resolved to do three things – write, play music, and, above all, educate about Israel.

At first, there were loose ends from my working life to tie up, scientific papers to complete, lectures to deliver, students to mentor. These tasks were rapidly disposed of. I could have continued my public health activities well into retirement had I been so inclined. I had been slotted in as a regular teacher of postgraduate doctors at two London medical schools. These were undemanding commitments that I rather enjoyed. An old colleague from my St Thomas's days contacted me from his home in Australia and suggested that I might like to run, on a voluntary basis, an online epidemiology course based on my innovative teaching tool, the clinico-epidemiological conference. I agreed and we tried the experiment on *People's Uni*, an open access online educational site, in 2014. It was moderately successful but not a sufficiently exciting experience on which to build a new mini-career.

From about 2012, I had been closely involved in planning the public health curriculum in Israel's newest medical school. This came about because a paediatric colleague of mine, Mary Randolph (who I hadn't realised was Jewish), called me one day in a state of panic: "Have you heard my news? I've just been appointed head of public health at the Bar Ilan medical school in the Galilee. Help!" So I did. Between us, we quickly developed an innovative and engaging programme for first year medical students; it included the clinico-epidemiological conference. For four decades, the Glasgow medical school had declined to implement my most revolutionary teaching tool; it took Bar Ilan about four minutes to decide to get it up and running. And it worked beautifully. I returned many times to Tsfat, the delightful little religious town nestling in the Galilee mountains where the medical school was based, to teach on the course, and it was always a satisfying experience.

Towards the end of my time in Glasgow, I had sketched out a tentative short-list of options for life after R day but had only the vaguest idea of how I might pass the time. I applied for a couple of locum posts in public health in London but neither they nor I found this a sufficiently enticing prospect, so I abandoned the idea. I didn't particularly need the money, as my university pension was quite generous, and I was filling my days successfully in any case. There were occasions when the *longueur* of vacant time threatened to become oppressive, but I shrugged them off, reminding myself that I was free to do whatever I wished with my life for the first time since I was aged three. Initially, my main objective was to train my children to drop any illusions they might harbour about my perpetual, unconditional availability as a babysitter. (Not that I ever minded grandfatherly duties – on the contrary, I seized every opportunity to fulfil them and was utterly besotted by my growing posse of grandchildren; I just needed to assert my independence at a vulnerable period of my life when time, that most precious of all commodities, too often vanishes with unexpected precipitousness, into the ether).

I could have opted to slump into a routine of late lie-ins, gentle walkabouts in the parks and streets of NW3, sampling at will any number of cafes, pubs, restaurants, concerts, plays and exhibitions. In short, I could have abandoned myself entirely to the languorous rhythm of a self-absorbed, hedonistic and undemanding London lifestyle. I wasn't averse to enjoying myself but I have always suffered a low boredom threshold and I knew that I'd need something more substantial to sustain my interest.

Instead, I chose a different course and strove to maintain a sense of strict daily discipline, rising at eight and buckling down to work by around nine. I'd had a trial run at this type of routine in the final months of my academic post, having made myself increasingly scarce in the office, so it wasn't an entirely new experience. In this way, I slipped comfortably into the role of writer, commentator and activist without consciously intending it. I kept a daily journal and drafted the occasional poem. Somehow there were always talks to prepare or articles or books to write, and I was seldom at a loose end. In fact, rather to my astonishment, I hit a productive literary seam almost from the start. Motivation was my secret weapon and there was one topic that motivated me above all else.

71

The conversations with my father in the final weeks of his life had re-ignited my determination to serve my homeland that was being traduced daily. This was no longer merely a matter of political commitment or even moral responsibility; it was a family tradition and one that I wished to sustain.

In 2015, London was home to about 250,000 Jews – sixty times the number in Glasgow. The range and richness of Jewish life in the capital was extraordinary. Upwards of 85% of Jews regarded Israel as central to their identity so it was hardly surprising that pro-Israel organisations abounded. They all had slightly different functions but there was much overlap, duplication, inefficiency and, inevitably, rivalry. The sense of territoriality between these agencies was often so strong that they point-blank refused to cooperate with each other at all.

*

The canard, pedalled by the Israel-haters, of an integrated, well-oiled and generously funded pro-Israel lobby that exerts untrammelled political power is not only a complete fabrication but a laughable one. Nevertheless, some *hasbara* (advocacy) groups do employ highly talented people who are tireless in their efforts to counter false propaganda and to disseminate positive messages about Israel.

There's a problem with this approach – it isn't working. The scale of the challenge is just too great. Demographically, Jews in the UK (and globally) are vastly outnumbered by Muslims, an ethno-religious population that is, tragically, almost universally antagonistic to Israel. And among Western liberal elites such as the media, trade unions, political parties and academe, Israel has become the new whipping boy, a handy (though wholly inappropriate) substitute for the old apartheid-era South Africa.

Ostensibly, antipathy to Israel is the mirror image of sympathy for the Palestinians but that view is questionable given the near-total silence of pro-Palestinian activists when the objects of their alleged sympathy are treated abominably by anyone other than Israelis. I first noticed this hypocrisy when King Hussein of Jordan killed thousands of Palestinians in 1970 (during "Black September"), and again when hundreds of thousands of Palestinians were kicked out of Kuwait, to barely a murmur of international protest, at the end of the first Gulf War in the 1990s. The same phenomenon was observable when Syria's Assad repeated the trick in 2014-20, ruthlessly barrel-bombing Palestinian refugee camps and causing thousands of civilian fatalities. By contrast, if a Palestinian child is killed accidentally in Gaza or the West Bank by an Israeli counter-terrorism unit, *The Guardian* will likely run the story on its front page. The hypocrisy is breathtaking yet unacknowledged. The evidence is there for anyone prepared to see it: the real purpose of the progressive fad of *Palestinianism* is less to do with promoting the welfare of Palestinians than with demonising Israel, truly the Jew among the nations.

*

What could I, a newly retired medical academic, offer those who were fighting this vicious propaganda war against the Jewish state? I was never under the illusion that I had the capacity, single-handedly, transform the ineffectual chaos of the London pro-Israel scene into a newer, leaner, meaner war machine. But I felt I had something unique to offer, or rather a combination of attributes. I was knowledgeable, had lived in Israel for nine years, had served in the army, and maintained close contact with the country. Moreover, as an academic I was used to public speaking, sometimes to highly critical audiences. Intellectually, I had always pursued an evidence-based approach to my work and strove do the same in relation to Israel and those who undertake *hasbara* on her behalf.

Let me press the pause button briefly. *Hasbara* literally means *explanation;* the word *hasbara* has recently become corrupted via the demonisation of its practitioners. Accordingly, it has unfairly acquired negative connotations – especially but far from exclusively – in virulently anti-Israel circles and is increasingly viewed as a depicting a peculiarly extreme form of political propaganda. My role is not to brainwash but to educate; the facts are so powerful that they speak for themselves. I am not a *hasbarista*, a propagandist, though I won't hesitate to challenge propaganda that is false.

In pursuit of my educational mission to set the record straight about Israel, I made an important discovery: an even greater trump card than my Israeli army service was my family background. Although my parents had started out as strong Zionists, from the 1950s onwards their position changed to the point where their three children entered adult life with either indifferent or hostile attitudes to Israel. In my case (as I've described), I refused initially to join Edinburgh's Jewish student society and was brow-beaten by my non-Jewish circle of friends into paying attention to media reporting of the build-up to the Six Day War. I was far from the stereotypical "brainwashed" Jewish kid (if such a being exists) who had never questioned Zionism. On the contrary, I was instinctively sceptical of the whole enterprise and only changed my view when I investigated the subject in greater depth.

My two younger siblings, products of the same parents and a near- identical family environment, remained resolutely remote from, and sometimes antipathetic to, Israel and all her works for most of their lives. So if any brainwashing occurred in our family, it was not in Israel's favour. I managed to persuade Julie and her husband to participate in my seventieth birthday celebrations in Tel Avi (and I suspect it was an eye-opener for her), but Melvyn remained steadfastly opposed to the idea.

Starting in that Edinburgh junior common room on a mild June evening in 1967, I charted a completely different course. My Zionism was, if anything, a rebellion against my upbringing not an extension of it. Anyone who challenges my support for Israel on the grounds that it is a conditioned reflex based on a diet of misinformation that they presume I must have been fed since childhood – an accusation that is frequently used to try to discredit Israel's supporters – is way off the mark.

My credentials for entering the fray were therefore unusually strong. I set about contacting and meeting leading people from Zionist groups in London to offer myself as a resource for the increasingly frenetic battle for hearts and minds that I discovered, to my horror, was being waged on a daily basis in the capital.

72

A couple of years earlier, I had met Luke Akenhead and Alan Jensen, two highly gifted (non-Jewish) leading lights within an impressive left-leaning organisation called BICRA – British Israel Communications and Research Association. This was a successor to the British Israel Public Affairs Council that had been set up by veteran *Guardian* (sic) journalist Terence Prittie in the 1960s when that newspaper viewed Zionism as a liberal cause worth supporting. Jensen invited me to write an expert report on Palestinian health for *Fathom*, BICRA's online house journal, as a response to the claims of Richard Horton, editor of *The Lancet*, that Israel had systematically undermined the health of the people of the West Bank and Gaza since 1967. Horton was a strong promoter of the narrative of an unconscionably evil Israeli oppression of the Palestinians that had become a central, unassailable article of faith in Europe's progressive circles.

Because I had worked in Beer Sheva in the 1980s and had witnessed at first-hand the huge Israeli investment in the healthcare infrastructure in nearby Gaza, I was fairly confident (though by no means certain) that Horton was wrong, and so it transpired. My report was long and detailed. I examined a vast volume of (mainly non-Israeli) data and all contradicted Horton's assertions; indeed, they pointed in precisely the opposite direction – Israel's actions over the decades had greatly improved Palestinian health as measured by all the standard indicators – including a steeply declining infant mortality rate and rising life expectancy. Israel had also improved the public health and healthcare infrastructure in West Bank and Gaza strip, thereby improving the quality of life of their inhabitants beyond recognition. Education (at all levels), housing and social services were all transformed.

The article took six months to complete and was published in late 2014, shortly after another round of IDF-Hamas fighting. We expected a furious counterattack from the usual suspects following its release, but none came. I'm fairly sure of the explanation: the case I had presented was unassailable. But it was largely ignored by both the medical and general media as it didn't fit the accepted narrative of Israeli wrongdoing.

I drew two lessons from this experience. First, the truth will (eventually) trump the lies and should be recorded for posterity, if for no other reason than to inform future historical research. Second, large numbers of educated people have no interest whatever in the truth; too often, inconvenient facts are simply swatted away by ideologues as irrelevant to their sacred cause, in this case that of Palestine. That such a closed and irrational mind-set can take hold of a substantial segment of the so-called intelligentsia in the 21st century is deeply shocking but that is what has happened, much as occurred a century or so earlier when distaste for Jews among the European middle classes became normalised and socially respectable.

I published a few other articles on Israel and, along with countless other activists, started a blog about the conflict. My writings ranged far and wide, from the need for evidence-based advocacy to analyses of political trends in Israel. These caught the eye of some influential people, including Israeli diplomats in London and pro-Israel groups around the country. A campus-based educational NGO called *StandByUs UK* offered me a natural home and I was soon appointed to its board with the grandiose-sounding but essentially meaningless title of Academic Director. I was soon in great demand as a speaker and, at one point, had to turn down numerous speaking invitations as my diary was full to bursting. I was gratified by this recognition and felt I was making some impact but I didn't get carried away as the bigger picture was bleaker than ever.

Public and political opinion had been steadily shifting against Israel across most of the world ever since Israel had had the temerity to the win the Six Day War of 1967, thereby transforming overnight her media image from David into Goliath. This process gained momentum in the 1970s when the Arab League realised that it could use oil to blackmail the rest of the world into aligning itself with the forces of anti-Israelism. (That should have been a major story in itself but, for some reason, journalists didn't care to write about it, or perhaps their editors or publishers were in thrall to the same financial pressures).

By the early twenty-first century, strident anti-Israelism had evolved into overt antisemitism. Jews were again being killed in Europe every year simply for the crime of being Jewish. In 2015, we witnessed shocking terrorist murders of journalists at the Charlie

Hebdo magazine in Paris, along with four Jewish shoppers in a kosher deli two days later, by Islamist gunmen. A BBC journalist, Tim Willcox, openly tried, during a live interview with a French Holocaust survivor, to link the deli killings to Israel by opining that "The Palestinians suffer hugely at Jewish hands as well" and was robustly defended by his employers in the face of an avalanche of complaints about this blatant racism.

By then, many European Jews felt their vulnerability was being deliberately ignored. Even President Obama saw fit to describe the Paris attack as random when it was patently nothing of the kind. Antisemitism, much of it fomented within sections of the growing Muslim community as well as on both the far right and far left, was on the rise across all of Europe. Around half of all racist attacks across the continent were directed at Jews (a pattern that was soon to be repeated in the United States) and yet Amnesty International, never slow to issue excoriating denunciations of Israel and western Islamophobia, declined to investigate antisemitism on the grounds that "we can't do everything."

For perhaps the first time in three generations, European Jews were fearful of their future and began to hide emblems of their identity, such as skullcaps and stars of David, from public view. That was unacceptable. We were winning some battles but losing the war. I felt we needed a new approach. The only snag was I had no idea what it might be.

73

When I review all my pro-Israel activities in recent years, the one of which I am most proud is a booklet on the Balfour Declaration that I drafted for *StandByUs*. It was published in late 2016, to the consternation of the Zionist Federation who protested vociferously, with history on their side, that the Declaration was theirs by right.

This won't make any sense to you unless you know what happened towards the end of World War One. On 2nd November 1917, the British War Cabinet issued a statement in the form of a letter from Lord Arthur James Balfour, the Foreign Secretary, to Lord Lionel Walter Rothschild, an Anglo-Jewish dignitary, for transmission to the Zionist Federation of Great Britain and Ireland. The letter stated that:

"His Majesty's government view with favour the establishment in Palestine of a national home for the Jewish people, and will use their best endeavours to facilitate the achievement of this object, it being clearly understood that nothing shall be done which may prejudice the civil and religious rights of existing non-Jewish communities in Palestine, or the rights and political status enjoyed by Jews in any other country."

The Balfour Declaration, as this document became known, was a ground-breaking British government statement of policy that recognised the profound and unbroken historical, religious and cultural connection of the Jewish people to the land from which they had been (largely) expelled by the Romans some 2,000 years earlier, thereby destroying Judea as a sovereign nation. (To add insult to injury, the imperial conquerors renamed the land Syria Palaestina, after the Jews' arch enemy, the Philistines, a seafaring people who had originated from Greece).

The British statement held tremendous symbolic significance for Jews, but it was much more than that. Its wording obligated the British government to use its "best endeavours" – meaning that they would implement all reasonable measures rather than merely offer support in principle – to achieve the objective of the establishment of a "national home for the Jewish people" in Palestine.

The historical and legal significance of the Declaration would become fully apparent in 1920 when it was incorporated, virtually word for word, into two major internationally binding agreements – the San Remo Resolution (often called the Jewish Magna Carta) and the League of Nations Mandate for Palestine that was given to the British Government later that year. That eventually led, through a devious and blood-drenched path, to the establishment of the modern State of Israel in May 1948.

Many allegedly expert commentators, including some who are sympathetic to Israel, have suggested that the Declaration was the foundational document of the Jewish state, and that its terms were only partially fulfilled in that Jewish aspirations were met while those of the Arab population of Palestine and the Middle East were not. Superficially, this is a plausible argument. But it's wrong.

The unpalatable fact is that the UK's enthusiasm for Zionism was so short-lived that if you blinked you missed it. Worse for admirers of the country of my birth, its government was effectively complicit in the Holocaust. If that statement shocks you, it should. British leaders, in a desperate attempt to appease Arab states, reneged on their internationally binding commitments to encourage Jewish immigration to Palestine and promote Jewish settlement there. A series of policy U-turns, culminating in the shameful 1939 white paper, severely restricted Jewish immigration, in the process condemning millions of Jews to a cruel fate at the hands of their Nazi persecutors. That was an unforgiveable moral crime that has yet to be acknowledged by any subsequent British government.

While the Declaration's first part (the establishment of the Jewish National Home) was technically achieved in 1948, it remains work in progress as most of Israel's neighbours – with the collusion of their external allies in the Arab League, Islamic Conference, United Nations and elsewhere – continue to seek her destruction, even if some employ circumlocutions to avoid being called to account. Without a strong army and the expenditure of huge and scarce resources on defence, Israel simply could not have survived. A demonised and delegitimised National Home, whose acceptance into the community of nations remains partial and conditional at best, can hardly be considered a successful expression of Balfour Declaration's declared intention. On the contrary, it continues to be challenged and threatened daily with annihilation. This is an affront to both the spirit and the letter of the Declaration (and is also, incidentally, a blatant breach of the UN charter).

The Declaration's second part (the protection of the civil and religious rights of the existing non-Jewish communities of Palestine) was meticulously fulfilled through Israel's effective constitution – the Declaration of Independence and related Basic Laws. The legal protection of minorities in Israel stands in marked contrast to the position of Jews in Arab states.

Critics of the Declaration complain that it was discriminatory in that it did not explicitly address Arab *national* ambitions. They perhaps have a point – or at least they might have had one except for the fact that history proves otherwise; subsequent to the San Remo resolution, no less than 22 Arab States were ultimately created. The first of these was a Palestinian Arab one, Transjordan, that was brought into being by the British in 1922 in territory that comprised the geographically larger Eastern portion of the original Mandatory Palestine – twenty-six years before Israel declared her independence.

The Declaration's third part (the protection of the status of existing Jewish communities in the Diaspora) was entirely ignored throughout the Arab world. Arab governments viciously turned on their Jewish citizens and actively expelled or encouraged the exodus of around 900,000 Jews (aka "Zionists") from countries across the Middle East and North Africa. To this day, none of these countries has accepted responsibility or offered an apology for this large-scale ethnic cleansing, let alone provided even minimal recompense to the victims.

It should be apparent to any fair-minded observer that, of the three principles enshrined in the Declaration, only the second (relating to Arab rights within Israel) has actually been fully fulfilled. Curiously, that is the only part that most commentators seem to think wasn't. The first and third parts – those relating to the status of Jewish people in their homeland and in the Diaspora respectively – have yet to be properly implemented and accepted by Israel's neighbours and by much of the international community.

In 2017, the Palestinian Authority and others sought to extract from the British government a retrospective apology for allegedly betraying the Palestinians a century earlier. Fortunately it never materialised; had that happened, it would have been a travesty. I believe my booklet may have made a modest contribution to that small victory for truth over falsehood.

74

StandByUs UK grew like topsy and now has a large global following. It is certainly proving its value – up to a point. But the fact remains that the legion of Israel-haters continues to grow year-on-year around the world. The election of US President Donald Trump in 2016 may appear to have changed the momentum in Israel's favour in the short-term – his transfer of the US embassy from Tel Aviv to Jerusalem, mandated by Congress many years earlier, was the fulfilment of a promise made by successive US presidents – but the central obstacle remains: the lack of a sufficiently statesmanlike Palestinian leadership willing and able to accept Jewish sovereignty behind any borders and thereby end the conflict. Even if that happy outcome were achieved, the agenda would simply move on to the (false) "apartheid" slur or some other battleground to which the bigots can rally their troops. This longest hatred isn't going away any time soon. We have to keep finding new and far more effective means of countering it.

Not only has antisemitism lingered, expanded and mutated into antiZionism, so has the related and disturbing phenomenon of Jewish self-abasement. That's not new, of course, but has been amplified, like so many other psychological disorders, by today's social media. In the twenty first century, as in earlier times, a minority of Jewish people deeply resent the biological and cultural reality of their ancestry and will do almost anything to distance themselves from it. Whether they are self-hating Jews (as many assume), or frightened souls who identify with the aggressor in a desperate (and, history proves, futile) form of self-defence, or are self-regarding guardians of what they view as their unassailable moral purity (that I suspect is closer to the truth), I feel sorry for their loss. They are on the wrong side of history in so many ways.

An example of the unconsciously antisemitic progressive Jew was the late Jonathan Miller who, in an interview with Norman Lebrecht, informed us, without a trace of irony, that he felt *Jew-ish* in the same way he felt *chimpanzee-ish*. The staggering arrogance and crass insensitivity of that statement revealed Miller's greatest blind spot – for himself and how others viewed him.

Who will stand up to the despicable narrative of the anti-Jewish, anti-Zionist or anti-Israel Jew? The silent majority of Jews (who else?) will have to do it but they will need the knowledge, tools and determination to ensure that they hit the target. That's one battleground, at least, to which I have long felt I might be able to bring some ammunition. By early 2015, I had begun to develop two principal ideas that I believed might help us, the Jews of the UK, regain the initiative and reclaim a truthful narrative. These were *strategic thinking* and *universalism*.

The former had been a recurring theme of my academic career while the latter epitomised one of my core moral values. Although I discovered excellent work being done by a range of groups and individuals in London, there was minimal inter-agency coordination and no evaluation of their impact. To me, trained in public health, these were glaring gaps. I proposed, in a brief paper, that we needed to formulate an overarching strategy urgently. It would comprise a long-term vision, a statement of fundamental values and principles, a small number of manageable goals, and some operational objectives with built-in timescales and budgets. Everything would be monitored, in terms of its impact, enabling us to evaluate our effectiveness and quickly remedy failings.

None of this was earth-shatteringly original and I didn't anticipate that it would be controversial. But it turned out that most activists, including some highly intelligent people, didn't have the first clue what I was talking about. Even the Israeli Ministry of Foreign Affairs didn't seem to have a strategy (though they may have simply declined to share it with me or anyone else). If I had to sum up the main elements of such a strategy in three words it would be these: *educate, defend, attack* (roughly in that order). That just about covers it. At the time of writing, I am struggling to achieve lift-off for the idea. I won't desist from trying.

By universalism, I mean that Israel is a worthy cause that should arouse the empathetic passions of every thinking, feeling human being. Too often, Zionism is labelled as narrowly tribal, a peculiarly Jewish obsession. That perception is both false and an ideological dead-end (as tribalism is largely yesterday's issue though populist politicians are working hard to revive it). And it's politically disastrous as our tribe is so much smaller than that of our opponents. If Israel's appeal is to widen, it has to be rebranded as a universal issue that should concern everyone. That shouldn't be too difficult as it happens to be true.

If the state of Israel is delegitimised, so can any country. If Israel is demonised, all of humanity is diminished. If Israel is libelled, it is an insult to all – starting with disadvantaged and oppressed minorities everywhere. Zionism, as the national liberation movement of the Jewish people, is a model for the liberation of all marginalised people. For some Jews, this is a difficult mind-set to enter for their attachment to Israel, their religion and culture *is* tribal. For most, however, it is likely to be second nature. Zionism has always viewed itself as a role model for all humanity and fulfilling that aspiration should be our take-home message to the sceptics. (In passing, I should mention that Judaism itself, contrary to popular myth, contains strong themes of universalism, notably the biblical missions of being *or lagoyim* – "a light unto the nations" and *tikkun olam* – "repairing the world").

I believe that combining a strategic approach with universalism could reap rewards in the propaganda war. Let me stress again that there is nothing original about either of these concepts. What is new is their application to the war of ideas that is currently raging around Israel and is entering a dangerous phase – possibly a tipping point. We can't afford to cede more ground in this existential struggle because Israel's current demonisation (fuelled, many Jews increasingly recognise, by atavistic racism) will translate rapidly into delegitimisation that, in turn, will lead – as her enemies fully intend – to her destruction. And, in consequence, to the weakening, perhaps terminally, of the Jewish people as a whole. We can't, under any circumstances, grant Hitler and his henchmen a posthumous victory.

That outcome is inconceivable. Defeat is not an option.

75

In 2016, I sold my Belsize Park flat to my troublesome neighbour for a good price on the eve of the Brexit referendum. I couldn't have predicted the result of the poll but property prices slumped thereafter so it turned out to be a shrewd decision. There was one small problem – I had nowhere to live.

After a short stay at my daughter Ilana's home while she and her family were visiting Israel, followed by two fairly catastrophic attempts to bond with women who offered me temporary accommodation, I rented a pleasant little flat in Mill Hill East (yes, such a place really does exist) before buying the spacious, lovely two-bedroomed home in central Finchley where I have resided since the summer of 2017. The location is further out of town than I would have liked but it's tolerable and I have everything I need on my doorstep. A tube station is a mere eight minutes' walk away and I have all the local facilities I need – including a couple of decent restaurants and a superb park with a fine children's playground. Besides, all my children and grandchildren live, like me, on the number thirteen London bus route.

I enjoy the regular company of all my family a great deal these days, now that my second son, Ethan, and his Sabra wife Galit, plus baby Amnon, have relocated from Israel where they married in a colourful Moroccan-style ceremony at the top of the Tel Aviv Azrieli Tower in 2017. That was the second family marriage with a matter of months as Pamela and her banker boyfriend, Mark, had tied the knot in a sedately elegant London hotel in 2016 and then produced baby Annie. That's seven grandchildren and counting – all of whom give me unalloyed, unconditional affection and pleasure. And a sort of immortality. It is impossible to describe the depth of my gratitude.

In 2019, I reached the biblically resonant milestone age of seventy and celebrated it in style, twice. The first was a spectacular afternoon tea at my eldest daughter's house to which I invited several family members to whom I owed hospitality plus a few more whom I hadn't seen for years. Then, some weeks later, I did it all again in Tel Aviv. I booked a deluxe hotel for all my children and their families, plus my sister and her husband. Both occasions were memorable (for me, at least) and my speeches were, I hope, suitably sentimental without being cloying.

Where am I now? (I recorded the following reflections during the Great Lockdown necessitated by the Covid-19 pandemic so take them with a large pinch of salt; life as we knew it may never return).

Activism and writing are my major preoccupations and I've no intention of easing up on either. The intellectual struggle against Israel's enemies is ceaseless and can be demoralising but I won't back down. I know that many others, whether Jewish or not, feel the same. My engagement with students via *StandByUs* is picking up momentum so I must be finding some success in tuning into their anxieties, thirst for knowledge and desire to change the world for the better. Nevertheless, I remain dissatisfied, constantly aware that I can and should do more. This is *the tension of the unfulfilled* (in the memorable words of a psychoanalyst friend of my father's) and it acts as a powerful motivator.

My writing is progressing. I wrote an autobiographical epic poem that I self-published and distributed to my children. I've no idea what they made of it and it doesn't really matter as its purpose was to put down a marker for posterity, a permanent reminder to future generations, that Daniel Steyne was here on earth and breathed and loved and laughed and cried and had opinions about all kinds of issues. In fulfilment of a lifelong ambition, I also wrote and self-published a thriller called *The Gold Dome* set primarily in the Middle East. It was fun. No, actually that's an exaggeration, it was surprisingly hard work, but surveying the finished product – warts and all – was satisfying).

My violin-playing is (I tell myself) better than ever, and I am regularly invited (in normal, non-pandemic times) to play first or second violin in string quartets. I keep fit by twice-weekly gym visits and, bar a couple of minor health scares, I've managed to stay physically and mentally fit in this reflective, autumnal phase of my existence. For that good fortune, I'm enormously grateful also.

I've no idea what comes next but that is the point of life, isn't it? That perpetual uncertainty is a sensation to cherish rather than fear. I take nothing for granted. If the past is a foreign country that I leave reluctantly, the future is an alien, star-studded universe that I am determined to explore and experience while I have the capacity. I will focus on doing whatever I can to make the most of whatever time remains and whatever fate throws at me. Throughout my entire life, I have been – and remain – unaccountably extremely lucky and have to keep reminding myself of that sweet reality every time I feel the old restlessness tugging at my peace of mind.

And that should be that. Except that it isn't, of course. It never will be. There are a few loose ends to tie up. Rather a lot in fact. They should keep me busy enough. I anticipate that some will bend easily to my attempts to do so while others will remain stiff and brittle and may even spring back and strike me with a stinging slap.

No matter. I have little option but to heed Socrates' (or was it Plato's?) admonition that an unexamined life isn't worth living. I will examine it, again and again, until there is nothing further left to see.

76

The toughest question any sentient Jew (and, I suggest, enlightened non-Jew as well) can and should pose is this: how can we stop the unstoppable, universal, primal, murderous Jew-hatred that has defied all previous attempts to eradicate it? Trying to find an answer has dominated my life for as long as I can remember. I was not alone. It could fairly be described as *the* Great Jewish Project, by which I mean the moral responsibility on all Jews to survive physically, culturally and nationally in the face of repeated attempts to annihilate them.

Actually, my angst was unnecessary. After three millennia or more of suffering, the Jewish people eventually formulated a highly effective response without me. By the end of the nineteenth century, Herzl and other Zionist thinkers had come with a plan that may be summarised as the Three Ss: self-determination, sovereignty and self-defence. Nevertheless, I felt a personal need to wrestle with the question and I eventually arrived at a simple answer. It boiled down to pursuing one overriding objective: doing everything in my power to ensure the Jewish state of Israel's continued existence as a healthy and secure democracy.

Over the course of my adult life, starting with that seminal war of 1967, all of this became increasingly obvious, the classic no-brainer. For many others – including some (though thankfully still a minority) in the Jewish community – neither the question nor the answer made sense. I listened carefully to their counterarguments and found them feeble and unconvincing. I didn't just disagree with their view; I knew in my heart and head that they were wrong, and dangerously so. My unshakeable conviction was that the Jewish people were entering a period of menace comparable to the 1930s.

Moreover, the daggers were pointing at all of humanity rather than merely Jews. Israel was just the canary in the mine. That's why Jews matter to everyone. History may not repeat itself precisely, but it rhymes (said Mark Twain, maybe) and historical mistakes are replicated endlessly. Our generation was critical of the preceding one for permitting, or at least opposing ineffectually, the insanity of political extremism when a brand of fascism known as National Socialism turned Europe into an incomprehensively barbaric slaughterhouse. Paradoxically, the strong Jewish dimension to these terrible events has obstructed frank discussion of these issues within the global Jewish community. The collective trauma was just too devastating.

My parents, in their youthful wisdom, were prepared to have that discussion and the need to act. They understood well the vile nature of the beast and opted unequivocally for Zionism, the only realistic Jewish response to genocide. After a prolonged spell of indifference (at best) in middle life, they (or at least my father) rediscovered the logic of Jewish self-determination in their later years, prompted perhaps by their elder son's proselytising. As I approach my maturity, I feel more impelled than ever to confront the forces of darkness, not least because I have a vested interest in seeking to protect my offspring and their families from the fate that befell their relatives within living memory.

*

None of these ruminations takes place in a vacuum. We are blessed with free will, but it has its limits. Complete freedom is an illusion. I understand that I am not and never have been a floating bundle of psychic energy that drifts and flits, like an intellectual libertine, from one interesting or attractive stimulus to the next. I am as tethered to my personality, circumstances and life experiences as the next person. And I recognise that those circumstances have, generally speaking, been exceptionally clement: I've had (to date) a mostly happy and productive life, free from serious disadvantage, disability or chronic illness. But I'm not complacent. Nobody can afford the luxury of resting on their laurels. Life is a fast-moving trajectory, a rollercoaster ride on a dizzyingly steep learning curve. Hold on tight and learn fast, or you're in trouble. You never know what deadly hazard – or heaven-sent opportunity – may lie in wait around the next bend.

That doesn't preclude glancing backwards occasionally. I feel the need to reflect on my progress so far. While my track record, personally and professionally, has been far from flawless, I believe that I have accomplished a great deal one way or another in my chosen career and am confident that my supporters and friends (just about) outnumber my detractors and enemies. Nowadays, I enjoy the pleasures of spending precious time with my delightful children and grandchildren. I regard myself as biologically young for my age with an unfulfilled future as well as a nostalgic past. In short, life was, is, and still could be, extremely pleasant and rewarding. What more could any man possibly want?

Well, rather a lot actually. I do want more and always will, until my last breath. That's the nature of the human condition, or at least mine. *The tension of the unfulfilled.* That's where life's trajectory has led me. It's a fact not a choice. It's what I've learned about the world and about my place in it. So far. Because I'm still learning, every single day.

What exactly do I desire for the future? I could enumerate some goals or aspirations: to contribute further to Israel-advocacy, to spend more time in the homeland, to write more articles, poems and books, to travel to Latin America and other far-flung places that I have never seen, and to leave my complicated financial affairs – and all the other miscellany I expect I'll be obliged to leave behind – in a healthy and manageable state for my children. These all look achievable ambitions. That doesn't mean that I'll achieve them. Or that I'll mind if I don't.

I have other lists. Here's one: the more elusive objectives lie in the realm of the spirit and emotions. I have discovered neither religion nor any variant of mystical belief systems in my dotage. Not that I've sought them out as I'm sceptical of their value. I'm interested in more earthly pleasures: to savour the flavours of good food, to rejoice in the sights and scents of spring, to continue to lose myself in chamber music as an improving violinist. Does that mean I'm a hedonist? Probably. And I'm absolutely fine with that.

Casting aside, for a moment, the quest for a modicum of significance, for the privilege of leaving a mark or two on life's pathway, I'd implore my Creator (if I thought He existed and was listening) to grant me this wish: to retain my capacity to enjoy life to the full until as close to the end as possible, up to and including the very last second before midnight.

Postscript

I don't pretend to have portrayed the totality of my life in this book. That would be impossible. Every human being is a complex animal whose existence comprises many distinct and interconnected strands. The two most obvious ones are work and family. The latter have featured prominently throughout this story in keeping with their overriding importance to me. I have referred to both at length at various points but (believe it or not) I have also striven to avoid burdening my reader with tedious or inappropriate detail.

Where am I now, this minute, on life's journey? I'd rather not contemplate the range of possible responses to that question. Others try to tell me, usually with oblique delicacy, that I am nearing the end, or at least the beginning of the end (rather than the end of the beginning, a position I would far rather occupy; thankfully I retain enough humility to recognise that assumption to be hubristic).

At the time of writing in 2020, we're holding our collective breath. The world is gripped by an unprecedented public health emergency, a pandemic due to a highly contagious coronavirus that causes a disease known as *Covid19*. The internet is buzzing with (probably fake) news that it may have originated from a Chinese biological warfare facility rather than from cross-species transmission (from bat to human) as the official narrative runs. It's most likely a spontaneous mutation of a previously harmless virus. We may never know its origin as China is hardly the model of an open, transparent society.

Whatever the cause, the effects are devastating; hundreds of thousands of people have died, and millions are unable to continue their normal lives. The high-risk groups for serious illness, death and long-term morbidity following infection are the elderly (meaning over the age of seventy – people like me) and those who suffer chronic disorders such as obesity, diabetes and cancer. Some ethnic groups (especially Blacks, Asians and Jews) appear to be at higher risk though the reasons are unclear. Thankfully, young children seem virtually unaffected even if infected.

Here in the UK, we've been in lockdown, of varying degree, for five months, confined to our homes for most of the day, and (for the first 12 weeks or so) allowed out occasionally only to shop and visit relatives. The restrictions are gradually easing at the time of writing but there's a general nervousness in the air. To date, the UK has suffered around 60,000 excess deaths (one of the highest mortality rates in the world) while the US has reached 150,000 (also one of the worst rates) and Israel has lost around 700 (which is still one of the lowest despite experiencing a second peak for which the public appear to have blamed government ineptitude). The global economy has not merely stalled but has ground to a halt and that will bring with a secondary public health calamity via financially starved public services, unemployment and poverty.

This is the greatest crisis the world has faced since the 2008 financial crash or perhaps even the Second World War. It's ironic that public health is the discipline at the epicentre of media attention and that I am no longer in a position to contribute. (I offered to return to work in the NHS but all they could offer me was a role as a contact tracer that I declined. I have a few well-honed skills in public health and that isn't one of them). Perhaps it's just as well: infectious disease control was never my strong point. Whatever happens, I am confident that human life won't end but there may be much pain for all of us before it recovers.

Yet some things never change. The antisemites are having a wonderful pandemic, blaming Jews (especially those of the Israeli variety) for the virus and claiming that the Israelis are unleashing it as another genocidal weapon against the Palestinians. While her enemies ratchet up their blood libels across all the main social media platforms, Israel is quietly coordinating her public health response with the Palestinian Authority to great effect: both populations have fared relatively well so far. Yet this is entirely ignored by the world's media, a remarkable phenomenon given that Israel contains more foreign correspondents per square kilometre than any other country. It seems that Israeli writer Matti Friedman was right – if a story reveals Israel in a positive light, bury it.

Putting that apocalyptic epidemiological event aside (and who would be so foolish as to do that?), here is where I think I have now reached. I've entered a new, mature phase of my life and am determined to remain as physically, mentally and socially active for as long as humanly possible. I can't foretell the future and so all predictions are pointless. But I don't apologise for aspiring to pass a couple more decades (at least) of high-quality living that may enable me to chalk up just a few more worthwhile accomplishments before calling it a day.

In my epic autobiographical poem, I drew on the metaphor of life as a flowing stream. Navigating gingerly in one direction or another, we pitch ourselves against a perpetually moving current that sometimes works in our favour and propels us along nicely but may equally turn around unexpectedly and sweep us away for ever. So here I stand, within hailing distance of the distal shore of that stream, perched on the latest shiny, slippery pebble (but not the last, I trust), surveying the swirling frothy eddies cascading prettily around me. I haven't fully crossed to the other side, nor do I wish to. Not yet.

In truth, not ever.